Bodies Adjacent

Also by Ardyth Kennelly

The Peaceable Kingdom (1949)
The Spur (1951)
Good Morning, Young Lady (1953)
Up Home (1955)
Marry Me, Carry Me (1956)
Variation West (2014)

Bodies Adjacent

Ardyth's Memoir & Egon's Journal

BY
Ardyth Kennelly
AND
Egon V. Ullman

SUNNYCROFT
BOOKS

PORTLAND, ORE.

Copyright © 2023 by Michael Massee, Timothy J. Pettibone, and Ardyth L. Morehouse

All rights reserved. This book or any portion thereof may not be reproduced, distributed, or transmitted in any form or by any means, including photocopying, recording, or other electronic or mechanical methods, without the prior written permission of the publisher, except in the case of brief quotations embodied in critical reviews and certain other noncommercial uses permitted by copyright law.

Cover photo: Ardyth and Egon, probably Christmas 1946.
All photos are from private family collections except as noted.

Cover design by Roberta Zeta

Publisher's Cataloging-in-Publication data:

Names: Kennelly, Ardyth, author. | Ullman, Egon V., author.
Title: Bodies adjacent : Ardyth's memoir & Egon's journal / by Ardyth Kennelly and Egon V. Ullman.
Description: Includes bibliographical references and index. | Portland, OR: Sunnycroft Books, 2023.
Identifiers: LCCN: 2023941526 | ISBN: 978-0-9904320-2-9 (paperback) | 978-0-9904320-3-6 (epub)
Subjects: LCSH Kennelly, Ardyth. | Ullman, Egon V. | Authors, American—20th century—Biography. | Marriage—Biography. | Physicians—Biography. | Austrian-Americans—Biography. | Jews—United States—Biography. | Portland (Or.)—Biography. | BISAC BIOGRAPHY & AUTOBIOGRAPHY / Personal memoirs
Classification: LCC PS3521.E5655 .B63 2023 | DDC 818/.5409—dc23

Library of Congress Control Number: 2023941526

SUNNYCROFT BOOKS
4110 SE Hawthorne Blvd. #749
Portland, Oregon 97214
www.sunnycroftbooks.com

Contents

Preface — page vii

Ardyth's Memoir, Part 1 — page 1

Egon's Journal — page 43

Ardyth's Memoir, Part 2 — page 147

Notes — page 187

Index of Names — page 223

Photos on pages 41 and 145

Preface

Ardyth Matilda Kennelly (1912–2005) was the author of five novels published between 1949 and 1956, including two best-sellers, and one published posthumously. In 1992, she wrote this poignant memoir—a love story, but also a eulogy and a lament—about her life with her second husband, the Austrian Jewish émigré Egon Victor Ullman (1894–1962). Egon had kept a record of their daily life on and off from 1947 to 1956, when Ardyth was writing and publishing her books, and she placed his journal in the middle of her memoir.

Ardyth's roots were in Salt Lake City, but she was born in tiny Glenada, Oregon, on the Siuslaw River near Florence. Her parents—James D. Kennelly from an Irish Catholic family and Lulu "Lula" Olsen from a Norwegian-Swedish Mormon family—returned to Utah when Ardyth was three years old. She grew up in Salt Lake City and Albany, Oregon; and except for a sojourn in New York City in 1963–64 and another in rural Polk County, Oregon, in 1969–72, she lived the rest of her life in Portland.

Ardyth began publishing poems and short stories at age fifteen. She gained national fame with her first novel, *The Peaceable Kingdom* (1949), which was based on the life of her maternal grandmother, Anna Olsen, a second wife in polygamy in late-nineteenth-century Utah. She also wrote *The Spur* (1951), a fictionalized account of the last days of John Wilkes Booth; *Good Morning, Young Lady* (1953), with a young heroine who meets the outlaw Butch Cassidy; *Up Home* (1955), a sequel to *The Peaceable Kingdom*; and *Marry Me, Carry Me* (1956), based probably on the early years of her mother's marriage. Her most ambitious book, written between 1977 and 1994 but not published until 2014, was *Variation West*, which follows four generations of a family in Utah against the background of the Mountain Meadows massacre of 1857.

Egon, an eye, ear, nose, and throat physician who was born in Vienna and graduated from the university there, had emigrated from Austria to Corvallis, Oregon, in 1926. He practiced as a physician and lectured at Oregon State College—where Ardyth was a student when he operated on her for a sinus infection in 1931. He moved his practice to Portland in 1932 and soon published a book, *Diet in Sinus Infections and Colds* (1933).

Ardyth moved from Albany to Portland in 1935 and married (for practical reasons) her friend Howard Scott Gibbs, while she and Egon began their affair. The following year, Egon published a book of poetry titled *Graver than Nonesuch*, dedicated "to her with whom I am gay"—no doubt Ardyth. After divorcing their respective spouses, the couple married on October 29, 1940.

Then followed two decades of life together—a life devoted to their shared love of books and passion for writing. Ardyth wrote the novels that brought her fame and some fortune, while Egon planned a book on the history of medicine and in 1954 published a biography of Albrecht von Graefe in the *American Journal of Ophthalmology*. He died suddenly on February 2, 1962.

Ardyth went to New York City to continue her writing career but returned to Portland after about two years, unable to find a publisher for her work. She developed a second career in the 1990s as a collage and mixed-media artist, and her strikingly original work commanded high prices at gallery showings. But even when stricken with partial blindness late in life, Ardyth never stopped writing.

*****

I want to express my thanks to Ardyth's sister Marion Kennelly Brownell (1915–2011) for preserving Ardyth's manuscripts and for sharing many memories with me; and to Marion's children—Michael Massee, Timothy Pettibone, and Ardyth Morehouse—for their unfailing support in the publication of their aunt's extraordinary work.

Nancy Trotic
Sunnycroft Books
September 2023

*Cold is active and transitive
into bodies adjacent,
as well as heat.*

— Francis Bacon

Ardyth's Memoir, Part 1

ON MARCH 2, 1962, I noted on its folder: EGON'S JOURNAL, 1947–1956. *Read by me one month to the day after his death. Can't stop crying. What could have possessed me not to know? This journal must be published someday.*

I don't know who I thought was going to carry out that order. I personally didn't expect to live long, we had no children, and I knew of no friends to put to such a proof. My mother, aged 80 in 1962, the same age I am now, couldn't have done it and wouldn't if she could. I was very bitter for quite a while that she would be the one to live (for four more years) and Egon be the one to die. How asinine that was of me. But for some unknown reason it just seemed like it had to be one or the other, him or her, as though they were the only two people left in the world.

When he collapsed that cold February afternoon in his office in the Kaiser Hospital and, despite the nearness of life-saving equipment and colleagues to work on him, died, and they came and got me, it seemed as if all the way there we were going under a hill or mountain or beneath the bed of a river, not on the open streets. It also seemed that I was under ordinance to render myself insensible to impression; why, I can't imagine. And even after returning home I stayed that way, as if cool itself was taking care of business.

Later I cried over the slightest thing. Too much stuff in the stores. A plane going over. The pointlessness. For weeks afterwards I would take Mother out to dinner and sit there in the booth and cry, and she hated it. I don't think she thought I ever really loved him, though she never said so. I think she thought that we had married him twenty-one years before this, in a manner of speaking—I at twenty-eight and she at fifty-eight and newly widowed—so we could be taken care of. And maybe that was partly true. Egon's age on our wedding day was forty-six, and I was pretty much taking him for granted by then as a young woman will an older man, especially if he has already been supporting her for several years.

Six, to be exact, during which his marriage went on as always and I myself did not stay single. His union was real, however, while mine was not. Mine, like the screen across the corner of my furnished room in front of a hot plate and dish cupboard, hid from view an association of occurrence, accident, and idea (begun in the air like mistletoe, then striking roots) more usually spoken of as "shacking up." As I use that now-quaint expression, I see that it implies not one but two grave offenses, sexual impurity and poverty. Adulterous conjunction in a *shack*. Whereas if terms like "castle-ing up" or "mansioning up" existed, only one transgression would come to mind, and that much tempered. Oscar Wilde would agree. He was the one who lived by the precept that "the man who calls a spade a spade should be compelled to use one"— which may have been one reason why on his deathbed he had hardly drawn his last breath when his body exploded with fluids from the ear, nose, mouth, and other orifices! and witnesses say the debris was appalling.

Some like to tell how as mere children the sound of a train whistle or a trumpeting circus elephant made them run away after adventure and the riches of the East. It was not like that with me. At twenty-two I was no more of a mind to leave the farm home in North Albany, Benton County, Oregon, that my kind stepfather had provided my mother, my younger sister Marion, and me for some twelve happy years than Sitting Bull was to trade the temperate zone for the frozen north. I had my own room up under the eaves, an old stove I could stuff with nice dry oak wood from the basement, hundred-watt light bulbs, an orange crate full of mostly textbooks (very good ones from three years of college), I could run downstairs for food, and I didn't even have to do any particular work.

This last perquisite was fairly recent. As a child I picked berries and hops and slid around on rotting leaves and mushy pericarps picking up knee-bruising walnuts; once I snipped beans in a cannery, and when I couldn't get out of it I helped about the house. But growing up and at the age of twenty selling a story to a New York magazine called *All-Story* for sixty dollars changed the entire vale of my life. From then on for the next two years, I was like a studio starlet on honorarium for some future explosion, some dazzling conversion into real fact; I was oxygen, hydrogen, carbon, and nitrogen waiting to combine into "vital properties." Or as

Emily Dickinson would have it, "Not what the stars have done, but what they still may do, is what upholds the sky!"

The only trouble was, all the upholding *I* was doing, upstairs reading from morning till night, either in the old Morris chair or piled up on my bed, or winding up and playing the old discarded phonograph, or out for a walk with sugar cubes in my pocket for the horses in the neighbors' fields, amounted to very little. And so it came about that the noiseless tenor of my days began to get noisier. Wasn't I supposed to be writing a book? *Riders of the Purple Sage*? *Girl of the Limberlost*? *Chickie*? Look at Ruby (my stepsister)—married, her own home, a job, a little boy. Marion (my sister)—engaged, working over in Albany in a beauty shop. Clarene and Freda (my cousins)—gone to Hollywood. Proust! if you want to cite an example, I didn't say, as I could see I had about reached my greatest heliocentric latitude. Then I did "a far, far better thing than I had ever done before." I packed.

THAT I REALLY WENT, stepped forth into the big wide Depression to seek my fortune in Portland without having to be pried loose from the doorjamb, was due in part to Marion bleaching my hair, the yellow she steeped into it going far to abstract the yellow from my belly, and in part to being able to get together thirty dollars. Helpful also was the news that my best friend Howard anticipated a move similar to mine as soon as his Albany job ran out, the Harris Tweed suit he had sent for arrived, and his waitress-sister and mother who cooked at the Elite Cafeteria agreed on a way of portioning out a few small loans to him while he set up in Portland as an artist.

And when I sorted through my stuff to see what to take with me, I found a forgotten announcement to the effect that Dr. Egon V. Ullman was moving his eye, ear, nose, and throat practice from Corvallis to Portland. The postmark on the envelope was two years old, but that was all right, he had probably gone through with the move and was still at the new address. Remember me, Doctor? You operated on me four years ago in the Corvallis General Hospital when I was a student at— I got your announcement. And as I too in recent days have pulled up stakes— Of course considering how much time has passed, you might well have— As Wordsworth said, "If Lucy should be dead!"—but I see you look just like yourself. So today as I was passing this building where you have your office, I thought—

Or not so much thought as went back in my mind to what a *rara avis* you really were down there in the heart of the valley, Doctor. As if Gloria Swanson's Count from that foreign land, instead of going to Hollywood to court Gloria, had landed in *Corvallis* and startled the town. No little mustache, no monocle or spats, but the accent, the dash, the luster of reputation! and didn't I see you making your rounds one morning (when I was your patient there in the hospital) in a *riding habit*? the first I ever saw in actual life. And how about the suppertime you looked in, in a *tuxedo*? going to the Portland Symphony's big concert at the college, the night nurse said, then to the private reception for the conductor? And how about Elissa Landi, the actress, that you met over in the old country? And while the Prince of Wales wasn't a *chum*, he did come to the clinic where you took your training to be a specialist, she told me that too. So as I was in the neighborhood, and as it is but human nature to aspire above rather than below one's station in—

I trended away. You can go into a store and say you're "just looking," but not a doctor's office. There you must have a reason. Actually, having been born with an eye condition called amblyopia ("lazy eye"), I *had* a reason but didn't know it, so I told myself it wasn't such a good idea anyway. Then as soon as I had decided that, why, here in front of me, within a display of books in J. K. Gill's window under a large placard on an easel saying BY OREGON AUTHORS, was the best reason in the world: a book called *Diet in Sinus Infections and Colds*, by Dr. Egon V. Ullmann! (What the others were I can't remember, some volumes of poetry? by Hazel Hall and Samuel L. Simpson,* *The White-Headed Eagle* by Richard G. Montgomery, *Desert Poems* by Ada Hastings Hedges, *A Short History of Oregon* by Dr. Horner? There weren't many Oregon authors then, not like the present day, when a vast patrician company, trying to bring order into the chaos of existence that otherwise would swallow them up in a maelstrom and carry them away without anybody knowing they ever lived—or for other reasons, including knowing how to run a word-processor—*write*.)

I ran into the store at once to inspect his book, published by Macmillan, second or third printing, then went running to his office, not to have him *autograph* it, for it did not occur to me to actually purchase a copy, but to *congratulate* him!

---

* My first Sunday in Portland I found out how to get out to the Lone Fir Cemetery on the streetcar and visited his grave. His poem "Beautiful Willamette," which we had to learn in grade school, I still loved after I grew up. And something just made me want to let him know I was here.

GREAT READERS, such as I have always been, feel about books the way the Mexican jumping bean feels about the dried seed-vessel he rattles around in. He is so attached to this veritable coffin that when given a chance to escape from it via a tiny window pricked out with a needle, he will not take it (as I found out when I once performed this good office) but will poke his head out, glare at the world, duck back down inside, and then with saliva or some other exudate seal up the opening *forever*. To great readers, one more book is one more brick to their ramparts, and that is why they can be fervent with an author even when they haven't read—or maybe even seen—what he's written! somewhat like Joan of Arc coming into contact with the King of France.

Was it a Thursday afternoon? I'm inclined to think so, as that is (or used to be) when doctors and dentists go shopping with their wives or play golf. Or did the economy or weather account for the fact that had I been a patient, I would have been the only one? Soon the office nurse stuck her head around the door and said she had finished and would be leaving now if that was all right. The shadows must have lengthened, the *Journal* clock struck . . .

My grandmother held one thing against my grandfather: he was a bragger. His whole family was like that, she said. Brag, brag, brag over nothing. And that afternoon, judging by the manner in which I went out of my way to mention the story I have already told you about that I sold for sixty dollars, and the page of poems and a story I had had printed (long before) in a Salt Lake City magazine called *The Improvement Era*, sponsored by the Mormon church and especially hospitable to contributors "of that ilk" (into which, willy-nilly, I was born, a third-generation Mormon), I was just like Grandpa. Braggadocio. But Egon looked pleased. Wonderful, he said.

The pursuit I was best at, reading, he also held in high esteem. And how glad I was as we talked on for the way I had traveled scrutinizingly through the textbooks in my orange crate and every other book I had been able to lay hands on during my sabbatical. Had he asked me, I could even have defined the word: a period of time during which you don't work your land, bill your debtors, commandeer your slaves, or do anything but devote yourself to the use and cultivation of reason.

But doing that and having it "take" are two different things, and as we walked, still deep in conversation, to a restaurant called the Oyster Loaf for dinner that early evening, I began to feel like an impostor who might be found out at any moment. What about roguish arithmetic? The subject matter of geography? All I could really locate in the world besides Oregon were England and France. And how about a foreign language? I knew a few phonetic expressions in Swedish, such as one meaning *ugh!* But music? Antiquity? Nothing. An aspersorium without a bottom, I hadn't read a single writer he quoted, could not pronounce *cum laude, editio princeps, trompe l'oeil,* and a million other indispensably requisite words. As we ate, I thought of the knight on horseback who, unawares, took off across frozen Lake Constance and when someone on the opposite shore said, "My God, man, you've crossed Lake Constance!" instantly fell dead of fright. But my case was different, I *knew* how thin the ice of my scholarship was! and expected to be engulfed at any moment.

But I wasn't, I got through dinner, even introduced my host to H. Phelps Putnam and Djuna Barnes, and as we left the restaurant and started for the apartment-hotel where he was living while his wife was in Europe, and where I would sit in the lobby and wait while he went up to his apartment to fetch a book called *The Enormous Land* by Arthur Schnitzler to lend me, I felt my sangfroid revive quite a bit. And by the time we set off on a little stroll up the Park Blocks to a seat in front of the Art Museum, I was as reboundant as Aldous Huxley in Hollywood when his *Encyclopedia Britannica,* which he had feared lost at sea, at last caught up with him.

LOOKING BACK, I can't see why I was so overjoyed that day to find an excuse to go running up to Egon's office. That is to say, in the light of my experience as his patient in the Corvallis hospital. For while it was fun to glimpse him there exotically going about his duties, contact with him had left much to be desired. He never made rounds without a nurse through whom he spoke like an Oracle through a drain pipe, and when patients spoke to *him,* what they said had to go back through the same conduit. But one day he appeared in my hospital doorway all by himself and said, "You write little stories." Temporarily bereft of the power of speech by this, I was marshaling my forces when I heard someone call to him from the corridor, he smiled, made as if to wave to me but didn't, then turned and was gone, leaving me limp.

The "little story" he had reference to would not be mentioned by either of us to the other in our lives again. And when remembrance of it—as I write this now—rose faint and dim, my first impulse was to repress it. But then I thought of E. M. Forster's pleading admonition to "only connect!" and thought I would try to do that, even if not for more than the *sake* of trying. My "little story" was written for an English Comp class and came out during my hospitalization (after a sinus operation) in a campus literary magazine called *The Manuscript*. What title I gave it I don't remember, or really what it was about, except that it took place in our neighborhood in Salt Lake City the year my father died, when I had just turned nine. But something in it I *do* remember and wish I didn't. And that is, that I put in, trying for "atmosphere" or I don't know what (for I seemed to be sure they had nothing to do with the story's datum), two little Jewish playmates that a bunch of us Mormon kids five or six to about eight years old, living in close proximity to the long-abandoned old municipal ball park, called Bertha Jew and Sarah Jew. "It's Bertha Jew's turn," we would screech out, or "Sarah Jew's turn!"—not to be hateful, but because like prehistoric children playing outside a bone-littered cave, we didn't know any better. And apparently the adults nearby who must have heard us didn't either, for nobody said a word. And the girls themselves, I hope, just considered the source.

But ten years later, when I wrote and put them in that "little story" Egon had reference to when he stood in my doorway, I wasn't a child anymore but eighteen years old, a college sophomore. And aesthetics, I fear, were not much involved. If my plot had been the old one of warring factions, in this case Mormons and Jews living in the same ghetto, hating each other, fighting, then growing to understand each other's differences and at last becoming friends, that would have been an excuse. But it was nothing like that at all, I didn't even know our locale was a ghetto. All I can think is that where habits of dismissal and discrimination run through the social and pietistic standards of where people live, it's like lead in the drinking water, a lot of the kids will grow up very dumb.

But *The Manuscript* was a college magazine, sponsored by the English Department and staffed by both student and faculty editors! Where was somebody's *blue pencil*? Did anyone's feelings get hurt?

And now to "only connect," if I can. Well—Bertha, Sarah, and Egon were all three Jews. Though raised as Egon was, being Jewish might not have seemed (though I found out later it did) such an actual fact to him as it did to them. In Salt Lake City, as is fairly well known, all non-Mormons of whatever persuasion are called Gentiles. So while Egon was stationed there at the airbase in World War II, that's what *he* was, which greatly amused him. I hope it amused Bertha and Sarah too, and that when we snotty Mormon kids called them Jew instead of Gentile, they just looked at each other and with their index finger next to their head made circles in the air.

THE YWCA HAD many conveniences, but before my week was out I moved to a furnished room in a once-handsome house on the Park Blocks. I didn't find a job but by degrees made sense of *The Enormous Land*, which turned out to be the human psyche, got my library card, and began to take out books, those Egon recommended but also others, developing in the process the stronger muscles Robinson Jeffers wrote that he did too when he carried stones for his tower. I turned, dog-eared, got peanut butter and honey, candle wax and lipstick on pages, collected words, and copied into a commonplace book such notions as Hobbes's "All evidence is conception, all conception is imagination and everything proceeds from sense," which I would try to grasp till sometimes when I stood up quickly I would almost faint, like a giraffe.

And the more my feebler, unruly mind became acquainted with Egon's strong and well-trained intellect, the more I would have jumped at the chance if he had asked me to go to Australia with him, the way the Professor asked Rita in the movie *Educating Rita*. But come to think of it, he *did* ask me and I *did* go, figuratively speaking, for many years. And did I come back educated? I came back like Rip Van Winkle down from the Catskills. You know how brilliant that was. What is education? Lafcadio Hearn said it is *what is left* after everything you have learned has dissipated into air. But say it never *does* dissipate, never *does* fuse or melt, so the gold is never extracted? What shall you do then? The next best thing is to quote, my dear, like sitting down when you are tired. Once in Altman's department store Emily Post, fatigued by shopping and unable to find a chair, sat down on the floor with her legs stretched out in front of her and her packages to either side, and sat there, too imperious to be challenged, till she was ready to get up again. Quoting is like that. A chair trundled up. Won't you sit down? Thank you, I think I shall, just here on a remark by William James to the effect that "experience is the state of having been occupied in the intercourse of life."

Ardyth's Memoir, Part 1

ON THE NIGHT WE occupied ourselves with both, intercourse *of* life and also for the first time with each other, it just so happened that Governor Huey Long of Louisiana was assassinated. When events take place together like that, and when on the same occasion even *more* first-time incidents coincide—tasting lobster in a dining room with classical musicians playing, and going to bed in a beautiful nightgown—it fixes the date, makes it red-letter, and one of these days I'm going to call the library and ask when Huey Long really did die by treacherous violence so I will know. It was a nightgown pretty enough for Mae Murray, and I took it into the bathroom and closed and locked the door, decorous in manner and conduct, as most young women were in those days, until in the process of putting it on I discovered I had broken out with red spots all over my body. Then I burst forth.

Egon put out his cigarette, calmly put on his glasses, inspected me, and said, "Have you ever before had such efflorescences?" I never had, but said I had a cousin who broke out in tomato season. When he determined that measles, allergy to lobster, and neurasthenia were probably what he called "quantités négligeables" and that my act of the late afternoon, shaving under my arms and immediately putting on a deodorant called Mum, which he insisted on being told about, was probably what had caused the reaction, he rolled his eyes up, shrugged, and said, "Americans." Then, very gently and kindly, "My child. Do not pay attention to advertising."

What time of the day or night Governor Long was shot I can't say, but it was late at night when we heard a paper boy calling EXTRA!!! through the Park Blocks, and Egon quickly threw on his clothes and ran out and bought a paper. When he came back, he sat down and smoked and read about what had happened. Deplorable, he said, but he also thought that Governor Long, if he had gone on long enough, might have become another Mussolini. I didn't know whether he would or not. I liked him. In the newsreels he looked like a handsomer and smarter Babe Ruth in civilian clothes, laughing and joking around. But he would turn serious, too, about the hardness of fate and circumstance on the poor, and that was a good trait in my eyes.

We had our first discussion about politics that night and found out we were both Democrats, but also that just to vote candidates into office was enough, we didn't want to go into it too much. As time went on, though, he would have to, discussing world politics and every other kind with the refugees from Austria and Germany who started coming, and I would be so proud to hear him, like the old Swedish woman who didn't know any English but when Brigham Young spoke, said in Swedish, "Oh, how beautiful that sounds!"

Poor Huey Long! and the hardness of fate and circumstance on *him*. Forever will his sad end be tied in with the other things I've mentioned, making the night they all took place together different from any other night that ever was, and somehow making "shacking up" different, too, from what I always supposed, and more like something nearly out of opera.

DUE TO THE ELITE RESTAURANT keeping him on as counterman for a month after they fired him, Howard couldn't get started on his career as soon as he planned, but he didn't mind, he'd have had to wait for his Harris Tweed in any case. Finally it came, and here he was in Portland, too hot in the suit because of the unusually warm autumn but looking splendid in it, and the rest of his outfit too, and the first thing I said to him when I saw him was that I had so much to tell him that if he hadn't come now, I'd have probably burst.

As high school freshmen, I think Howard and I recognized each other as fellow spirits, but what I would call our *fraternal* friendship only began when we rode back and forth to Oregon State together from our homes in Albany and North Albany with three other kids, at a cost per rider of eight dollars a month. We spent a lot of time together then, waiting around for everyone to show up, eating our lunches in the car, taking strolls on the campus, often skipping school on Friday afternoons to go to the matinee at the Whiteside theater. Having spent a lot of his life in the company of his mother, his sister, and the waitresses who sometimes roomed with them, Howard was easy to be with, you could just say whatever came into your head and it would sound all right.

We told each other what we wanted to be. I used to say a librarian (but that wasn't so, my actual life's ambition was never to work), and he wanted to paint like the greatest painters, such as George Inness. We also admired the gangsters of those days, "Schemer" Drucci, Dutch Schultz, Pretty Boy Floyd, and I think wished we could be gangsters ourselves. I'm sure I told him what I hated about my looks, and one day he told me there was something about himself that just made him sick but he didn't know what to do about it, and that was his eyebrows, which were plucked. Oh, come on, I said, because when I looked at them, they weren't in a thin line or anything like that, which the pain in his voice would make you think.

Across the bridge of his nose, though, where wild hairs usually grow, there weren't any, that space was cleared and smooth. The brows themselves were slightly shaped, too—not terribly, but enough to take any boy who had eyebrows like that out of the all-boy category. I was sort of startled. Still, I couldn't see why they would bother him so much, especially when all he had to do to remedy the situation was to let them grow back in. But he said he couldn't do that. He had been trying since the previous summer, but every time they started to grow in, bristly and going in every direction, he couldn't stand it, he had to pull them out. Well, I said, to comfort him, for I could see he really felt terrible about it, they're not conspicuous. Why, if you hadn't mentioned them, I wouldn't even have *noticed*. (And that was true; young girls only pay attention to themselves.) Now, however, I did notice surreptitiously, and saw that a pattern seemed to be fixed. The bridge of his nose stayed smooth, his eyebrows stayed slightly shaped. And they stayed exactly like that for the rest of his life.

I have said we often skipped school on Friday afternoons and went to the matinee, and once we saw a movie called *The Wet Parade*. It was about an alcoholic father, an abused mother, and a young son (Robert Young; it must have been one of the first pictures he ever made), I think the father finally killed the mother. It was very tragic. I could see out of the corner of my eye that Howard was crying, and when it was over and the lights came on, he said for us to just stay where we were till the theater emptied, he didn't want anyone to see him with his eyes all swollen and red. We took a side street up to the campus parking lot and walked slow, so as to let the hour get later and the kids we rode with less apt to notice. I had cried, too, but not like him, and he said it hit so close to home that he could hardly bear it. His dad drank like the father in the movie, he said, "and he gets mean and awful and—disgusting—and he forces himself on my mother, and sometimes I could just kill him!" I said something sympathetic like, Gee. But what he had said didn't mean all that much to me, we never spoke of it again, and it was years before I realized that "forces himself on my mother" must have meant sexually, and that that might have had something to do with how Howard was.

What that way was, was as if Sex didn't exist, but that was not unusual in the early thirties. Pretending it didn't was one of the earmarks of respectability. The word "sex" was considered as nasty as any word you could think of. The expression "to *have* sex" hadn't even been invented, I don't believe, and any behavior deviating from heterosexuality or from the "missionary position" during close encounters of the first kind was thought perverted by most of society and labeled pathological by much of the medical profession. Howard and I never discussed anything physical, we cloaked in euphemisms even finding a restroom, and as much as we could acted like disembodied spirits. Of finances, our lack of them, we could speak freely; I would pay my half for the movies we went to and the big Mr. Goodbars we bought to eat while we watched Marlene Dietrich and Gary Cooper in *Morocco*, Lawrence Tibbett and Lupe Vélez in *The Cuban Love Song*, Norma Shearer in *Private Lives*, and others too numerous to mention. We talked movies the way the Lake Poets talked poetry, as though the Desiderium of all nations had come.

I couldn't go to college for what would have been my senior year, and Howard couldn't either. But as he lived in Linn County while I lived across the river in Benton, we didn't see each other much for the two years we both "laid around the house," as it was called locally, except once in a while we would meet halfway and go for a walk. We talked a lot on the phone, though, almost every day, and when we saw each other in Portland, it was as if we had just been to a matinee or had a class together the hour before. After we shook hands, what we did was go and have coffee at Jack Cody's restaurant (your own coffee pot, the height of elegance and sophistication), I heard about the housekeeping room he had rented two blocks from the Portland Hotel, his art, and how he had saved up for his Harris Tweed suit, and he heard everything about me. I was just *dying* to tell.

WHEN EGON SAW my room for the first time, with the high ceilings and closed-off fireplace and the wallpapered partitions standing around, he said it looked just like a set for *Mademoiselle Modiste*. And when Howard saw it and I told him what Egon had said, he said he bet it did, the partitions looked like big hat-boxes standing around. He loved it, but he said he liked his room better, it had a wonderful north light and mine didn't, but of course I didn't need a north light. We had lots to catch up on, more than I even told him, for I was thinking of something in the back of my mind that I didn't want to broach too soon and maybe put the kibosh on. Does that sound suspicious? like bats among birds that ever fly by twilight?

By this time several weeks had passed; I wouldn't say I was used to Egon, but I felt calm with him, like Dr. Aziz in *A Passage to India* with his first true English friend, Mr. Fielding. Beyond that, however, our state of feeling with regard to each other was such that it manifested itself in warm attachment, and when I found out what a bother the prevention of uterine conception was and how liable to demonstrate that even if Hobbes said so, all conception was *not* imagination, it occurred to me that it might be the better part of valor to get married. Not to Egon, of course, for as I say, he was already married (and his wife would soon be returning), but to Howard, if I could get him to do it. He knew all about Egon and me, even to the rash I had broken out with on the night Huey Long was assassinated. But having heard many tales of woe from his sister and her chums about men being such rats and getting what they want and then you never hear from them again, he could hardly believe I was getting my rent paid and everything. Not that we were talking great sums, but as he said, a lot of girls didn't even get a phone call. So I was lucky, but it could end any minute, like *Back Street*. I didn't think it was going to, though; something told me it would last a long time. And that, I told Howard, was why I wanted to marry *him*.

Did I tell him that? I can't remember the wording, can't recall how I broached the subject, if he was shocked, aghast, fell back gasping or what. I am sure I gave him a list of reasons why he couldn't do himself more of a favor. It wouldn't cost anything, would make him more interesting, insure his staying footloose, he would always have drawer and closet space, he could keep his own hours, wouldn't have to talk if he didn't want to, would never have to pay somebody else's bills. Besides, I might have said, although most great artists prefer to stay single, when you're talking about *our* class—I wouldn't have said working class, redneck, proletarian, for such a designation would have nearly killed him—after a certain age, unless you have an iron-clad reason, such as being your family's sole support, if you stay single you become a nuisance, people ask questions, you're more of a detriment than an asset, whereas if you get married, all those problems are solved. I may also have mentioned that I once heard him say he was never going to get married. So if that was the case, the best thing he could do to be *sure* he never would was to marry me. Then if a girl proposed, he could say, in the words of the old song,

> *I can't get away*
> *To marry you today,*
> *My wife won't let me!*

I'm not sure I said any of that precisely, but that would have been the gist.

"And besides, Howard dear," I could have said but don't think I did, "you're so picky and critical, you never could find anybody to suit you anyway."

That observation I based on the way he dealt with the movie actresses. No matter how beautiful they might be, there was always something wrong. Gloria Swanson had that snouty nose. Jeanette MacDonald had too big a chin. Marlene Dietrich's forehead was too high. Norma Shearer had little eyes. Greta Garbo's lips were too thin. Marion Davies had poor teeth. Clara Bow's neck was too short. He confined himself to the movie population, for which I was very glad, as I would have hated to have him start in on me, and he never said a derogatory word about his plain sister and her friends. But the movie stars got both barrels and there was no appeal.

I DON'T REMEMBER HIM accepting my proposal in so many words, but when the time came, as it seemed to do in no great while, there he was, there *we* were in front of a one-eyed minister in a church parlor with a three-footed upright piano (books were stacked in under the corner where the fourth foot should have been) getting married. Such marriages, I understand, are called "white" marriages and are, and have been from time immemorial, entered into all over the world. But not knowing ordure from Shinola, as the saying goes, I honestly thought I invented it. I also didn't know Howard was a homosexual. That is God's truth. Having run across Oscar Wilde's lamentable story in my reading, I knew there was such a thing as certain individuals only liking their own sex, especially when their own sex was young, thin, blond, petulant, rich, and an English lord, but the implication seemed to be that after Oscar served his sentence in Reading Gaol for sodomitical behavior and went over to Dieppe and Paris and points south to die, that kind of put a stop to the whole business. It was like some crazy invention that just didn't make it and was taken off the market.

Now, when we know so much about sex and its adjuncts, it really seems strange to say that though I knew him so well, with respect to Howard I was like Martin Eden with his ethereal girlfriend. Martin just couldn't imagine her on a chamber utensil, and if I had ever thought of doing such a thing, which of course I never did, I couldn't have imagined *Howard* on one either. He was rather large and tried to maintain a tan. But buttoned into his ROTC uniform, which Oregon State boys had to wear once a week, he would suddenly become as pale and fragile as Aubrey Beardsley about to die of TB. He hated sports, perspiration, and getting his hands dirty, and loved movies, magazines—the kind beauty shops subscribe to—bands like Paul Whiteman's and Ferde Grofé's, the Book of the Month, "cultural" radio programs, and trifling rumors from New York or Hollywood, all these matters being what we mostly talked about. But I saw no reason why these preferences should keep him from having the appropriate excellences of the usual male. In the Depression, his never taking a girl out on a date was not so unusual, especially as his sights were set so high.

From what I told a somewhat bemused Egon about Howard a few days before my marriage, which was everything I knew about him up until that time, I am sure he surmised that he was not a particularly heterosexual person. But he didn't say so, or tell me any of the things which would soon come out in books like *Goodbye to Berlin* and which he, as a doctor and generic European, must surely have seen or known himself, firsthand, about "different" styles of getting through the night. And as questions to ask didn't seem to occur to me, the subject of Howard was disposed of quite quickly.

But wouldn't you think Egon would have felt some disquiet in the face of such machinations? Not at all. Curiously dreamy, he saw me go earnestly ahead, like Thomas Ferguson inventing the buttonhook. And when he came up to the Multnomah Hotel to the room I had taken for just that one night under my new married name, Mrs. Howard Scott Gibbs, and spent my wedding night with me, perhaps he wasn't in Portland anymore but back where he came from, Vienna, in a vain, empty, unsubstantial play by von Hoffmannsthal or Schnitzler. I didn't have the sense to know it then—he was so almost Rotarian about America, so proud of having left Austria *before* Hitler, so quick to disparage his old life—but of all the expatriates, he was the one who most embodied

Vienna. *Die Fledermaus, Der Rosenkavalier, Anatol*—he was any one and all of them personified. And I guess that was why when I intrigued myself and my old friend Howard into a phony marriage, instead of looking askance, Egon was as carried away as only a wry, sportive, cynical Viennese in a tight little Viennese suit and gold watch chain and handmade wingtips from a shop along the Ringstrasse could be. And don't forget the cigarette holder. And the fedora.

WHERE HOWARD SPENT our wedding night I don't know, but I think by himself in his new quarters, listening to the little Philco radio he brought from home. I could be wrong. He never told his relatives how the land really lay. I'm sure of that because one afternoon many years later, long after Egon and I were married, Howard's mother, Mrs. Gibbs, came and had coffee. And while Mother was in the kitchen, Mrs. Gibbs said she'd always been so sorry that things hadn't worked out for Howard and me. "But I always laid that to the Depression," she said. "I always thought you kids would have made it if it hadn't been for that." She was a sweet woman. I felt so sad and ashamed I didn't know what to say. I could have cried, really. But all I did was nod and look away.

I never told anyone how the land really lay, either.

And now look.

Robert Frost's old Witch of Coös did somewhat the same thing as I'm doing now the night a traveler sought shelter with her and her elderly son. As the three sat by the fire, she blabbed secrets the family had kept for forty years—of murder, of a grave in the cellar, of the skeleton that tried to come upstairs but she knocked it back down, striking its hand off—she saw one of the finger bones in her button box just the other day— Her son tried to shut her up, but she wouldn't stop. It was all so long ago! she said. So silly. "I don't remember why we ever cared."

Anyway, Howard didn't make much use of his north light. By the next summer he had moved to San Francisco, where I imagine he could let himself be his true self—the parfit gentle knight he was meant to be, studious, courteous, generous, and gay. Whenever he came north to visit his folks, he usually dropped in on us, and in fact early in Egon's journal he makes mention of the fact that we have seen him. After Egon died, we stayed in touch. Howard never married again, had some success as an artist but more as a bartender for many years in the renowned Palace Hotel.

He acquired a house, lived a romantic life, and died at the age of about seventy on a trip to Marrakesh, where on instructions from his sister he was buried. I was sorry to hear that, as I heard him say more than once that he wanted to be buried beside his mother in the old pioneer graveyard in Peoria, Oregon.

E. M. FORSTER WAS on the right track. Once you try "only connecting," there's considerable satisfaction in it. But I do have to say it's easier said than done. Take what I would like to do now: contrast another couple with Egon and me, hoping with a little mythology to represent an equation identical in certain coordinates—though a hundred years apart—with us.

First, the other couple.

When the Hudson's Bay Company moved from Astoria to a spot up the Columbia not then called Vancouver but soon to be, they left their old station open as an aid to navigation until further notice, and in charge of one man, a clerk by the name of Mountstuart Elphinstone. A "younger son," like many another adventurer, this young Englishman had asked for the job, hoping that the isolation would throw his life into a fresh perspective, and the stillness (after the exodus of bluff company men, hunters, traders, French voyageurs, a small body of redcoats, and all but a few Clatsop Indian servants) would spur him on to some propitious thinking. With duties to perform, letters to write, a diary to keep up, a spyglass, a shelf of books, and of course the interesting flora and fauna of the region to examine, he did not fear low spirits or ennui until he noticed a few weeks later that the substance of most of his propitious thinking was going towards how to kill himself without disgracing his ancient name.

Then one day a party of Siuslaw Indians arrived at the fort with baskets and a carved canoe for barter with the Hudson's Bay Company. Apprised in a speech by Mountstuart in Chinook Jargon, in which he was not very fluent, of the company's move, then given directions as to how to get to the new location by the Clatsops, whom he summoned for that purpose to his side, the Siuslaws, after warming themselves briefly at a bonfire and eating a few handfuls of something from the rush vessels the women carried, went on. All except one member of the party. Dressed in deerskin and a tule rain cape and wearing a tule hat adorned with a pileated woodpecker's topknot, she seated herself on a stump in front of the fort and—waited. No one noticed her, the Clatsops smoking and gambling behind the building, or Mountstuart being dull and dejected in his quarters.

Why did she stay? The site was a forsaken one. Impetuous love? When Mountstuart Elphinstone came out to speak to her party, did she view him "with a wild surmise," like Vivien Leigh first seeing Rhett Butler? Was she coming down with something? In a snit with relatives?

It is easy to be in a snit with relatives. Many may be lintheads, and others possess a nerve one would hate to have in a tooth. Perhaps that very morning a cousin had said to her, "You know, Tupso"—that was the girl's name, Tupso—"the shamans have discovered that what we call 'intelligence' is really seven or eight different *kinds* of intelligence, spatial, mathematical, verbal, mechanical, kinetic, and so on, and since you have only one, the kind needed to tell stories and sing songs around the campfire, why, you are not, as the tribe seems to think, intelligent at all! In fact, you are basically a moron."

Thank you, dear. A cheerful companion shortens the miles.

Was she tired? Like Emily Post that time in Altman's?

Harassed by a warrior standing on her moccasins? Tearing her beech-bark underbodice?

When Mountstuart came out, as was his wont, to step up onto the very stump she was sitting on to watch the sunset and make himself feel worse, he was surprised to see her. "Madam, may I inquire what you are doing here?" he said, fixing on her a searching gaze. A Clatsop's visage may have looked to him like a chocolate-chip cookie, but *born on the Sabbath day* said this Siuslaw face. She told him what she was doing, but he didn't understand her. Then he told her what *he* was doing, which was suddenly feeling lighter and gayer than he had for weeks and requesting the pleasure of her company inside the fort to supper, but she didn't understand him. However, they talked some more and pretty soon, as miraculously as Cuchulain in a blinding flash able to translate the blackbird's song and Helen Keller all of a sudden empowered to grasp the meaning of the word "water," they knew perfectly what each other was saying. And soon after that they became a couple. They "shacked up."

Mountstuart, anxious to fix once more the identity his exile had diffused and refer himself again to his proper species, taught Tupso comparative grammar and shared with her what he knew of the "trade" language of the area, a hybrid speech of English and

French terms built upon words spoken by the Chinook and other tribes, the better for him and her to hold intercourse. When the insufficiency of both English and the Jargon weighed on him like a scorching day, he would plunge into the cool dialect of his hierarchically ordered social class and Tupso would wait for him on the bank, reproaching him with silence for abstractions far beyond her, such as primogeniture, rank, function, damned outrage, office, estate, and attainment. Then he would return to the light, familiar chat she liked best and say whatever came into his head, such as that Euripides had said that "the first requisite to happiness is that a man be born in a famous city." To explain "famous" and "city" took time, but when he felt she understood, he told her that he himself had been born in famous London, *such* a city and *so* famous that in medieval days if a bondman "attached to the soil" could get away, reach London, and live there for one year, he was a free man! "Free" took some defining, and when he said that a free *serf* was a free man but that a free *younger son* was an oxymoron, Tupso sighed with exasperation.

"I was *ten times* as smart as he was," Mountstuart said. "Why, at Oxford—" Thinking out loud, remembering, he would not take time to tell her what things *were*—Balliol, Greats, Sent Down—or Service in Orange that got his father's father's father endowed with estate and title by an English king who couldn't speak a word of English! "So don't despair, my dear. And now two words that sound alike. Signet. In ring. And cygnet. Baby swan. 'So doth the swan her downy cygnets save!' Fairholme was our country house in Sussex. That's where we had the swans. And we had— Well, no matter. When I came away, it was from London. 'Dear God! the very houses seem asleep. And all that mighty heart is lying still...' At daybreak when we started out for Wapping, I thought—oh, God! Will I ever see it again?"

WHETHER IT WAS THE first requisite to happiness for a *girl* to be born in a famous city Euripides did not say, but Tupso was happy enough to be born where she was, in the deep dark Siuslaw forest. Trees there (smelling like cedar chests and Christmas Night and eucalyptus globulus) rose up off the forest floor and kept on going, some so big around that twelve little Indians holding hands couldn't reach around them or skip within their undergrowth of manzanita, salal, thimbleberries, ferns, and rotting logs (asleep in lycopods and moss) that once were part of templed majesty. The sun never did get through in certain places to the surface of the ground, so under your feet it squished like a spilled-on shag carpet. Footpaths ran where they wanted, where the deer decided, and humans came afterwards to chop back boughs and branches, break off sprays of leaves, and tramp down brushwood along those ways and locate close at hand their villages, small as a musquash town, four or five cedar longhouses, thirty or forty people, everyone related to everyone else.

Forest clans were as different in many ways from other Indian tribes as the materialist from him who thinks all things exist but as ideas in the seat of consciousness. Beginnings meant little to them, the calling into existence of the world, the reason for being alive, they would have been a big disappointment to Joseph Campbell. *When* things happened did not interest them, only the event, the hills catching on fire, the Siuslaw in flood, news from the dunes of a beached whale. But to think today of how they were and believed is to little purpose, they are all gone now, shadows as they were amongst the trees. The deer decided to stay, but not with the old assurance anymore of sole possessors of the property, more like the homeless on our city streets, nervous and ill at ease. And of course the ghosts did not go elsewhere and can be glimpsed sometimes against the vacant rain . . .

THE COLOR OF TUPSO'S irises and pupils were the same, coal black, running into each other as she listened.

"I never thought it was so bad to kill the King of France!"

Oh, no. The King of France? Was very good.

"The swan, my dear, in classical mythology was sacred to Apollo and Venus. And as I started to say—at Fairholme— Cruel and frowning universe! Untenable life! Why should the swans and everything belong to *him*? Oh, I beg you, listen. Or I shall die."

I do, I listen. What do you want from me?

SHE DID, SHE LISTENED, and like me, like any forest dryad, understood that understanding was a multitude of mixed solemnities. I say "forest dryad" in a joking way. But it's a fact that *I* also started life in the Siuslaw woods, probably not fifty feet from the longhouse where Tupso was born. It was still a wilderness, but the part down close to the Siuslaw, where you could look across the river and see the little town of Florence, Oregon, thought of itself as enough of an entity to have a name. And so it had one, the founder's oldest children's names, Glen and Ada, put together to make GLENADA. I brought Glenada's population up to 117, and if the *Titanic* had not gone down the very night I was born, taking up the whole front page and almost the whole next edition of the *Florence Gazette*, I am sure that fact would have been given prominence.

Glenada was a town, all right. Just deeper in the woods than Florence, that's all, and a little more lost, and no such thing upon it as a piece of ground bounded by four streets. But a wagon road went through it, it had clearings, chimneys with smoke coming out, good clotheslines, coal-oil lamps, and people didn't just run out into the woods, they had privies, with patterns cut out high enough so that if a hobo (as unlikely as a gryphon) or a bear came by, they couldn't rare up and look in through the star shapes or the crescent moon. I didn't stay in Glenada long enough for me to learn to use our privy. By the time I was six months old my folks, "city people" as they considered themselves, born and raised in Salt Lake City, had pulled up stakes and left, never again to live in the wilds.

Nevertheless, for the purpose of "only connecting," I am going to consider Tupso and myself to be sisters under the skin, two Siuslaw girls about on a par with one another. Or on a par when you think who we "shacked up" with, Tupso with her London-born, Oxford-educated, displaced Mountstuart Elphinstone, me with my Vienna-born, University of Vienna–educated, displaced Egon Victor Ullman. I don't say the two displacements were the same. The Englishman's elder brother inheriting all the family's wealth and holdings, even the swans, was what had stuck in Mountstuart's craw, while what had stuck in Egon's— But when I went to match our talk, or Egon's and my talk when we first knew each other, with the couple's a hundred years earlier, I realized that when Mountstuart begged Tupso to understand him, it was with *words*, while Egon begged me with *silence*.

I don't mean we didn't converse, I just mean we were like the people in T. S. Eliot's poem who would "come and go, talking of Michelangelo." We talked books, talked about the trivial round, the common task, that *day*, Egon being for a long time the way I imagine state's witnesses resettled by the CIA or FBI must be. No past, like Adam. But I was like that too, as though ignorance and poverty and not being as good-looking as one was obliged to be were old crimes to be kept from sight. And all these years later, I think I know what Egon had to hide: the scar that anti-semitism in

Vienna, even *before* Hitler, had left on him. The *surprise* of his wounds! I could be wrong, but all during the Hitler years, with the refugees arriving here, with all that was in the papers and on the radio, why did he never act as if it had anything to do with him? I don't mean he pretended to be a *Gentile*. Or that he didn't pitch in and help his fellow Jews. He did, in every way he could. But standing apart and, if you will pardon the big long word, desynonymized. It was really strange.

TUPSO PROBABLY FOUND out a lot more about Mountstuart than she ever knew she did. Of course if she lived long enough, lived to be eighty— Things gradually dawn on a person. The half-settled phrase, the partially located proper name, the barely grasped revelation, remembered for how it sounded, not for what it said, as the years go on stand clear, as when a fog lifts and you can say, yes, that meant *that*. When Tupso heard about London and its wonders, no doubt partly in sign language and maybe by means of a triangulated map drawn in the dirt with a stick, and I heard about Vienna, which I somehow missed seeing and hearing even the *name* of in grammar-school geography, we both probably thought the same thing: big deal. For just as the sun couldn't get through to Tupso's and my Siuslaw forest floor, so the meaning of famous cities and famous cultures couldn't get through to the matted growth of the fallow-land of our minds.

History tells us that Pocahontas got to go to London but never came back, because she took sick and died and was buried over there. Tupso didn't get to travel. When the Hudson's Bay Company closed the Astoria station, which they did within the year (the navigation thereabouts having become of more interest to the encroaching Americans than to the English), and ordered Mountstuart Elphinstone to report to headquarters in Vancouver, he took her with him. And that is all we know. But it is not beyond the bounds of reason to think they may have grown old together, considering how soon that happened in those days.

I missed out on travel, too. I don't know if our lives would have been different if I'd seen where Egon was raised and met his folks. He met mine, but that was the same as if Mountstuart had met Tupso's fellow tribesmen. Fine, honey, but let them camp out in back. That would be the older contingent, the ones like apple dolls. Our younger generations have been to colleges and on exchange scholarships all over the known world, they run computers, cars, planes, boats, businesses, races, there are no flies on them.

I ONCE SAW AN interesting documentary on PBS. It was about sleep. Scientists from Johns Hopkins and elsewhere, and in Europe, were finally going to solve the mystery of why we sleep. The studies went on for years, volunteers grew gray hooked up to machines and sleeping with the light on, records piled up of the spasmodic movements under dreamers' eyelids, graphs accumulated, systems of chemical and mathematical tie-ups, curves of equation, variations. At last it was done. Each scientist was asked to sum up his work. Finally there was just one man left to interview, in Scotland I believe it was, a renowned worker in the field, and the interviewer said to him, "And now, sir, do you feel that after all this work has been done, we know why we sleep?" The scientist looked at him for a long moment and then he said, "My dear chap, we don't even know *why we are awake.*"

I have mentioned that study to different ones, and when I get to the part about how we don't even know why we are awake, they can't stand it. "Why, of course we know!" they say crossly. And some act really angry and say, "That's crazy."

SINCE I STARTED these pages, one reason *I'm* awake is to fly backwards, like the gooney bird, and see the past, especially Egon under the vagaries, trials, and tribulations of an existence I had so little understanding of. Now that it's too late, after the horse has been stolen, so to speak, and when I could as easily make the *amende honorable* to our old duplex as to him, I read books, I look at pictures, I bought a Rand McNally VideoTrip Guide to Vienna and went on a sightseeing tour, fifty minutes running time. But the fiacre with the matched greys and the coachman didn't traverse the right *strasses* or *gasses*, and the guide, disembodied like the voice in the ear of a holy fool, didn't point out the right landmarks. Mostly I wanted to see where Egon lived, but I had my eye peeled for a few other prominent objects in the townscape as well, such as:

"The most beautiful insane asylum in the world!" the Empress Elisabeth said when her doting husband asked her what she wanted for her birthday. Started the next day, it took ten years to build and decorate, and she had been in her grave (stabbed to death by an assassin) almost that long herself by that time. But St. Leopold on the Steinhof, the most ravishing monument to madness ever built, would have been a perfect present for Her Beautiful Majesty, especially since her profound melancholy, hysteria, narcissism, and anorexia would have made her as eligible for admission as any mental case in Vienna.

"Heartbreak Hotel!" I and many others would say was our favorite Elvis song. And as a *real* Heartbreak Hotel (Herzeleide Haus) actually exists in Vienna, the least the Rand McNally VideoTrip could do for us American tourists would be to take us past it. There the brilliant young philosopher and author of *Sex and Character*, Otto Weininger, killed himself at age twenty-three. But the place was already called Heartbreak Hotel when he moved in.

"Kornhäusel's Synagogue!" you can say to refute the physicist who insists that "what the eye doesn't see and the mind doesn't know, doesn't exist." Because, listen. When Joseph II (the monarch you saw in the movie *Amadeus*) was Emperor of the Austro-Hungarian Empire, the Jewish community in Vienna went to him to ask to be allowed to build a synagogue. "Of course," he said. He was very tolerant. "But there are rules. Your synagogue can't stand off to itself like an architectural structure. It has to be concealed from the street. And a big residential building has to be built in front of it." The brilliant architect Kornhäusel took the commission, followed the game rules, did a great job, and as soon as the Jews figured out how to bypass the building he put up in *front* of it, how to get into a position to *see* it, and then how to get *into* their synagogue, they were delighted. And the Gentiles were delighted, too, because "what the eye doesn't see and the mind doesn't know, doesn't exist." Not.

"The Sühnhaus!" Sigmund Freud said when the cabinet-maker asked where to deliver the new cradle. The cabinet-maker may have drawn back in awe and superstition when he heard the name, as the Sühnhaus, meaning House of Atonement, an apartment building, had just been built on the tragic spot where the Ring Theater used to stand before it burned down a few years earlier, killing hundreds of people. The new building would exorcise the spot, His Majesty thought, but folks were leery of moving in until word went round that several Excellencies would be dwelling there. Dr. and Mrs. Sigmund Freud signed up early, and their first child (and the building's first baby) was born in their apartment a few weeks after they settled in, prompting the Emperor to pen a note of congratulation for bringing *life* into the world where *death* had once triumphed. But the child was hardly out of swaddling clothes when the Emperor raised the rent and the Freuds moved out. Otherwise, psychoanalysis might have been born at the Sühnhaus, too.

IN THE EARLY 1920s, it became sort of a fad for general practitioners from the United States to travel to the great European centers for six-week courses in the medical "specialties" at the renowned universities and clinics. These courses were expensive, but the certificate the American doctor received at the end, to frame and hang up in his office, more than paid for itself over time. Egon taught a course in ophthalmology to some of these doctors, and in 1925 one of his "pupils" was a Dr. William Johnson from Corvallis, Oregon. Before long, Dr. Johnson had become a personal friend, the wives met and liked each other, and soon emigration and a partnership for Egon in Dr. Johnson's Corvallis clinic were being talked of. Then an agreement of sorts was come to, and when Dr. Johnson returned home, he initiated the course of action which after almost two years resulted in Egon and his wife coming to America.

The Rand McNally VideoTrip guide to Vienna leaves much to be desired. Never did I get to see the Baroque apartment house where Egon was raised. When he got married, he moved, of course, but his folks still lived there, and that would have been the last place he went before leaving, to tell them goodbye. If we could have driven past there, I'd have thought of that, his coming out and just standing there looking up and down the street and wondering if he would ever see any of it again and what was going to happen. Then a fiacre would drive up, maybe the very one (for it looked very old) that I got out of when the fifty minutes' running time of the VideoTrip was up, he would get in and tell the driver, "To the station."

VIENNA WAS STILL beautiful in late 1926 when Egon set forth, still civilization's most important repository of art, architecture, science, and learning, still a capital, though no longer called by anyone "the most gilded, Baroque, and capricious dream that history has ever known." But Egon must have caught glimpses of it in his childhood, when it was really like that.

What plenty! What deliciousness! How bravely attended were the monarchs, dynasts, and princes—what rooms full of gold and silver, gems and jewels, beautiful palaces, ample territories, fields, rivers, fountains, parks, lawns, living statues, living sprinkling systems, living music. Honors, medals, beribboned chests, beards, mustaches, flowing sideburns, the snap of heels brought sharply together, the air kissed softly above fair white hands. The Wienerwald to stroll in on a summer's day. Summer wine. Organ grinders. Dobosche torte. Wiener schnitzel so exquisite you could sit on it and not get grease on your pants. The Riesenrad, the Ferris wheel, turning around higher in the air than storks fly back from Africa, divisioned like a railway-carriage for the likes of Mrs. Mahler, Wittgenstein, the Third Man. Yes, the greatest city. Happiness to see the light of day there, amongst the sportive throngs of ultra-conservative Viennese, whether Gentile or Jew! full of anxiety about correctness, protectively doubtful and questioning, suspicious of every motive. Oh, no, you say, that couldn't be the Viennese. Light-hearted, airy, offhand, addicted to social pleasures, that was how *they* were. The Great Waltz, the Merry Widow, the Student Prince! Then why was the town so full of exophthalmia, that condition where the eyes bulge out and you can see the whites all around, more so than anywhere else in the civilized world? Why weren't people allowed to do something they weren't very good at? Play the piano? Sing? Be second-rate? Where did all the connoisseurs come from? They didn't attend performances but sat like tribunals on a chair of state, a place of judgement and decision. The concert, ballet, opera, or play that came before them they heard and tried like cases in a Court of Justice. But the reason for that was, and is today, as the French murderer and anarchist Émile Henry said, "There are no innocent bourgeois."

And thus it was that in Vienna, eating *en famille* was not a time to intrude on what might be forming in people's minds. Freud refused to compromise his thoughts by speaking at table. If he happened to notice an empty chair, he would look at his wife, raise his eyebrows, point with his knife or fork at it, and she would tell him why the son, daughter, sister-in-law, tutor, or governess wasn't sitting in it. And it had better be good.

As for many years the emperors of the Austro-Hungarian Empire seemed to have nothing in particular against anyone, and as the nobility went along with the rulers, and the common people went along with the nobility, life in Vienna, on the surface at least, was not such a hardship for Jews as it might have been elsewhere. If they wanted to assimilate with the Gentiles and make it outside the ghetto, they were welcome to try. Many did, scientists, artists, the intelligentsia, "modern" men who believed that an end to religion meant an end to strife. But the price was high. Assimilating meant giving up in many ways their proprium, their selfhood, the unique and vital culture of their people, close family ties, the Torah, the direct line to God, the Sabbath. Language and ritual were lost too, "next year in Jerusalem," the whole scene. That was the first generation. The Jews that came after, such as Egon, those who were *born* into the world of the Gentiles, were supposed to have been spared the pain.

Egon's father, a dermatologist specializing in venereal diseases and the first physician in Vienna to own an X-ray machine (with which, like many of X-ray's first wielders, he did more than a little harm, according to his son), had made the break in early manhood. In classic German he said, you take the good with the bad, right? What are you going to do? He made a good living, many of his clientele being titled persons who paid by the year and for whom he provided their own waiting room apart from the common patients. He read papers before the Medical Society, on grand occasions could pin a row of medals on his chest, including two from Aegean kings. He was assimilated, had privileges, but not the one of being Herr Professor Doktor at the University. Oh, well.

Egon had every advantage. And all he knew about being a Jew was what he and his friends, mostly also Jewish (true assimilation being easier said than done), heard in the form of slurs and insults from Gentile schoolmates and even teachers. For this world their parents were trying to enter, and into which they themselves thought they had been born, was pogrom-minded. And in spite of the ruling class's kind bienséance toward the Jews, which many of the lower orders also adopted (as they would a fashion, like eating ice cream with a fork), discrimination was rife, and the atmosphere was that of psychological, cultural, and social alienation. You can't go home again, but you can't really go anywhere else either, except to limbo "large and broad, since called the Paradise of Fools."

But a paradise nevertheless their famous city was. The vast *empire*, like a tree so loaded with fruit that it breaks its own boughs, had long since ruined itself with its own greatness, splintered and broken apart. But Vienna stayed huge, puffed up, gorgeous, a veritable whirligig of gaseous politics, commerce, finance, industry, and laws laid down for pure and flawless workmanship. Nothing would happen to *it*. It was like Carl Sandburg's poem:

> *The doors were cedar*
> *and the panels strips of gold*

> *and the girls were golden girls*
> *and the panels read and the girls chanted:*
>> *We are the greatest city,*
>> *the greatest nation:*
>> *nothing like us ever was.**

But things go round, they ebb and flow. Archduke Franz Ferdinand, nephew to the Emperor and next in line to the throne, a relative the Emperor never could stand anyway, went to Sarajevo and got himself assassinated, and his morganatic wife with him. The stuff hit the fan. World War I sprang full grown, like Minerva, out of the head of Kaiser Wilhelm of Germany, which meant that everybody in the world got into it but a few Patagonian Welshmen. The good old Austrian Emperor died in the midst, never knowing his side had lost, or seeing his empire forlorn, incult and horrid, possessed by petty princes, the great families extinguished and rooted out. The country never quite became a haunt of ravens and wild hogs, or a receptacle of wild beasts, or buried in its own ruins, but a Corporal making his way upwards even then saw to it that it came close. And the famous city of Vienna itself after the war?

> *The doors are twisted on broken hinges.*
> *Sheets of rain swish through on the wind*
>> *where the golden girls ran and the panels read:*
>> *We are the greatest city,*
>> *the greatest nation,*
>> *nothing like us ever was.*

In Sandburg's poem, the great city he's talking about finally disappears off the face of the earth. "And even the writing of the rat footprints," he says,

> *tells us nothing, nothing at all*
> *about the greatest city, the greatest nation*
> *where the strong men listened*
> *and the women warbled: Nothing like us ever was.*

But of course nothing like that happened to Vienna, and even the little bit left of the empire stayed viable enough to vote to become a republic in 1920. The people took over. That should fix everything, right? Vox populi. But for eight hundred years they have been a family of juveniles under a strict but loving father.

---

* From "Four Preludes on Playthings of the Wind."

Now that father, the last of a long line, is dead and they are on their own, the nicest kids you would ever want to meet when things were going good and they had plenty. But when the tide turned, something else. Distressed, forsaken, left to the rage of beggary, chill winds, starvation, nastiness, and sickness, to irksomeness and prices no one could pay with wagonloads of pretty paper money, the nice kids took on beasthood, the rank, condition, and nature of beasts. And whom (even before the fluttering Gypsies) did they rive and rend? The Jews.

No surprise there, because for fifteen hundred years Church and State, banding together, had prepared the way. Contempt was traditional in all circles, hatred showed itself in many forms, and the systematic harrying of Jews was thought to be based on the innate moral feeling of mankind. Then two or three monarchs in a row, possessed of mental light and free from prejudice, had worked some changes. So had modern Christianity, more New Testament than Old, and Science advancing farther by the day. Little by little the Jews left the ghettos and dispersed about the town. Most people shrugged and let it go at that. But some did not, brought up in corrupt opinion.

Vienna had her share of these, in slow combustion, smoldering and smoking and on their guard. They watched and objected to everything. Jews out of their neighborhoods, out of their proper clothing. Opening doctor's and lawyer's offices, music studios, businesses. Pretending they didn't kill Christ! Pretending not to have inherited "racial" traits such as being too good in arithmetic! Making believe they didn't want to get hold of all the money and control the world! In days of prosperity, these anti-semites had other things to think about than the Jews. They might spit and hiss, mutter a medieval insult or two as they passed or jostled someone whose looks they didn't like off a curb, but actions like these were more on the q.t., like flashing.

But when the Emperor died, and the war was lost and the roof fell in, then no more Mr. Nice Guy. Out they came in droves. And when the Corporal I mentioned before, made as big as King Kong by state-of-the-art amplifiers, lights, and cameras—no, Kong was a piker in comparison—when he screeched his harsh screaming cry, they raced forward to help him with his plans for totalitarian tyranny, rearming the Reich and laying waste to as much as they could of the known world. Of course it took more than the natural-born goons of Vienna to do all that, but eventually they had plenty of company—peasants, laborers, small traders, shopkeepers, bureaucrats in uniform and out, rulers, religious leaders, businessmen, industrialists, and even some members of the intelligentsia—all but one little lame boy who couldn't keep up and so was left behind. And what was to be, would be.

I have a pretty good idea of the sequences now. But when Egon and I first got together, I was Tupso all over again. My radio was tuned to the music stations. At the movies, when the newsreel came on, I went to the ladies' room. My magazine of choice was *Vogue*. It didn't take much longer to read the paper than to drink a cup of coffee and smoke a cigarette. The world was just—out there. As usual. Raising Cain. But as the song said,

> *What's to do about it?*
> *Let's put out the lights*
> *and go to sleep!*

When Egon wasn't with me, which was of course a lot of the time, he must have talked about newscasts, front-page stuff, what columnists had to say, editorials and so on. I know he did because of the friends he used to take long strolls with up towards the zoo or on the Reed College campus on Thursday afternoons or Sunday mornings—a young man named Richard Neuberger, whose folks had a restaurant and were Egon's patients; a professor named Dr. Goldenweiser; a man named Dr. Steiner whose father was a friend of Tolstoy's. They must have had big discussions about what was really going on. Egon liked to talk and argue, I found out when the refugees started coming and I saw and heard him with them.

But the way he and *I* talked was like a couple of shepherds on the slopes of Mount Olympus, or Keats and Shelley, or Peaches and Daddy Browning, or Paul and Virginia. Was it I who set the tone? Maybe. Did Tupso? Maybe not. We each in our day put ourself in the way of what we wanted to happen. That, I admit. But Mountstuart could have just gone back into the fort and left Tupso sitting on that stump. And after we shook hands and I congratulated Egon on his book, he could have ushered me out. That would have been as far as we could go. I always think of us needing them, but maybe it was the other way around. Maybe it was like Jack Chance that autumn after sizing up the young poet:

> *Under his hat I saw his eyes*
> *Measuring without disguise*

Ardyth's Memoir, Part 1

The ripeness of my house,
And measuring myself, and he
Turned in and approached and spoke to me.
He had decided undismayed
This was the place for Chance, and I
The [one] for him; and so he stayed.*

Maybe it was really like that, them picking *us* out and us not knowing. For our very dumbness. The comfort of that. Archduke Franz Ferdinand had his choice among ten princesses of the blood but picked Sophie Chotek, a minor countess, whose bier when he and she were murdered in Sarajevo and lay in state would be two feet lower than his. They might even have deceived us. Mountstuart might not have been a "younger son" at all, but a highwayman on the lam. And Egon never *telling* me of the tough times in Vienna through the years, and all the misery even for people with servants, about the beastliness to the Jews even *before* Hitler (I thought Hitler started the whole thing, little knowing he just plugged into something already existing, like you'd plug a dryer into PGE's huge current), was in a way a deception. I'd have been kinder, softer, different, had I known.

Why did he want me to be dumb and not know? But here was how he made things seem: that he left Vienna not to *get away* from something but to *reach out* to a superior life in America. Nothing was wrong with Vienna or Austria, except in comparison with the United States, which was everything great put together. Like you'd say, Earth is okay but Heaven is better. Why he would adopt such a pose I can't imagine. But of course I can. Pride. That *he* picked the time to leave. Nobody did it for him. And it is true that when he emigrated, it was done of his own free will. And after the refugees started coming, there was sort of a cachet to that. *They* had to get out, *he* didn't, and I soon saw, or thought I saw, him kind of lording it over them on account of that. But an exile is an exile. The difference is so small between the exile from the paternal roof (me), the person whose prolonged absence from his native land is voluntary (Egon), and those compelled by dire circumstance to flee for their lives (our refugee friends) as hardly to exist. And no real exile—which all of us were, really, each in his or her own way—had any more true psychological security than any other.

When I say he lorded it over the refugees (he also gave affi-

---

* From "Ballad of a Strange Thing," by H. Phelps Putnam.

davits and worked tirelessly to find niches for them), I mean he did what Grandma hated so in Grandpa: he bragged. As an aborigine, this bothered me, it didn't seem like manners, finally I told him, stop it. But he kept on, why should they be homesick and sad? Everything over here was perfect, everything over there was terrible. (Now he had changed his tune about that and admitted to conditions of adverse fortune, of trials and afflictions beyond counting, but always as if he had stood above them and they never had anything to do with him.) He would take these stands, that Gershwin was better than Brahms, the Packard was better than the Daimler, the washing machine and vacuum cleaner were better than human servants, mass-produced shoes were better than custom-made. "But there *are* shoemakers in Portland who can make shoes?" The questioner would sound anxious. Oh, certainly, Egon would say, with the careless little shrug I found out was Viennese, but who would want to go to them when you can walk in and buy a pair of Florsheims? Some of the refugees had brought plaster casts of their feet with them, little knowing they had as much chance of custom-ordering a pair of shoes over here as bespeaking a new pair of gonads.

If Egon detected the slightest hint of criticism in questions about our customs, he would resent it greatly. Why did we ruin our desserts and candies by putting *salt* in them? the newcomers asked. Why, because *salt* enhanced the *sugar* and made American desserts and candies the best in the world, that's why, he said. And the stories of gagging and throwing up he didn't believe for a minute, that was just the Viennese for you.

I always sided with them against him. For a few years, until they found "their right homes and their right passions," I and they saw a good deal of each other, not with close familiarity, I regret to say, more like the way I think Tupso might have socialized with a boatload of Mountstuart's London connexions. I never felt at ease the way I should have or learned their ways, which to me were sometimes baffling. For example, here they were, exiles in a strange land, but they hardly got their hats and coats off before they began sorting themselves out into the exact same social strata as had prevailed at home, the furrier and little tradesman (anyone nearer the bottom than that hadn't got out in the first place) discreetly snubbed by the lawyer, doctor, and professor, their wives and families falling into the proper slots beside them. They were all in this together but kept their distances.

Gemütlich was what they were to me, of course, as they'd have been to Gauguin's saronged brown ladies, Lafcadio Hearn's geishas, or even Tupso, had she been offering them tea and a slice of (salty) pineapple upside-down cake and not able to understand whether their "Thank you!" meant *yes, thank you,* or *no, thank you,* for it could have been either one. (I never did find out which was which.) They were all bilingual, so much so that I hardly felt even *lingual* in comparison. But I think there was another reason for my unease, and that was that these people at my table and under my roof were my first bourgeoisie *up close* (except Egon, who didn't count because by this time he was my husband). They took me aback, almost classic examples, as they seemed to be, of the haughtily contemptuous middle section of society that up until the French Revolution had had their place between the really high and the really low. We never had a distinct middle class like that in this country. I felt I was seeing the eighteenth-century apothecary, solicitor, Madame Bovary, her husband— No, I'm just saying that now. At that time they were just a bunch of strangers with much better manners than mine or anyone's I'd ever known. There were several young students, and with these, so poised, speaking English, I always felt like *I* was the refugee and they were the ones at home. But that was the old glittering culture for you, stretching clear back to the Greeks and Romans, that turned out finished products while so many of us, no matter what Emerson said, were just the hides drying on the fence or the raw lumber that would saw up full of knot-holes. I didn't think that then, I think it now. But Egon kept bragging. And I was such a dummy, never looking beyond what he *said.*

It took me years (really almost up until I started writing this) to realize that the disparaging way he spoke of Vienna after the refugees started arriving was just a pose, the cover-up of an irrational love attachment to the city of his birth. His "hatred" was Masetto's in *Don Giovanni* for Zerlina. She had betrayed him, so he hated her. But he hated her because he really loved her. Not that I mean to say that all Egon's bragging about *America* was phony. He really did passionately believe that this country was "the last best hope of earth," the bonfire in the night, the perfect security against wild beasts. The day after Pearl Harbor he ran down and enlisted, and served in the Air Force Medical Corps until the last day of the war. Maybe he even liked salt in things that were supposed to be sweet. Maybe the only way he could live was like people given new identities by the CIA or the FBI.

But as his father's old colleague Freud said, to the degree that you try to repress your memories, to that degree will they dominate your life. And that was why Egon ended up the most hopelessly Viennese of all the exiles, I think. He would have laughed at that and been surprised at me for saying so, in a tone I'd have meant to be tender. I wasn't usually tender, Tupso wasn't either, I don't suppose, maybe the cold Siuslaw forest, the sullen river, had something to do with that. Treat 'em rough and tell 'em nothing. You came over here of your own free will, didn't you? Nobody shipped you over here a prisoner in chains? So why are you grieving inside yourself till one of these days it's going to kill you? Don't tell me, honey. I can't do one damn thing.

IN WHAT I THINK OF as my *Mademoiselle Modiste* days, things cost so little that here in Portland, and I suppose all across the country, even common tradesmen, doctors, and lawyers, not just rich men, could keep what was known as a mistress. You could get a very decent furnished room for ten dollars a month, coffee was twenty-five cents a pound, cigarettes fifteen cents a pack (Wings eventually came down to about eight cents), a ticket to the movies cost ten cents, clothes and furnishings in proportion. So I wasn't very expensive. Considering how demanding I became, and greedy, and conjoining a lot of my thoughts with extension, I'm surprised I never importuned for things. But I never did. Egon would ask how much everything was going to come to, rent, phone, lights (if they weren't furnished, which they usually were), the groceries, the newspaper, etc., I'd have it written down and added up, and he would leave me that much. I must have had walking-around money too, for cosmetics, to get my hair bleached, the movies, cigarettes, and coffee at various stopping places in the downtown area. Oh, yes, and typewriter paper and rent (about two dollars a month) for a typewriter. Later on I owned one.

So in other words, for the six years before Egon and I got married, he was keeping me. I didn't go around spreading the news, as to be "kept" in those days was a very déclassé thing, unless by King Carol of Roumania. Family and friends lived seventy-five miles away, they had no way of knowing about my life, that I wasn't toeing the mark whatsoever and was sleeping till ten almost every day. Never did I mention this, but if asked said I worked at the library (part time) and did "free lance" typing, etc.

Actually nobody cared, I was far away and not such an intimate to the family. Of course later, when I hadn't *worked* my way up but by marrying Egon and writing a book got a slight boost upwards, why, there was more looking me up. But that wouldn't happen for quite some time.

The year before Egon's and my wedding, while he was being divorced and I was divorcing Howard, Mother became a widow and came up to Portland to live with me, and that made a big difference. She was very hospitable and sent word to one and all the relatives to say they should come and visit us. The twenty-five-cents-a-pound coffee went very quickly then, and whole sacks of flour. By that time, I lived in a small apartment (up a notch from the furnished room) with a good little gas stove, and Mother baked all the Swedish breads and coffee cakes that Scandinavians like with coffee. The Viennese like them, too.

It seems so strange to think of it now, when everyone knows everything, but in those times, Mother came and lived under my roof (she was left penniless and had nowhere else to go, she had three other children but none of them could have taken her in) and did not know that Egon was paying the bills. That is, she did know, but she thought he was "backing" me the way a maestro will "back" a promising singer or violin pupil, and not by word or deed did we let her know any different. Egon called upon me like the Gentleman Caller in *The Glass Menagerie*, and we never could get together except if she went to visit relatives in Albany or California. For that was another thing that was cheap, bus travel, about two-fifty for a round-trip ticket to Albany. How could she *not* have known? But there were pockets left about the world of Victorianism then, and I really don't think she did. It was like me not suspecting for many years that Howard was a homosexual.

By this time, with Mother being there and expenses being more, not a lot more but some, and Egon paying for everything but hardly able to get together with me even to kiss me the sweet way people used to kiss (like Jeanette MacDonald and Nelson Eddy), and me not using the typewriter or doing much of anything at all except reading, Egon was starting to get a little impatient for me to get out and get a job. Knowing how this horrified me, I don't think he came out and said so in so many words, but very casually mentioned that he had heard that there was such a thing as a WPA Writer's Project because he had a patient who had a cousin who was on it, and maybe I wouldn't mind doing something like that.

I was quite startled, but then he said that this patient had said that some of Oregon's "famous" writers were on it, which might make it interesting for me. So I applied and was poor enough and met some of the other qualifications, and then there I was amongst the famous, dear little Eleanor Allen the poetess, who immediately began to call me Fiorella, Howard McKinley Corning, Claire Churchill, Ada Hastings Hedges, and many others. It was fun to see them and for us to banter and smoke and drink coffee together. But it was hard for me to do something regular like that. Not that it was so regular, you could roam around town and do about what you wanted, but you did have to sign in in the morning.

LONG AFTER I was grown, an old family friend, Mrs. Gregory, while talking of something else, happened to mention that I was the most spoiled girl she had ever seen. "Your mother just spoiled you to death," Mrs. Gregory said. I was amazed to hear that, for everyone knew that my younger sister, Marion, the baby of the family, was Mother's favorite, and wasn't the favorite the one who got spoiled? Marion was truly beautiful, kind, sweet, smart, a talented musician, she made up darling songs and didn't have a lazy bone in her body. She had also married the catch of the valley down around Corvallis, a young and handsome farmer boy named Kenneth Pettibone, who had been elected National President of the Future Farmers of America and had his picture taken at the White House with President Herbert Hoover. "Are you sure you're not talking about Marion?" I said. "No, you. I watched with my own eyes," Mrs. Gregory said. "Your mother spoiled you so much it was just ridiculous."

Well, I was sick a lot as a girl growing up and Mother would fix these pretty trays, and before permanents she would curl my and Marion's hair with a curling iron stuck in a lamp chimney, being careful to put her own hand under the hot curl as she released it so it wouldn't fall down and burn our neck. She washed and ironed school clothes. Anything you were doing she would take out of your hands and do herself, because you were so clumsy and she could do it better. When I finally began using my typewriter in earnest, if she had known how to type she would have taken *that* out of my hands and done that.

And in fact when my first book came out partly based on stuff from her childhood, she read it (skipping the parts where I "went on and on") and said, "But I do wish somebody would write it how it *really was*." She said this more than once through the years, and finally I said to her, "Well, why don't you write it? Just by hand, on your tablet with the lines, like you write a letter to Aunt Fanny or Aunt Laura—just like you talk—and I will pay you two cents a word, like the magazines pay." And so she did, I kept the pages, and if this were a real book I would put them here to show how different the story *teller* is from the story *writer*. She *told* the most enchanting stories in the world—I used many of them and could have never in this world been a writer without her—and I'm sure she thought if you could *tell* them, you could *write* them easy as pie. But much to her surprise, it didn't work that way. At the time of the above conversation, my books had come out, she was getting on for seventy and she couldn't stand it not to make a stab at somebody doing it *right*. But "everything" only used up a handful of her lined tablet pages, pages which turned out to be like a locked front door you bang and kick against but it won't open, you can't get in. And so she saw that and waited awhile, and then quietly gave up. But I know she never thought I did the writing job any better than I made pie-crust or ironed shirts, but there was nothing to be done about it now. Nobody in the family except Marion liked anything I wrote, few members were readers, and certainly not of anything (clear through) by me.

Mother didn't mean any harm when she snatched what you were doing out of your hands so as to do it properly. She would have snatched me out of God's hands when he was making me, I'm sure, if she could have done so, for she never thought he did as good a job as he could have. Her idea of a perfect daughter was one who was beautiful enough to go in the movies or marry a rich man. Those two things were all that counted. Oh, yes, and to be good to your mother. To be a singer on the stage would have been all right also, or a dancer like Ginger Rogers. But beautiful was the first requirement, and all the rest would follow. Look at Marion, her fine marriage, everyone said Kenneth would be rich someday.

I was five feet, ten inches tall. Tall girls were looked down on in those days. My legs were too long. Mother and I would sit across the room from each other having coffee and she would study my legs, they were too long from the knee to the ankle, she decided, and she would say how if she could just operate and take about four inches off the bone in that stretch of my legs, they would be just perfect. In later years she read about an operation like that being performed in Sweden or somewhere, a tall girl being shortened by taking four inches out of her femurs, and she was just exultant. "That's *exactly* what I'd have done with you!" she said. And she would have, too.

She tried to help me get rid of the freckles I inherited from my Irish father. "The first time he came down to our house with the Fagergren boy, I thought he was the freckledest thing I ever laid eyes on!" But by keeping out of the sun as much as possible and putting on freckle cream at night (which I have since found out had carcinogenic mercury in it, which even fifty years after the last application I still look for to kill me), they didn't show too much.

Mormons are bitter against cigarettes and Mother was Mormon raised, but she was glad when she found out I smoked, as I had big heavy aunts and smoking does keep you thin. She didn't want me to get fat, too freckled, stand up too straight and lose Egon. She didn't say so and maybe she didn't even think it, but her whole attitude seemed to be that if ever there was a goose to be plucked it was him, and she warded off anybody who might interfere. There weren't many who would have, just a few acquaintances and a fellow or two from the Writer's Project making fifty-eight dollars a month like I was (this was the year between her coming to live with me and my marrying Egon). Losers, nobodies. About a week before the wedding I burst out, "But I don't love him!" and she didn't say a thing, just looked disgusted. I liked Egon, though, and after both of our divorces came through and we married and moved to a beautiful rented house that Mother just reveled in, I liked him even more, and then as the years went by and he *was* such a goose to pluck and such a darling, I was like the girl in the story who married for what she could get out of it, but when fate went against her short, nondescript, middle-aged husband, she got a job and supported him, because by that time she loved him so much she would have died for him. That was how I was exactly, and I still feel the same. Not that I ever had to support him, because if I had, I think I would have first tried to talk him into jumping off the bridge with me hand in hand.

In later times, as I got more smart-alecky, I began to think he was kind of a wimp. But if he did become so, it was my fault, always decrying physical activity and inveigling him into a sybaritic kind of life, that being more conducive to conversation. Had he had a different companion, I think he'd have played tennis, even climbed mountains. He did so in his youth, in lederhosen and a hat with a feather in it, swam heroically, and at the estate of a patient of his father's he learned to ride Arabian horses, and jump. I've seen pictures of him taking fences, riding boots, riding habit, a riding crop, the whole deal.

When he came to Corvallis, his best friend was the officer who trained the cavalry of the ROTC. He rode and jumped all the time. His other friends were the head of the music department at the college and his wife, who taught piano; and the Dean of Women, a somewhat elderly widow. They all could speak German, had been to Europe many times, arranged their furniture like a Biedermeier parlor, and in those first years to be with them and their friends in their little gatherings must have felt quite like home. When his wife Gretel joined him after he had found a place to live and they got settled, she rode too. As her folks had raised horses for the Austrian army, she might even have jumped. I know she liked to climb and once climbed Mount Hood. In the summer she wore a dirndl. From photographs, I see she happily became one of the Corvallis "kultur" group, though they were older than Egon and she.

He'd have been better off with regular exercise, I realize that now, but with me he just lolled more while we drank coffee and smoked and talked and read. What it was kind of like was the Magic Mountain. We had just gone up there for a visit, neither of us meant to stay, and the next thing we knew, six—ten—fourteen years had gone by. No, wait, we weren't up there the whole time. When World War II started he was one of the first to enlist, was commissioned as a major and soon was in the Air Force in the medical department, head of EENT, the eye, ear, nose, and throat section of whatever base he was assigned to. He was in it from the beginning and stayed to the end. I was with him most of the time, finding and fixing up living quarters, trying out recipes, paying people for their ration stamps for coffee and cigarettes, but not really being of the help I now realize an officer's wife should have been. Just as I couldn't write Mother's stories right, I couldn't seem to get my wartime role right.

In Newport News, for instance, where I naturally had never been before, I set about finding somewhere for us to live and soon, in a dirty, picturesque alley, found us two rooms in a shabby house with a rickety dark staircase where we would have had to share the bathroom with about ten other people. It was perfect—cheap, an important consideration, as we were sending Mother money (she had moved in with her sister down in California) and

Egon was paying alimony, and I could visualize it all home-decorated. I was about to give the straight-backed old Southern gentleman who showed it to me and who either owned the place or was in charge, a check when all of a sudden he said, "What line of work did you say your husband was in?" "Oh, he's not in any line of *work*," I said, "he's a major in the army, in the Medical Corps, and we've just been stationed here." The old man stared at me and then just got furious, I thought he was going to hit me. "A *major*?" he said, "in the U.S. *Army* and you're down here in this area to rent *accommodations*? What in the world are you thinking of? Don't *rank* mean nothing? Don't *respect* mean nothing? What kind of officer can the man be to have a woman like you?"

I didn't argue, just felt ashamed I had to be told things like that, then left. Maybe we stayed in a hotel. We weren't in Newport News long. I wonder what the old gentleman would have thought if he could have seen us together, Egon always wanting to loosen his tie and wear his cap on the side of his head and walk along meditating with his hands clasped behind him like Felix the Cat, and me with my bleached hair and three-quarter-length lynx coat (fur coats weren't that expensive then), as many inches taller than Egon as Mother wanted to remove from my femurs.

When the war was over, we could finally go back where we started from, and the G.I. Bill made it easy to buy a house, two stories, four bedrooms, one bathroom, big corner lot, fifty-two hundred dollars, about five hundred down. "We'll live here forever." Of course we didn't, but moved five more times. Each time we would love where we were, and I would overturn the whole thing like a harrow a grouse's nest in a field. Egon's journal starts at the third of those last five abodes, when I have finished an actual novel and a schoolgirl is typing it. When she brings it back, he will decide which publisher to send it to, as I just read old English books such as Burton's *Anatomy of Melancholy* and know little about "the trade." But he had a book called *Diet in Sinus Infections and Colds* published by Macmillan in 1933, so he knows a lot about it, every little detail.

He will tell you now how our life was for the next nine years. His book (for his journal *is* a book, and a good one—he wanted so much to be truly an author like Santayana or Logan Pearsall Smith or the guy who wrote *Jurgen*, belles lettres, not just medical stuff) ends during the first year of his illness. He would have six more years to live after that. But read it, please, and we'll talk again.

James D. and Lulu Kennelly with children Jimmy, Ardyth, Marion (on James's lap), and Grace, 1915

Sisters Marion and Ardyth Kennelly, 1917

Lulu and Hiram Parker at the Parker home in North Albany, about 1923

Egon Ullman in Corvallis. (Photo courtesy of Oregon State University Archives.)

Ardyth with Howard Gibbs at a Parker reunion, 1936

Ardyth at her typewriter, probably in the late 1940s

Egon's Journal

From MEMORY, READING *and* LISTENING:
les petits riens of my observations

SUNDAY, NOVEMBER 23, 1947

The other day Ardyth suggested I keep a record of our daily life. She really meant, or so I imagine, of her life. I did not answer at once, in fact I cannot now remember whether I answered at all. How can one person record another one's doings if these doings are mostly not on the surface and consist for the most part of thinking, feeling and loving?

But when, last night, she read to me the produce of her last three days' work, I began to see the light and knew that all she wanted, really, was to put to paper from day to day all the little things that are usually forgotten before the words have died, the food has been eaten or the door closed behind the guest. The things, the important ones, the hundred indecisions, visions and decisions that compose the final pattern of one's life, are usually remembered or can be reconstructed well enough. But for the little things, one might as well—if one cares at all, and who doesn't?—keep notes, if for no other reason than to come back to one's younger days some time later when the doings become rarer and the thinkings less strong. Moreover, two people like us, who do talk so much about important things and significant people who have for the greater part died before we were born, and whose one partner startled the other at the outset more than once by asserting that all of her real friends are dead and every one of her lovers has been buried, deserve to leave more of a mark behind in their house than old slippers, cracked coffee cups and a library.

Since last night I knew that Ardyth is a novelist. That she is a writer with a style all her own and an imagination as apart as her hair and her eyes and her wit. But that her medium would be the novel on a large canvas I knew only since yesterday, because she read to me a whole long passage with characters more alive and near than those met in my waking hours.

Today I have seen her only briefly—in the bathtub, all soaped and laughing; she was working all day upstairs and came down only to take a bath and have dinner. She tried a new dress on that Mother had made for her—except the buttonholes, which she usually buys at the Singer Sewing Machine Co.—out of grass-green striped material with a bustle below the waist. She looked so sweet in it I wanted to be a baby kangaroo resting easy in the ventral pouch of her bustle while she grazed through the house.

But my time flew by with reading a biographical essay on Flaubert by Somerset Maugham and some pages of Osbert Sitwell's *Great Morning*.

Since Ardyth is writing a novel, I feel I should bring myself up in the tradition and read some newer novels myself. How else could I judge a novel? It has been so long since I've read fiction. (If one does not consider much of the medical and scientific literature so.) Yet I feel that Ardyth will be read—most of all by women. One half—the top half—of the reading world is anyway composed of women. Somewhere I read "Women, once our superiors, now our equals!" In the literature of fiction, I'm sure, women, once our equals, are on a fair way to become our superiors.

I am glad Violet, our cat, is recovering from a bad case of hair-balls in her stomach. She hasn't been feeling good lately and hasn't eaten for five days. Each time she tried to, she vomited within minutes after the last swallow. The veterinary suggested I massage her stomach. I did and she liked it and purred each time. I took her in my lap and squeezed her in the hope to inch the hairball a little further toward the exit. It is distressing how one becomes attached to a little cat. She is now squatting in front of me on the table and follows with movements of her head and railroad nystagmus in her eyes the moves of the typewriter. Ardyth told me often how the cat was helping her to write. She has almost become superstitious about the cat. She is given to superstitions anyway, especially since she read the life of Mrs. Blavatzky.

I am pleased, though, really, I need not take the cat to the dog and cat hospital. The last time we had her there, because we went out of town for a few days, she came home sick and lorn. The girl there told me when I came to get her that she would not eat at all. Animal patients, like children, cry and howl and scream too much for me, I am sure mostly of fright. I at least, when I can't cure or improve the vision of my patients, don't let them suffer if I can help it. However, I speak as though I would know the veterinarians. How bold of me, I hardly know my own colleagues. But that's another chapter.

TUESDAY, NOVEMBER 25, 1947

This morning I overslept and completely forgot my appointment with my dentist. So I quietly slipped on my shirt and suit, kissed Ardyth (I always do before leaving the house) and rushed downtown. On the way back I stopped and had a shave and a quick breakfast and then still had time left. I returned home to get some books and found Ardyth dressed in my G.I. pants, huge black socks and one of my T-shirts, drinking coffee. She was going to scrub the floor in the kitchen, much to my dismay, because whenever she does I feel utterly distressed. But, she says, it's the Norwegian in her that makes her do it. I dressed her little finger, which she had cut while opening a can of coffee earlier, and found it not half as bad as she made me believe when she told me of the accident. But all women like to exaggerate a little, particularly when it comes to their health.

While I inspected the finger all around and tried to make as much as was necessary and as little as was good of the whole affair, she told me of the things she had read last night in a book about 10,000 wonderful things. Most wonderful of all were the cries of the street vendors of Egypt, who peddled their wares, beans, roots, cottons and figs, by calling on the maidens of the Nile and the bulls of the country. She loved that with a twinkle in her eyes. And then she told me of the doings of the fat French monks in the Middle Ages who started the day at two in the morning with a prayer called "cockcrowing." I interrupted her, saying, "They sure started early." She laughed by saying, "Damn early for a cock! But isn't that a wonderful book?"

I had to leave for the hospital, and Ardyth was eager to begin cleaning the house for the Thanksgiving party. I kissed her on the flattened-up-together hair, which made her exclaim, "What a shame you have to see me in this outfit." I really wouldn't have paid any attention if it hadn't been for my G.I. pants and my only pair of winter socks for cold weather.

CHRISTMAS DAY, 1947

The two of us are alone. Ardyth's mother left for Marion's, and we did not go after all. Ardyth sent a trunkful of toys, books and other things along, and both of us hope Mother will have so good a time of it that she stays a real long time.

Ardyth housecleaned most of the day and engaged me for minor tasks in between, like emptying the vacuum cleaner, moving furniture, rolling up the carpets and bringing her hammer and nails to wherever she fastened things to the wall (a great pastime of hers). I used to wince for every hole she made, and felt when I saw a row of them like they were aimed at my heart. At some places the holes looked like those in a shooting gallery. But time has taught me not to pay any more attention than I would to a pool of water that has been spilled on the floor, because after things get back into place again, or rather to a new, more becoming corner or spot in the house, everything looks beautiful and so fitting, as though that was the only place in the whole big house where it was meant for.

With each housecleaning, minor and sometimes major, rearrangements take place which at first invariably confuse me. If I try weakly to ask why, or offer an alternative which at the time seems to me to be more practical, I am usually cut short with a "Who is the mamma in the house?" which makes me abide and pay no further attention. Once in a great while it has happened in the past, not in this but in another house or two, that I came home at night and walked into our bedroom to take off rain-soaked clothes before presenting myself, only to find out that where the bed used to stand there was a desk, and my clothes cabinet had moved without telling me to another room. I used to be frightened by such unforeseen and surprising moves. But I found out that such changes take place in complete order, and no more than a question is necessary to get me the full information as to where my house robe or my stockings or tax receipts will be kept from now on.

After things were in their place, we sat down to a cup of coffee and talked it all over. I am always ahead of Ardyth with my coffee because I like it warm, almost hot, and when I drink it fairly fast it tastes to me like a wonderful coffee candy such as I used to get from my grandfather forty-five years ago, while Ardyth takes her time and sips it slowly, very slowly indeed, being perfectly happy in holding the cup for an hour or so in her hand, without ever spilling a drop but always minding, sort of, my getting ahead of her. She no longer smokes now, after having indulged for the past ten years rather heavily, because she found out that cigarettes caused her heart "to jump" or "to thump" or "to thud," as she changes calling it with the changing sensations, meaning of course extrasystole of the heart.

I mentioned George Sartin's *History of Science* and the interesting fact that there are so few biographies available of scientists, while every poet, artist and writer, even though he might be only of local interest, finds soon at least one, if not a series of, biographers. Is it that the scientists who dominate today's scene so completely have not discovered yet the secret of how to dominate our hearts? Ardyth, of course, was at once sympathetic with the lack of biographies of scientists, saying that even if they existed, no one would be interested. But that was only her emotional reaction. But I went on that we must consider that any life is interesting, even that of John O'Brien, for instance, who dies today suddenly in Boston while he was watching a wrestling match. Neither of us, I said, has any interest in wrestling, and yet we feel sorry and are curious. What did he die of? Probably he was a heart case and wrestling overexcited him. There was, I felt sure, a story behind this sudden death, as behind everything if one takes the trouble to go after it.

It is just as moving a story to follow the struggle of a scientist, his trying to solve the mysteries of nature, his tragic failures and his occasional triumphs, as it is to write a biography of a poet or, as far as that is concerned, of any person. But the scientist, in most cases, presents himself to us in an indirect way, very mediate, and often leaves nothing behind but a few scanty data or formulas. How he arrived at them is much more difficult to guess or to ascertain than the birth of a tragedy or that of a literary work. Of course no method, whichever used, is precise, but it surely is more difficult to write a readable life of Newton than a life of Sir Francis Drake or Francis Thompson. The story is often told of how Sir Walter Raleigh, on receiving no one knows how many different accounts of an incident which he had witnessed from his own window at the Tower, laughed at the idea of his writing a history of the world. And yet he did write one!

Of many a scientist I know no more than his name, if that much. Think of Domagk (I am not sure whether I spell his name right), the discoverer of sulfanilamide. All I know is that he received a Nobel prize and was not allowed by Hitler to accept it. Did he contribute enough to the happiness of mankind to be remembered? Was his discovery an accident? Hardly so. How and why did he make it, and why was it he who made it? Did he have any idiosyncrasies, was he ever in love, did he have a mother-in-law or a father who dominated him? Wouldn't it be worthwhile to examine the ways of his behaviour, his ways of checking and rechecking, finding and abandoning results and finally, most interesting of all, his ways of expressing himself, in his fine style?

Ardyth listened but, I could see, with impatience. Finally she said: "Who is interested? What emotions can hide themselves behind a formula, an equation, a recipe, a pill? It takes more than an experiment or mathematical speculation to make people feel that there was a man. A Samuel Johnson, a Lincoln, a Keats, those are the ones I want to laugh with and cry, they give us the only values mankind is interested in. Why, one story of Lincoln, one line of Keats, one tantrum of Dr. Johnson is worth all the chemistry and mathematics you can talk about."

I did not answer, because I knew we understood what each of us meant. As far as she was concerned, she was willing to accept the scientists' contributions as they came, as boon or as menace, as the case may be. But also, as far as she had any say about the matter, the artist may lack the profound training and the scientific comprehension, he may not make a good philosopher according to academic standards, but his intuitive intensity, his patient obsession, and the quality of his imagination entitle him to rank with the great Prometheuses of all ages, those who are bent on changing the world as inexorably as their rulers appear set on its destruction.

It occurs to me how much was missed by my failing to keep a diary from the time I met Ardyth. I feel that if I had done that, the thing would have had a beginning, and the happenings of the past ten years would have made a fascinating story, while as I begin now, it seems I am starting in the middle and will have to fall back every so often to the past in order to explain the present. Yet that is, of course, so with everything one begins, for one always has to begin somehow in the middle, because there has always been one love before the first one. Nor is there any story or event that ever ends, really, since it only needs another mood or impression—or if necessary, another reporter—to continue as though no end was really intended.

Egon's Journal

It is interesting enough to put down on paper—from day to day—the happenings and thoughts of a period in our lives when Ardyth has finally settled down to write. To follow her while she is writing and to see what will come of it. What being printed, published and being read will do to her—and possibly money—or not being published, not being read. I am sure, though, that she never will quit writing—even though the book she is working on now might not be what I think it is—for her life is one of devotion to writing, so true and so sincere as to admit no doubt, ever. She has the enviable gift to recollect her past and reminisce in the most minute details, almost from the day she was born.

When I search my memory for events and feelings belonging to my earlier boyhood, up to the age of fifteen, I find for the most part a blank. There are only stray images, like those of early childhood, with no sense of any consecutive interests, any affections or sorrows. And yet I know that my feelings in those years were intense, that I was solitary and unhappy, out of humor with everything that surrounded me and attached only to a sort of dream life fed on books. I was not precocious. I may have had in some ways more ability than the average boy, but it was lavished on boyish thoughts and a certain backwardness or unwillingness to accept the reality of my environment.

Why have I forgotten all those years? The causes are no doubt physical, but the effects may be expressed in literary terms. The past cannot be reenacted except in the language of, and with the contrast imposed by, the present. Especially the feelings of children, although intense at the time, are not ordinarily long-lived or deeply rooted. We stamp our feet, we cry desperately or we silently hate, for not being allowed to do this or to have that, always for something "do not." But these objects are trifles. If we remembered those occasions, they would seem now indifferent; we should be ashamed to confess those feelings, or we should laugh them off, as if the things that now preoccupy us, if we outgrew them, could seem to us more momentous than vast portions of the past; almost all our dreams, particular conversations and thoughts, become unrecoverable. Our accepted, organized, practically compulsory habits shut them out. But these habits themselves will change, more or less, with time and with circumstances. Even what we still think we remember will be remembered differently, so that a man's memory may almost become the art of continually varying and misrepresenting his past, according to his interest in the present. This, when it is not intentional or dishonest, involves no deception. Things truly wear those aspects to one another. A point of view or a special light in seeing things are not distortions. They are conditions of vision, and spirit can see nothing not focused in some living eye.

More than once in my life I have crossed a desert in all that regards myself, my thoughts or my unhappiness, so that when I look back over the years I see objects, I see public events, I see people and places, but I do not see myself. My inner life, as I recall it, seems to be concentrated in a few oases, in a few halting places, like bus depots where the busy traveller stopped to rest, to think, to decide, to be himself or to love. I say the busy traveller because those years' long stretches of spiritual emptiness were filled with daily actions and, I presume, feelings, with later studying medicine and practicing the art and science of it. Yet all was done under a sort of mechanical stimulus, the school bell, the examinations, the daily tasks. Old thoughts, familiar faces and voices, until the school bell rang again or the water was turned off. Of my self in those years I have no recollections. For some periods, it is as though I had not existed at all, or only as a mechanical sensorium, an activated apparatus, doing its work under my name.

That is what I tried to tell you, darling Ardyth, last night when you urged me to reminisce and I could produce practically nothing to please you.

I am glad you liked the lobster. I did, too.

December 27, 1947

In trying to keep a record of one's days, the choice of what to put down and what to leave out is, I am sure, the secret of all readable journals, and I mean readable not necessarily by strangers, commonly called "the reader," but by oneself at a later time.

We had the visit of Ardyth's first husband, Howard Gibbs, and his friend Ring Rees. They came yesterday, unexpectedly and suddenly, and left as they came. The first sight of Howard, I know, made Ardyth jump with joy, because he had remained the same good friend after her divorce that he was before her marriage, and if nothing else it is always heartwarming to see and meet an old friend. But both fellows were quite intoxicated when they entered, and instead of trying to find anew the old understanding and feeling of nearness, these were taken for granted beforehand and the time was spent with making drinks and fussing about the ice cubes and the choice of liquor and glasses.

Finally we asked them to come to dinner with us, because Ardyth was not prepared for dinner guests. It was by that time 6:30, and we were hungry. But Howard, as well as Ring, who had started their drinking undoubtedly in the early hours of the day, seemed to feel no need for food—only whiskey, and more of it. So when we finally got to the restaurant, Ring did not eat at all except a small piece of herring, which served him merely as a come-on for more whiskey, and Howard reluctantly ate a Beef à la Stroganoff, with relish but all the time with a swallow of straight Bourbon in between swallows. The conversation was accordingly defective, if there was one at all, or limited to commonplaces. The only thing that could not be missed was that Howard looked poorly—he must have lost fifteen pounds since I saw him last two years ago—and showed signs of getting older—no gray hair, to be sure, but deepening lines in his face, particularly around his eyes; and that he had no money. Or else why did he make such a point of needing to change his rail ticket for a bus ticket, which would take all the time he would otherwise have spent with us. Yet notwithstanding his being broke, he brought Ardyth a sweet-smelling corsage, and for me a large red buttonhole carnation.

After dinner they left—I think they had to meet an actress—before Howard went on to San Francisco and Ring to more whiskey or to his ninety-year-old father. When he proudly told me of his father's birthday, I said, "How wonderful, that's just the age when one begins to love one's father again like when we were children." He said, "How did you know, but it's true, up until fifteen years ago my father and I were fighting all the time and couldn't get along at all."

Ardyth and I drove up to Freddy's to receive our Christmas presents. We did not hit it off with him exactly on Christmas day, because Ardyth has lately been irked and irritated somehow by Freddy, and I had all I could do to prevent her from breaking off with him entirely. I don't think she really meant it when she threatened it to me, and I couldn't bear the thought of hurting the boy to his core. After all, it was as much her fault as his that he perpetuated all those traits that do make for a difficult friendship—loquacity, never knowing when to take leave at night, telephoning at all hours to say nothing for an intolerably long time and pervading the very air with his own deepening frustrations. Her fault because she does not think it does ever any good to try to change anybody's ways, and because she feels that almost all friends are such not because they have been carefully chosen, but rather because they were wished on us like our little cat—and somehow we have to put up with them. And that, of course, is true with most people's friends who become so because they are neighbors, or happen to have gone to school with us, or lay in the bed next to us in the hospital. How many of us are privileged to really choose our friends, and if we were, how often would the choice be a happy one?

Freddy (and his tiny mother) received us with the expectation of one who now has set his mind to have fun by seeing the other fellow having fun for what he has done for him. There were three packages displayed on the coffee table, unmistakably to be spotted at once, and wrapped up with care and time and indulgence. One from him for Ardyth, one from him for me and one from his mother for both of us. But before we got to receiving the gifts, Ardyth felt glad how well the tiny mother looked in a dress she had sent her for Christmas, not overlooking the fact that it was bounds too big for her and offering to take it back for a smaller size. Of course everybody knew that there was no smaller size except in the children's department, and the children's department naturally did not carry such dresses. I cannot now remember what was agreed upon except that the dress was very becoming and that son and mother were pleased.

Freddy's presents are always welcome. We know he confines himself to books, and he knows us well enough never to make a mistake in his choices. Only his generosity is embarrassing, for how can a man who works in the post office, as he does, afford to spend so much? A life of Samuel Johnson, Edwin A. Robinson's letters to Harry de Forest Smith, Morris' Postscript to the past fifty years, Van Wyck Brooks' Whitman and Melville, two novels and one book on murders in Los Angeles? He watched us carefully for months about our likes and dislikes, which he is familiar with anyhow, and knows our library. But it is always touching to see to what trouble he goes to get just what we would like best and what, in his opinion, we need most.

While we admired the books, he played Gershwin's piano concerto and set me wild to buy it. In fact, I know I must have it, because for some queer reason I prick up my ears and brighten with pleasure whenever I hear Gershwin and wince when Wagner and yawn when Mozart is played. Don't ask me why.

On Christmas day Ardyth had housecleaning and rearranged things. I love it—when it is over. But at first I am always baffled and often bewildered. For most of the time my room, my desk, my things are in order—only for me. There are pants hanging where I put them, letters, notes, checks, bills, waiting to be dealt with or to be put in order, and all those things which take a positive delight in getting in my way perpetually until I want them, when they vanish like smoke and watch me from some hide-out while I vainly search for them all over the place instead of wishing them further away. There accumulate those remarkable conglomerations of things, those bastards sprung from cohabitation of impossible objects—in a word, hell for a woman who when in a housecleaning mood wants to see everything "in its place." After it's all over, when I come unsuspectingly back to the habit of looking for things where I think they are, I find some are on my side and are lying there as good as gold, while most of them have been naughty and are now having fun behind my back.

The desk I write on is now in our bedroom, and everything, once I know about it all, is so inviting—I could go on writing forever if it were not for this ball-bearing pencil I write with, which scratches so loudly that I can use it for almost nothing except listening to it.

NEW YEAR'S DAY, 1948

The holidays were so filled with social engagements—how odd for us!—that there was not even a half an hour to sit down and recollect. Ardyth was throughout at her best. She looked, with the additional ten pounds put on in the past two months, at her very, very best. Calm, enchanting, endearing and beautiful as ever any woman, and so witty. Not one single outbreak of Irish anger in all these days, full of plans and good intentions. Whenever people fall for her charms, she becomes frightened and confides later that she *really* does not love them as much as they might think she does, and is afraid that sometime, sooner or later, she might be caught in anger and spoil the picture. Actually she never does, because what little of the deep, ever-whirling emotional pool of her comes to the surface, I absorb like a shock absorber, and she always makes up. In fact, I hardly ever mind these interplays, because I think right then and there of the sweetness of making up. She has not written at all since Christmas and blames it on the fact that she misses smoking, given up by her without apparent hardship about three weeks ago. But I know that's not the reason. It was simply too many people about, and telephone calls and presents.

One more event—George Stern's wedding—on the eleventh, with the reception in our house, and I hope peace and calm will return to 2015 SW Park. I am glad I insisted on Eva sending a housecleaner up the following day. Ardyth would have thought nothing otherwise of washing, cleaning and scrubbing for two days afterward.

New Year's eve we spent at the Sawards with Frink, Waknitz, Malbin, Button and us present, each with his wife, of course. It was the first opportunity to get acquainted really since I have been working with these men (now just two years).

All the women drew immediately together around one table and the men around another—and Ardyth. It was the first time I saw her surrounded by husbands while the wives watched from across the room with approval and interest, for she entertained all of them by her inimitable gift for listening. Only her face, her eyes and her smile were speaking, which obviously was enough to keep the conversation going til three in the morning and cause each member of the group to entertain the rest with the best stories one could think of. The few times, though, Ardyth told a story, the mystery of her story-telling talent was apparent.

I have tried to read a few pages through Motley's *Knock on Any Door*, which Freddy gave us for Christmas as a typical American novel and whose front page carries his dedication: "Live fast, die young, and have a good-looking corpse." My first reaction to this motto was of course to live slowly, die old and have a little withered-looking corpse. Only a romantic dreamer like Freddy, with his Oblomov nature, could be attracted with such a Wildean thought. Moreover, only these frustrated, always-talking and never-doing people would mistake such a book as expressing anything characteristic. Squalid conditions, base motifs, entanglements with the law and life in the gutter have always interested writers. But never before have writers found so much satisfaction in presenting such characters without ever balancing out the whole impression of the book with a hint at the other—the good life, and proceed on the assumption that depraved people are the typical ones and symbolic for our times. Dickens, with all his shady characters, knew better than to tear the reader down to their lowest instincts and never lost sight of the good in man. In fact, there is less life in the gutter in our time and country than there ever was before, but the urge to tickle the lust for sensation is so great in the writer, and gullibility so pitiful in the reader, that no subject is distasteful enough and no method cheap enough not to try.

Freddy glories when he talks of it. No wonder he is afraid of life. His apprehensions and distrusts are so deep-seated, his hunger to be tortured, frightened and distraught is so intense, that he avoids a movie, a book or a conversation which might point toward a more positive side of life. I know he can't believe that Ardyth is writing in earnest, he calls her explicitly at times she told him she is working and pays no more attention to it than to any human endeavor that is made with an earnest purpose. He would love to live in splendor and hear people say: Here goes Mr. Jacobson—but never would the thought enter his mind to give—or to earn the attention of his fellow men by doing something. When we talk about books, I even suspect him of not saying his *own* opinion but merely repeating what one or the other critic had written about it, because in giving his own opinion he would have to work his own brain, and he is afraid of even doing that.

Sometimes when I hear him talk to Ardyth about a play or book, I feel like Henry IV, who greeted the tardy Crillon after a great victory had been gained with these words: "Hang yourself, brave Crillon! we fought at Arques, and you were not there."

Tomorrow morning at eight I have to demonstrate a few interesting cases to the house-staff—a deaf-mute child who learned to talk, and a patient with a malignant pterygium on his right eye, on whom I have performed a graft from his lip to his eye and so cured the condition. I have done this once before in the army, using a piece of the patient's foreskin. In this case, I did not want to repeat this procedure, because the skin of the penis pigments after it is exposed to light for long and gives the impression of freckles.

JANUARY 2, 1948

Eight to nine, demonstration of patients to the house-staff. From 9:30 to 5:00 I saw patients without meeting one interesting case; I hope it wasn't me who was not interested!

At five I stopped at the bakery to pick up a loaf of rye bread. Then dinner with Ardyth while she discussed with me different wedding punches she is considering serving at the reception after George's wedding. The one she liked best cost $140. I am not sure whether George will like it so well when he hears about it. At eight

I took Ardyth to her dancing lesson at Murphy's. This time she had Mr. Newberry as teacher, who can dance like a dream but who can't talk well. Until recently she danced with Mr. Derby, who can't dance but can talk like a dream? I have not met either one.

Now, at home, she is ironing my shirts while I write and came in only once, poor girl, to express her anger at soiling the collar of a freshly ironed shirt with blood from another cut of her little finger. I wonder how she manages to cut always the little finger.

In a very little while we shall go to bed and eat apples.

JANUARY 4, 1948

These days with us alone in the house are heaven. Ardyth is happier and quieter when her mother is absent. She wants to redecorate the upstairs and rent it out so as not to have room at all in the house for a guest or an occasional friend. But in reality this is meant to mean that Mother cannot stay in the house. She wants to have her live a few blocks away in an apartment of her own and we give her an allowance for living. I fear that this won't solve the problem any more than past efforts, because in that case Ardyth will feel obligated every minute of the day to inquire whether Mother needs something, or to simply "run over and see how Mother is." We talked much about the problems of mothers in general and how many lives are simply ruined by the egotism and domineering of the old ladies. It makes me feel sometimes as though all the world's troubles are due to the mothers.

Toward evening we went out for dinner and stopped at Jack Cody's. It's a perfectly wonderfully built place with all the modernities of a restaurant, but without the better cooking. Things taste kind of stale there. The place was full, and as my eyes wandered about I remarked to Ardyth how homely the female guests appeared. If one had to take an inventory of female beauty in this place, one would have to conclude that American women are outright homely. But then, I said, "Beauty is only skin deep," to which she replied: "But oogliness goes down to the bone."

Much as both of us like lobster, we refrained from ordering it because of the price, two and a half dollars a plate, and let it go with an order of ham with champagne sauce. It did not taste like either, and we agreed that the best food is still the one at home. And home we went, leaving the lure of the movies aside and reassuring each other of the comforts and beauties of our house. (Especially so since I found out in the morning that a house across

JANUARY 17, 1948

the street on Park Avenue, a house one-third as big as ours and without oil heat, has been put on sale and the price is $3,000 more than what we paid for ours.)

Ever since Christmas the days have been crowded with doings and meetings, and best of all work. The most talked-about event was George Stern's wedding (probably the least important), with the never-mentioned work of Ardyth in the background, but ever present and permeating every inch of the house. The novel progresses so natural and so artless as to make the tremendous emotional effort she makes appear to be completely absent. Yesterday evening, at the reading of one of the best chapters, she cried so bitterly, with the tears running down her cheeks and her eyes turning red, that we had to interrupt for a while. It was all about the cow Bonnie having been sold.

For a few days before and right after the wedding, the telephone rang ever so often during the day, and the women, the little women for whom Ardyth has such true understanding and compassion, bothered her so much that I had a hard time of it, for she is so glad to see me come home that she grasps the first opportunity to show her wrath about being annoyed by Mrs. Stern or Claire, or whoever else, to me. The poor girl is so worked up at such times, which often do coincide with her premenstrual time, that she suffers the tortures of a saint. During such an outburst of anger, she made it known to me, without mincing words, that the telephone is the invention of the devil, that it is her mortal enemy and should be torn off the wall. The next day I went to the telephone office and had our number taken off the list and made it an unpublished one. Only the hospital hence can call me. They will come on the 20th of January and make the change.

I acted at George's wedding as the best man, with Ardyth taking a sort of mother's role, since Eva the bride is an orphan. Outside of us and the couple to be married, there were only three people present: George's mother, her sister and the sister's husband, Uncle Alfred, who used to be ages ago a clerk at the Austrian Embassy in Tien Tsin. But that was a long time ago. Now he is 72. He gave George a beautifully carved teak wood chest, which he had kept from his old days in China, as a wedding gift.

We went first to Mother Stern's apartment to get the bride and her ladies-in-waiting. George went behind us with Uncle Alfred.

When we arrived at the synagogue at 5 p.m., the schammes, who greeted us with a gesture as if he was saying who in the hell is this? did not know a thing about the wedding. I thought that strange, and, not caring much for the rabbi anyway, I blamed the delay right away on him.

The schammes, as a recent German refugee, could not talk a word of English. He showed us into the library, mumbling something like "Ich weiss nicht warum." [I don't know why.] The library had a stone floor and was neither heated nor lighted. It was too dark to look at books and too cold to sit down. No one spoke a word until after a while Ardyth, trying to make conversation, said, "What an interesting room." But no one took her up on it, and everybody shivered and looked pale. I guess our party looked more like it was going to a funeral than to a wedding. I thought so particularly when George, in a low whisper, confessed to me he had diarrhea.

After waiting about fifteen minutes for the rabbi, I asked the schammes to call him on the phone and ask him whether he had forgotten the wedding. But the schammes could not use the phone, since he did not speak English. So finally I made George telephone, and he came back quickly, announcing that it was all a mistake and that the wedding was to take place in the rabbi's home. Everybody felt relieved—mostly, I think, because everybody knew it would be warm there.

So we drove up to the hill of the rabbi's pretentious mansion and there were greeted by the landlord with the words: "Since when don't you understand English, George?" Poor George, I'm sure, felt more diarrhea, but tried to laugh it off. All of us rearranged again the flowers in our buttonholes and the ladies their corsages as we were graciously shown into the library by the rabbi's wife.

The room where, the rabbi immediately informed us, many a marriage had been performed was really impressive. It was one of those precious dark oakwood libraries built into the walls and over the doors up to the ceiling, with modest lights contained within the shelves and filled completely with the complete works of all the great writers one can think of. Expensively bound pig's-leather tomes in excellent condition, especially ordered, if not made to order, and put up in such a way as to obviously impress the eye more than invite one to read there.

The rabbi went right to work and arrayed us in a half-circle with Mother Stern, her sister and Ardyth behind, and I to the right of George with Uncle Alfred flanking the bride on the left. As I listened to the well-greased voice of the rabbi, I noticed his well-nourished wife back in a dark corner watching him with the utmost admiration and could not help wondering how she would not by now be bored to hear his words over and over again. As for myself, I performed well, I think, as the best man and guarded the ring til I was asked to turn it over. Yet while he wedded the couple, I could not repress thinking of Ogden Nash's poem:

> *To all things clergic*
> *I am allergic.*

When it came to signing the papers, Ardyth, who had witnessed her first Jewish wedding, stepped forward to the little desk on the wall and fully expected to sign her name as one of the witnesses for the bride. She was sorely disappointed when the rabbi completely ignored her, for she knew not at the time that women cannot officiate in any function in affairs of the Jewish church. This, of course, needed later a good deal of explanation on my part, and I can vouch that my explanations did not satisfy her.

We arrived home just in time to greet the first congratulants—Uncle George and Aunt Anna from Albany, who had come all the way to attend the reception, which Ardyth had prepared in our house to repay the kindness of the Sterns in past years, and more specifically for their invitation to stay with them after she came back to Portland two years ago, until she could find an apartment.

As I think back now, I am sure that the punch Ardyth had made for the occasion was more of an attraction than the newly married couple, because the bride did not say hardly a word all evening, and George the groom spent a good deal of the time in our bathroom. But the punch was spoken of as much as drunk by every one of the hundred-odd guests. It was a fishhouse punch which George Washington loved to serve to his guests in Virginia. Here is the recipe:

> 3 bottles rum
> 2 bottles brandy
> 14 oz. peach liqueur
> 2¼ cups lemon juice
> 2 cups sugar syrup
> 6 bottles sparkling Burgundy
> 4 bottles Champagne

It was, of course, George's reception, and we furnished but the house and its hospitality, so that we did not know half of the people who soon milled through the rooms. But if we had looked like a party to a funeral two hours earlier, we soon began to feel like [we were] celebrating V-E day on Times Square, with all attempts at getting acquainted by conversation abandoned and taking the presence of everybody, known or unknown, for granted, patting shoulders, cheering and fraternizing. Soon one of the carpets was removed and Ardyth led the dancing, with all the charm and grace her person radiates at all times she feels kindly toward mankind. Looking at her smilingly, I foresaw that in a day or two she'll ask me whether I, too, sometimes love people on Tuesday and loathe them on Wednesday. But I pushed the thought aside as fast as it came and gloried in her glory.

The last to go, as always, was Freddy and a fellow by the name of Bob Blauer, a furrier in George's department who was so drunk that I had to cool him off before letting him go out of the house by establishing him in a children's chair safely anchored against the railing of the front porch of the house, in the cold of the night.

When the last guest had left, Ardyth beamed, because she knew her efforts as a hostess had been better than successful and that she had really made a contribution by turning the affair into a real festivity. She was tired, however, and her feet were numb on the sides of her soles. She had bought for the occasion some flat-heeled shoes so as to look not too incongruous in height attending the wedding of probably one of the shortest families in Portland. But the shoes were one size too small, as it turned out, and squeezed her feet considerably. Before turning in, I had to reassure her that the feeling on that part of the body is not very important and will come back soon.

We went to bed, and as she stretched out with a good feeling of physical fatigue and satisfaction that it was over, I comforted her, like Solomon, with apples, for she was sick with love, and she enjoyed the tart gaiety of a green apple.

January 18, 1948

Ardyth is the best housekeeper you ever saw. Today she has the sewing fury and mended, buttonholed, pressed and altered her wardrobe all day long—a rare sight, because I don't remember the last time she had a needle and thread in her hand.

Of course, it always was her mother who with pride fixed her clothes and ran the sewing machine at all hours, many of those latter spent by moving the machine from room to room and corner to corner. Half of the time of Mother's existence is spent by moving—either things around, or herself from place to place. I don't believe that she has ever slept longer than a few weeks in a row in a bed that remained in the same place in the room. Sometimes the bed is moved as often as three times in a week, once the head turning east, then west and then southwest, each time arranging the lamp, with miles of extension cords, and the family photographs, neatly pasted on a board or in a frame around the walls, so that she can help herself to light and the sight of her beloved ones with the least effort. But, like an efficiency expert, she always finds a better way which would make her spend less energy in using bed, sewing machine and family photographs and never counts that she exerts her strength a thousand times more by moving and fixing the furniture every little while than possibly turning her head a little more to look at her mother's photo or stretching out her arm an inch longer to turn on or out the light, which by the way she never does anyway, because it is left burning always, rain or shine.

Some of that restlessness, of course, transfers itself to Ardyth, if Mother is in the house; and no matter how helpful she is, she does cause, merely by her presence, an extra effort on Ardyth's part to please her. I don't know how successful Ardyth will be this time in keeping Mother content in California.

JANUARY 20, 1948

If more people would have their telephones taken out of their homes, I believe we'd have less neurotics. It is astounding how much calmer Ardyth is since she is left alone. We now have no interruptions of empty inquiries from people who use the phone just to pass the time.

After a pause of a week, Ardyth sat down to write again. I am watching what influence the book will have upon her who is writing it, and during that very writing. For I am sure that as the book issues from her, it will modify the course of her life.

Like all introspectives, she loves to go into things and tells me often about her physical discomforts, which appear and disappear with endless variety, like the figures in a kaleidoscope—and, as these do with children, hold her forever in a spell of amazed or surprised anxiety. These discomforts make her talkative and often produce reminiscences of her childhood back to a time when she was no older than eighteen months. At such occasions she likes to read to me Montaigne or Marcus Aurelius and other masters of introspection, lately Edwin Robinson's letters. The latter, of course—closer to her time, if not contemporary—rings closer to home, since he, like she, suffered greatly from his inconsistencies, whereas Montaigne, though melancholy, was a passionately amused spectator of self. If introspection for Montaigne, Proust and others has been an art, even though as an attempt to objective study, to Ardyth it is forever but a punitive expedition, during which she is tormented by her vanity or idiosyncrasies and sundry human weaknesses. Only yesterday she told me that her melancholy differs profoundly from that in the writings of most contemporaries in that it is not at all caused by the change in the American scene, a loss of faith or despair in the future, but is definitely connected with the physical cycles of womanhood, and she conceded that her depressed moods seem a little in excess of the circumstances, as T. S. Eliot said of Hamlet.

Last night, in bed, she told me she was going to take a Shakespeare course one evening a week, having never taken one during her years in college. The idea for it came while reading *Untriangulated Stars* with a piece of the last apple in the house in her mouth. Somewhere in these letters Robinson refers to the apologia of Socrates and builds up the context of the paragraph on associations with it.

She: What does a-p-o-l-o-g-i-a mean?
Me: Apologia of what?
She: A-p-o-l-o-g-i- a.
Me: Why, that's apology, don't you know? When Socrates was accused of heresy and had to face the judges, he—
She: Apologized.
Me: No! he denied—
She: Oh, he denied flatly—I see.

JANUARY 26, 1948

The coldest day of the year is never the one with the lowest temperature recorded, but the one when the wind sweeps down the Columbia Valley from the East and enters the house through every finest slit, slot and crack of doors and windows. You feel cold then, even if the thermometer registers 80 degrees in the room. Such days mean actual physical suffering for Ardyth, who has a somewhat unstable thermic system anyway. Today, while the full moon is out and the wind is howling, she is ill with cold and squats over the furnace opening in the living room inhaling the hot air with her inferior parts. Even on warmer days she loves to do that—in a standing position, though, when after a meal she suddenly feels freezing. Most people feel comfortably warm after dinner. Not she. Her skin pales and often goes into gooseflesh—I have seen her teeth chatter—and she begins to complain bitterly about being cold until, after half an hour or so with the furnace going and with the help of a cup of coffee, she recovers.

Tonight she promised to attend an evening class on Shakespeare at the Extension at Lincoln High School. But I kept her at home. After a long day of writing—eight beautiful pages—and one hour "wasted" with diarrhea, a rare happening with her, I thought she had done her share and deserved to stretch out and take it easy. I read her some biographical notes on William James from Matthiessen's book and we discussed Pragmatism.

She found the meaning of James' thoughts to be almost "childish," commenting how strange it is that men can devote their lives to explaining things that are really self-evident and need not be talked much about—and become famous with it. She did not think I—or James, rather—told her anything new. She concludes whimsically that she always "joined the procession and was willing to face the music and take the risk." With this quotation, she happily returned to her newly discovered book on the assassination of Lincoln by the Negro John E. Washington: *They Knew Lincoln*.

SUNDAY, FEBRUARY 1, 1948

The time with the telephone lasted exactly three days. For three days there were no calls and Ardyth thought she had the problem licked. On Thursday I came home and found her ironing my shirts, dissolved in tears. Claire had called up and Ardyth could hardly speak over the phone, feeling betrayed and spied upon. In her mood, being alone at home and feeling tense and unwell on the fourteenth day of her monthly gale, she abandoned reason and allowed her emotions to magnify this little incident, where no harm was meant, to become an obsession. For two or three hours she cried to herself and honestly felt as though the world had come to a stop. As often in instances that arise suddenly, without warning, her first impulse was to run away, escape, leave—she knew not where—just go away. For a moment she felt the urge to commit suicide to "end it all," but after a while her better self asserted itself and she got out the dampened shirts and ironed one after another until I came home, when every thought, feeling, impulse and sentiment came out with tears and heartbreaking self-reproach. As so often, she tried to explain the whole episode by going back to her days as a girl, her being jealous of Marion, her younger sister, and her difficult times after her father's sudden death.

Claire, innocently but persistently, had pursued finding our new telephone number by calling the hospital often enough that the night operator, the only one I had not spoken to myself not to give out our new number, had given it to her. The much better way, of course, would have been for me simply to tell the people who call Ardyth habitually not to call over the phone, but that would not do—it might have hurt their feelings. So I had to go all the way to making a change in the phone set-up.

The following day Ardyth felt better and asked me to read up, in the library, on the newer aspects of the menstrual cycle with respect to hormones, because she felt sure her feelings and violent emotional breakdowns were due to some compelling cause that had to do with ovulation. With all her intellectual grace, she tried to show me how fully aware she was of her being unreasonable so often, toward me as well as toward things in general, but also how hopelessly helpless she felt in the struggle between "the good and the wicked" in her. It is, of course, this struggle within herself, the passion never to be surprised and be seen by anybody when she is not prepared and dressed and made up for company, that is the core of a certain vein of her personality which approaches eccentricity, and I find it very attractive. In fact I know, like Henry Adams knew it of Clover, that Ardyth rules me as only an American woman can rule men, and I cower before her.

Friday we went shopping and bought some lingerie and house clothes for Ardyth. When we came home she dressed up with these new acquisitions and played with each piece, skirts, sweaters, jackets, nightgowns, bed jacket and slips, like a very young girl—or all women?—and no one would have suspected that here is a grand person, a great artist, a wonderful woman with wisdom and love to whom people flock to find, in talking to her, a moment of peace and security. Like a child she strutted before the mirror and gloried in the line and the fit of the clothes, which really was but her own charm and beauty, and suddenly all was good and hopeful and peace. And when we settled down, she blamed the change within her on a little pill of promone, a progesterol hormone, which I found recommended for women who become tense around the middle of the period and had brought home for her from the hospital.

In the evening she read to me eighteen pages she had written in the last two days and brought me so completely under the spell of her style that I did not know whether it was the story, or the way she put words together, or the way she read them to me. I felt absolutely enchanted with her.

MAY 2, 1948

It is soothing to be alone—the two of us, I mean. Mother is in Albany for one of the birthdays of Uncle George. She never misses one or forgets it.

Ardyth and I get along so much more easily when we are alone, because there is no one else to consider in the house and, I suppose, she can give me her undivided attention. I must be jealous or resentful somehow if she talks or listens with endless patience and kindness to the old lady's never-ending reminiscences of long past days. How Mrs. Hansen baked cherry pie or Uncle Arthur died of pneumonia or Mrs. Peacock lived to be a hundred without ever leaving her room for thirty years. I feel so much freer when we are alone because I am rarely scolded, if ever, or dealt with impatiently, which is always or often the case if Ardyth resents Mother. She never lets her feel or notice it, but if she can no longer stand reminiscences which contain hints of discontentment with the present, she turns her impatience on me. Knowing that, from observation as well as bedtime-whispered confessions, I remain unruffled and go about my little tasks in the house in as unconcerned a way as possible.

So today, with Uncle George's birthday, we are at ease and discussed all morning Chopin's Études, Viennese coffee houses, Lana Turner's marriage to Topping, and plans for the future. Moreover and foremost, we talked about the novel, which is now completed and has to be gone over before the final draft is typed. We will get a typist for this. Ardyth discussed the title several times with me and seems not to be able to get around the temporary working title of "Love Is a Local Anguish," taken from a letter of Coleridge to Southey. She read me the letter the other day.

Sometimes at night she is reading about Lincoln's assassination, which holds an everlasting fascination for her. I had to take the book away from her and suggested she not read it at night because she gets so terribly excited about it that she cannot go to sleep, especially lately, since she plays with the idea of writing a Lincoln novel, or rather the story of the manhunt for Booth. I am enchanted with the idea of her doing it.

Another cause for nightly interruptions of her sleep are her toenails of the big toes. She squeezed both her big toes during the wedding reception for George Stern way back in January when she wore new, too-small shoes. Soon thereafter the nails of the big toes turned black. Due to her habit of wearing a kind of sandal in the house from which the big toes stick out, she traumatizes these very toetips repeatedly and lately got especially the left big toe so aroused that it sometimes cannot stand the pressure of the blanket at night and keeps her (and me) awake. Her with pain, me with mixed feelings—anger, pity, the urge of the physician in me to amputate the toenail and my impatience with the foolish vanity of women. But then we fall asleep after a while and I forget her big toes till the next night comes. I wonder. She would not even show it to me until very, very recently. She'd show me anything, anything rather than her big toe, she often said with tears in her eyes. Yet when I finally saw it, I found that it was a perfectly good old-fashioned big toe with a bruise and discolored nail and nothing to be ashamed of.

November 27, 1948

"Love Is a Local Anguish" went out to Houghton Mifflin on my birthday, September 22. It took Sylvia Carl, a high school girl from a close-by apartment house, two months and ten days to type it, for she could work only half days, helping her father paint and paper the apartment or the mother to keep house the other half. But she did well, and there were few corrections to be made.

During the time Sylvia was typing the MS, we moved to an apartment on Montgomery Street after having sold the house on Park Street to a Mrs. Hazen, who died about ten days after she and her husband moved in. Mrs. Hazen was a sweet old lady who had swollen legs when we first met her four weeks earlier, very definite ideas on the order of wallpaper and an immediate liking, if not love, for Ardyth. Indeed, we later learned from her husband that on the last day she could still talk, three days before she died, she talked about Ardyth and how she was looking forward to a rummage sale she had proposed the two of them would hold with the things they wanted to discard, worthless furniture, kitchen utensils and the sundry worthless bric-a-brac all women spend their money on when they only intend to spend time. But it never came to it. Mrs. Hazen died prematurely at an advanced age, leaving her lonely husband alone in the huge, newly papered—and what paper!—house, and most of our discarded furniture went to Spada, a newly acquired friend.

Ardyth was again in her element—decorating a new apartment. Papering the walls pale pink, the ceilings silver, painting the built-in library to match the walls and discussing the new furniture with Mr. Cohen filled her days. Mother, of course, was at her side with brush and broom and hammer and crossbar, and the more the two women went into it, the more uneasy I grew. I can't stand the smell of fresh paint, it makes me truly sick to my stomach, and I grow sad when I see one after another of my pants, socks and shirts being exposed to Ardyth's concoctions of Mr. Fuller's paints. But there they went, no matter how much I sighed or how faintly I protested, for painted everything must be as long as there is paint in the house, and if there wasn't any more paint, I had to go down and buy some more, special colors, indigo, vermilion, cobalt.

Then I was surprised by the delivery of an old but very beautiful china closet with mirrors and curved glass plates which had cost practically nothing at all. Two months later I wondered why Ardyth had no money at all in October, but none, none at all, and having by then become used to the very nice china closet, the way it was put up so that the mirror effect was at its best, it never came to my mind that she could have possibly paid more for it than she had told me at first, and had earmarked her October money—all of it, mind you (like in "Life with Father"), in August! so that I was—as usual—pressed for money more than I had anticipated.

By the time the apartment was finished it was truly elegant, inviting and radiating Ardyth's personality all over. Charms and simples in the kitchen, indigo-colored chest and pinkly fringed bedspreads in the bedroom, an impressively arranged library in a room overlooking town and mountains—three living rooms in a row with the double doors removed between them, and a picture gallery of old prints over the bathtub. Over the toilet hung a self-drawn angel with a striking likeness of Ardyth, the black nail that kept it on the wall used as eye.

There was only one flaw in the apartment—Violet, the cat. From the day the new cherry-red carpet and the specially designed couch to match it were delivered, she began scratching and clawing the wool out of them. Whenever I was present, I protested by clapping my hands or hissing or shouting, or making myself felt in the quickest way my reflexes would make me do. But soon I learned that that was not the way to do with a cat—not with Ardyth's cat, anyway, for I was told that it was making the cat nervous.

Of course, my heart bled when I saw the expensive furniture become more ragged and frayed as time went on, but since I could not stay home all the time to hold Violet in my lap or keep her, one way or the other, from pulling thread after thread out of the costly cloth—my protestations to Violet became weaker and meeker by the week, particularly since I noticed that she helped Ardyth writing her second book. In all sincerity, the cat never behaved as well and helpfully as during the hours Ardyth spent in the studio at the long, specially built desk with room enough for her and many, many spread-out papers, the typewriter and dictionaries, writing about the time when John Wilkes Booth shared the hour with Lincoln. Then Violet crouched peacefully somewhere on the large desk and followed Ardyth's hand as she put the words down line by line—hour after hour.

About the middle of October, at a time when we thought it much too soon to hear about the book, since everybody knows that first novels are reported on by the publishers after at least two months or maybe longer, the managing editor of Houghton Mifflin was sincerely interested in the book, thought it incredible that it should be her first, and asked for information about Ardyth past and present and the book's background. Ardyth wrote her promptly in response, and on November 6th a letter arrived from H.M. offering her a contract with, by the way, some very pleasant content. Mrs. de Santillana, who signed as managing editor, asked for Ardyth's consent to the terms of the offer, which contained a $500.00 advance in royalties—and promised then to send the contract for signature. This was three weeks ago today. Today my girl is a little nervous because she has received neither contract nor a word since.

DECEMBER 11, 1948

Ardyth received her contract for "Love Is a Local Anguish" on December 4, signed it, returned it and is now waiting for the check of $500 advance payment which is due at the signing of the contract. It'll come just in time for Christmas, not to buy things for herself—or me, God no—to buy things for her little people whom she would not let down even if I had to go broke Christmas, birthdays or anytime.

The acceptance of a first novel today is a great event in anybody's life. It is thought of as an accomplishment in itself. As for me, and I think Ardyth too, we think of it only as the latter. She could not fail, and more events will follow. The managing editor of Houghton Mifflin enjoys corresponding with her and closes her letter (received today) with the words "Do let us hear from you whenever you feel like it." We like it! With three letters exchanged, she made a real friend with Mrs. de Santillana (editor) the way she did with my mother across 7,000 miles, so that Mother wrote me she loves Ardyth more than any other child-in-law, without ever having seen her. How she would have loved her had she lived to meet her!

The placing of the book has not changed Ardyth at all. It has only brought to the fore two traits that I knew so well all these years, traits needing just that sort of encouragement: the passion to write and the even greater one to live. To write so that all the people will love her and to live so that she can love all the people.

Lately she has met a few Italians. Last August I thought of writing a memorial for the centennial of Corti's discovery of the organ of hearing. In search of someone to help me translate Corti's writing, I found a young Italian professor of philosophy who teaches at the University of Portland. We became friends, and I asked Spada to the house. Ardyth likes that young, proud, Catholic Florentine now, sends him real paprika or a bit of cake whenever we have guests and she cooked more than we could eat, and likes to be led by him through the museum whenever there are European pictures on exhibit. He in turn introduced her to a Reed student, Falbo, who promptly borrowed a good and rare edition of Ossian from our library and makes her think he is a poet. I doubt it very much, for if he were he would not write a "thesis" on Leopardi but would produce some poems instead.

Well, Spada and Falbo are good friends, and, being single and cooking for themselves, have won a soft spot in Ardyth's heart. Today I came home after a hectic day in the clinic, and as I opened the door I saw my girl all fixed up, dressed, makeup and everything. "I am going over to Spada's now." "Oh," said I, "it's raining hard, do you want me to take you over?" "Yes, of course, please." As I drove her down, she took my hand and said: "Darling, I got beautiful thick lamb chops for dinner and asparagus. But now I have to go. I sort of invited myself."

"Why did you do that?" I asked.

"Because before I married you, I never led a proper life."

"I see," I answered, "so now you want to have an improper life."

"Yes," and we laughed.

Ardyth is well along with the Booth, and as if to soothe any bad feelings I would have about that visit with Spada, she added: "You know in January I am going into seclusion" (to write the book). I acquiesced.

The attitude of many of her friends has become more, shall I say, formal, since she is going to be published. Before that everybody loved her—now they do that, of course, but she takes on proportion in the eyes of people like Freddy or my sister or her aunts.

New Year's Day, 1949

Christmas over with, it was decided that Ardyth would go down to Santa Monica to finish the Booth. People don't leave her alone here and keep on calling her on the phone. I told her I cannot take the phone out. They have to be able to get me from the hospital. But I would not object to her going down south. I bought the ticket and we began telling everybody she was leaving. We went to the Good Will and bought a large trunk for the many books and things she was to take along, and packed it full. Her departure was set for New Year's Eve, and she was to arrive on the second of January. On Christmas Eve we sat in the library and looked at each other. The room was lovely, dimly lit with red lights, and the view of the city overwhelming, with all lights on and the air clear for a change.

"I wish I didn't have to leave you alone," she suddenly said.

"You don't have to, if you don't want to," I said. "Yet now that we have decided upon it, I think it is really the best thing for you to go and come back in two months, the Booth all done and nothing more on your mind. Look, you'll be all ready for the first book to get going, you can then go with Mother to Salt Lake City to look things over for the next novel, and moreover I'll buy you a new outfit of clothes."

"I'd much rather stay here if nobody would bother me. How about telling everybody I am gone and I stay here?"

"That's an idea, and I'll help you all I can. I'll accept invitations about once a week, and you write everybody a card from Santa Monica, sending the cards first to Mother. How do you think Mother would feel about it? Would she be hurt?"

"I'll fix it with her right now."

She called Mother in Salt Lake City, where she was spending the holidays with Aunt Tekla. Mother didn't quite like it, but Ardyth can always appease her mother.

Next she explained how she was fixing the little dining room into a study and how she was not going to leave the house until the Booth was written. She told me how glad she felt that she left the Booth story, about a month or so ago, just at a spot where she had Booth and Davy at Dr. Mudd's, where they spent the last night of their lives in a bed, and how she felt they were safe there until she could get to them again in about a week or so. She had the same feeling she used to have before going to pick hops as a child. She knew she was going to have to make a great effort and would feel sweetly tired, even exhausted, at night so that she would want to go to bed almost before sunset, maybe without supper if she was too tired. But the next morning she would be fresh and never would miss a day.

In order to make the deception complete, I went to Lilly and borrowed a small suitcase for the trip, and Ardyth sat down and wrote a number of cards and letters. It all looked authentic, and Ardyth, for all people know, left last night for Santa Monica.

I am soooo happy. I have her with me, can look out for her, even wash the dishes, and she is reading to me what she wrote the day before every evening after dinner. We unpacked the trunk last night and put the books back on the shelves.

I made her promise me that every evening she will come with me for a little ride in the car and possibly a half an hour walking up in the hills. Today she is at work and I will go to Dr. George's New Year's Egg Nog afternoon. Tomorrow I have to see Professor Woodbridge in the hospital to study his detached retina. I will operate on him within a week. In the afternoon I might see "Hamlet" with Olivier. I cannot afford to miss *that*.

JANUARY 9, 1949

Today I took the first 25 pages of "The Wounded Name" to Sylvia for the last typing. Ardyth does not want to give her more at a time because she would go crazy if they were lost, since she has only that one corrected copy.

She is all closeted now, officially absent in Santa Monica, and hasn't seen a soul except me for the past ten days. She gets up in the morning at seven exact, about ten minutes before I push myself out of bed, prepares our breakfast and then smokes a cigarette with me. At exactly eight she is at her table, our dining room table with two boards put in, and begins to type the pages she had written by longhand the day before. This she can do while somebody is in the house. So I can remain until the time comes for me to go, about 8:45 or 9 o'clock. But not even I can remain when she does her real writing. I could never explain that fact. Mother bothers her even more. Yet in the evening when I come home, she tells me over and over that she feels like she was in a cell of a jail and points out how many good books have been written in jail, quoting Cervantes, Wilde, Dostojewski, O'Henry and others.

She works through, without a minute's pause, til the clock says noon. Then she goes out in the kitchen and makes herself an omelette with apricot jam and a cup of coffee. But now she can't enjoy this as much anymore, probably because of the repetition, and asked me today to bring home some kosher corned beef and Cheddar cheese for sandwiches. After thirty minutes she is back again for work and never stops til 5 o'clock in the afternoon. When I come home at that time, she looks like she has been putting up fruit all day, with sweat on her face and sort of bedraggled, apologizing for her looks and imploring me not to look at her. But I reassure her of the truth that no woman ever looked lovelier than she right now, after all this travail. That pleases her no end, notwithstanding her protests.

Usually about that time I unpack whatever I had brought home, steaks, vegetables, a bottle of five-year-old imported Chianti and maybe a movie magazine for her to look at. Also I give her the mail, which she does not go down in the morning to remove from the box. It's mostly from Marion or Mother, but occasionally a message from a friend who wants to know more about her book or herself. Then she makes dinner for us while I catch my breath from a full day's work, or just from running up the long parapet and stairs of the house, and as we sit down she reminds me that I have forgotten to put the water on the table or to pour the wine, definitely my business.

During the meal we glory in the success of having deceived our friends about her whereabouts, and maybe the telephone rings and somebody inquires whether I have news from her and how long she is going to stay. I have learned by now the role of a bachelor so well that I am not even tempted any longer to make a mistake in what I say. I usually tell of how warm or cold it is in Los Angeles and how Mother is, so as to make my words sound more authentic, and when I return to the table we both laugh heartily.

This noon I made the omelette while she was running the vacuum cleaner, and when I opened the lid of the pan, I noticed that the omelette was beginning to collapse rather than to be high, as she likes it. When I served it, I asked her what would have become of it if I had left it much longer on the stove. "Why," she said, "it would become smaller and smaller until it's all gone." "Well," I said, and we roared.

Last night I saw "Hamlet" with Olivier. Freddy finally persuaded me to go with him and I went, although I hated to leave her all evening alone. But somehow I have to accept invitations, or else my refusals would arouse suspicious questions at once. I was glad I saw "Hamlet" at this point. It made me aware of the parallels in the characters of Booth and Hamlet, and moreover showed me her wonderful gift of association by choosing the title of the book from Hamlet's last speech.

FEBRUARY 6, 1949

Ardyth put the finis to the Booth this noon and changed the title to "The Spur."

In a letter to her mother, she enclosed the text of two telegrams to be sent from Santa Monica to Freddy and Mrs. Stern announcing the finishing of the book and her return soon.

In the evening, when I came home and she had read me the last ten pages, she became suddenly melancholic such as I have rarely seen her. She would not talk for a long time. When I finally asked what was bothering her, she said she was afraid she had failed, and cried. She slept restlessly that night.

FEBRUARY 7, 1949

Ever since she began writing the last pages, her bowels closed up and she is terribly constipated. Throughout the years, we had a saying that if all her organs rebelled, sometimes one or sometimes the other, at least her bowels did their part without ever quarreling. But apparently this time it's their turn.

We are snowed in, with several inches of snow having fallen last night. The sixth consecutive day of severe winter in Portland! I don't know whether I'll be able to go to the office.

MARCH 1, 1949

Everything went according to schedule, even if pain, agony and frequent crying accompanied it. On February tenth we went to Seattle. There were several reasons for this. To begin with, I wanted real bad for Ardyth to get out of the apartment for a few days, because she had been closed in for almost six weeks without seeing a soul except me and the cat. Then there was a letter from Diggory Venn asking for pictures for the book-jacket, and lastly I had promised Ardyth to get her a spring outfit as soon as the book was finished. In the back of her mind, meanwhile, was always the face-saving gesture to "have been away and have come back home," so that she did not, after all, lie to her friends about having been away. We returned on the fourteenth, and Ardyth began calling up a few friends. It took her several days to meet the world again, but she made the adjustment remarkably quickly. Only her bowels remained still uncooperative, until three days ago she told me that she found she has to eat more cooked vegetables. Which was O.K. with me.

On the 20th of February I got the manuscript typed and ready for the last corrections. Ardyth sat up that night until 4 o'clock to get it in shape and wrap it up, without forgetting to put her father's square knot in, and address it to Houghton Mifflin. I took it to the Express, not without feeling like an uncle who is sending his nephew out in the world.

On February 24th we received the pictures which Kassowitz made in Seattle and were gratified to find them as good as we had hoped for, and we mailed them to Mr. Venn.

We had a little party for the professor of literature Dr. MacRae, Dr. Jones and Father Scheberle. Charles Lee and his mother, as well as Freddy and Dr. Spada, were also with us. Ardyth hoped so much for good conversation and a real jolly time. But little came true of it. Only the food was good, and Ardyth's looks. She wore a new, light brown silk dress with something floating over her bottom and looked like a fairy. But we learned little except various complaints from the professors, who stayed nevertheless until 2:30 in the morning. At least we went to bed feeling that *they* had a good time.

I am having a little tiff with Dr. Mossman. I think I must call it insubordination. When I mentioned it tonight to Ardyth, to hear and get her advice, I am sorry to say she blamed it all on me. I felt real bad and asked her how in the world she could ever put up with me if I really was as fickle and prevaricating as she said I am. She waved my protest aside, saying that that is what *she* loves in me, but she doubts whether others will. In fact she said it was my stories, true and imagined, that made her love me. I am thinking about that all the time while she is at dinner with Dr. Spada and Mr. Potassio, treated to spaghetti. I don't care much for Dr. Spada, since he is getting fat and thinks I don't know that Ardyth went there for dinner.

NOVEMBER 11, 1949

"The Peaceable Kingdom" was published on November 7, 1949, with some fanfare, at least here locally in Portland, and if the wires of Paul Brooks indicate anything, in the East too. The British rights were sold on publication day to Victor Gollancz, and the first review I read in the New York Herald Tribune of November 6th was very good.

But the whole fuss, with parties, praise and publicity, made Ardyth sick—first she got a cold which refused to yield its moisture to Thephorin tablets—and then, after all the noise of the three days of feting were over, she broke down with crying and a deep melancholy. When she saw, with some surprise, that I had enjoyed the whole thing with "Viennese" gusto, she cried the harder and confessed that she felt so terrible because not even the success of her first book could "stop the pain in her heart," the pain of living! She cannot get over having been so lonely in her teenage years—then over not belonging—then over not being loved—not even now, when she has begun to rise.

I bought a beautiful, pure 18th-century copy tea table and brought it home in the car. She did not pay too much attention—at first. But after I made a nice fire and the tears calmed down, she looked and showed me signs of approval and forgetting her pain.

"Pull up your sleeves and please help me," she said calmly as she surveyed the room, and within no time at all we were pushing the furniture around like professional huskies. That always brings her back to reality.

NOVEMBER 20, 1949

Ardyth is working downstairs, in her new but not yet fixed-up studio, on a syndicated article on anonymous photographs of her collection.

I am sitting upstairs in hunting shirt and whiskers whiling the time away with paying unreasonable plumber bills, keeping account books and thinking the situation over.

The first thing that comes to my mind is the new house at 2029 SW Montgomery Drive that we bought and moved into on October 26th, 1949! If things work out, I will consider this one of the major events in our life, because for the first time in our married life and the unmarried that preceded it for six years, Ardyth seems genuinely happy with the surroundings. Think of it—we lived in 33-odd places together before we moved in here, and with each move we knew, as we fixed up the place—apartment or house, as the case was, rented or bought—that it would be only for a while, until she got tired of it and we would move on to the next one.

But this house seems to be different. At first she did not want to move in, and was not even looking for a place. We just went for a ride in search of a place for Marion, Mother and the boys (they have become our charge since Marion's husband Kenneth disappeared from the visible surface of the world with some $70,000 in July of this year) and were looking for a house for them, to be bought with the first money Ardyth was to receive from the Literary Guild. Driving along Montgomery Drive on a beautiful Indian summer Sunday morning, I saw a "sale" sign in front of the door, stopped and went into the house, Ardyth refusing to even look at it because with her distaste for being promoted, she never wanted to live in Portland Heights.

An old lady with a heavy Irish brogue took me around, and I was at once enchanted with the glassed-in rooms and sunshine that came through the trees, which still showed enough foliage to make the sun, as it came in the rooms through the lace curtains, a warmly welcoming friend. I was in the house only a few minutes before I hurried out to the car and got the whole family in to see it. "You simply *must* see this one," I said, with apparently enough enthusiasm in my voice to have Ardyth and the rest come out of the car instantly.

She was at once enchanted with the house—location, architectural layout, and the old lady from County Clare in Ireland, Mary Wallace. Mrs. Wallace and Ardyth hit it off within a few minutes, and when I showed her a newspaper clipping about *The Peaceable Kingdom*, we closed the deal. We could move in on an earnest money payment of $250 and agreed to pay out the house in full, $15,000, as soon as the Literary Guild pays. (Within 90 days from now, I do hope.) As soon as we have the title, we will redo and refurnish the whole house, build a garage and fix the sloping grounds in the back. The floor beneath the main floor holds a carpeted studio with a fireplace and an open terrace, a small but sufficiently large built-in library, and room enough for desks, couch, coffee table, etc., which makes Ardyth completely happy to work in. I consider this house as a very important contribution for her future work, the more so since she repeatedly tells me of the happiness that, she is sure, lies within its walls.

DECEMBER 12, 1949

Yesterday, after reading aloud the chapter on addictions in Salter's *Conditioned Reflex Therapy*, both of us quit smoking. Now, 24 hours later, I for my part still long for a cigarette, and Ardyth seems to get over her craving apparently by warning me never to take up smoking again, or telling me (and herself) how happy she is about our decision. To make things worse (for me), she put me on a 1,500 calorie diet, and between not smoking and going hungry, I feel melancholy, irritable and uneasy.

Since I am on vacation for the month of December and so spend most of the time at home, I have ample time on hand. To pass that time with less uneasiness, I am washing with the new Bendix or drying with the new dryer or ironing with the new ironer. I just nibble at it — Ardyth loves it all so much that she asked Marion to bring over her laundry and that of the boys to keep us busy.

This afternoon we are leaving for Albany, Ore., where the mayor has declared Ardyth Kennelly Day (tomorrow), December 13. She is supposed to get the key to the city, but I am looking forward more eagerly to a basket of Albany produce promised by the Chamber of Commerce.

Ardyth is reading *McTeague* by Frank Norris and apparently likes it, being impressed by it. I am still plowing through Parrington's *Main Trends* . . .

DECEMBER 22, 1949

Both of us quit smoking exactly twelve days ago. Ardyth seems to be much more of a hero than I am, because I have since puffed away three times at a cigarette, while she never once did. However, I think I too will entirely overcome that craving, which still makes itself felt every once in a while. For hours on end I can go without even thinking of it.

What made us do it? She was reading to me one of her famous books on how to improve, relax, lose one's phobias and so on. This time it was *Conditioned Reflex Therapy* by Andrew Salter. Somewhere in the chapter on addictions, he makes the statement that each pack of cigarettes smoked costs the smoker eleven hours and fourteen minutes of his life. He does not say how he arrived at these figures, but we were so tremendously impressed and apparently cared so much for not losing any more precious minutes or hours of our lives that we decided to quit smoking right then and there.

Yesterday the Mark Twain Society made Ardyth an Honorary Life Member.

I am buying a lot of books these days and have accumulated an entertaining lot of reference works. Since our books are still downstairs stored in boxes, we now have at least the pleasure of having these *Information Please*s on hand, because there is hardly an hour that Ardyth does not ask me, or vice versa, about the meaning of a word or the habitat of a snake or the wedding customs among some faraway tribe.

I also brought home the second volume of Santayana's autobiography, *The Middle Span*, and Ardyth tells me that it is by far the best of all he had ever written. I liked *Persons and Places* real well and thought it of rare beauty, but she said it was too cold and ice-frosted. But this one she is really enthusiastic about.

I have read Edna Ferber's *Cimarron* and did not much care for it. Too journalistic and without kick for me.

I have been on vacation for the past ten days and still will be until the second of January. Ardyth makes good use of my vacation by making me wash (I love to with the new Bendix and dryer) and run down for the groceries. Today I am going with a big order. The family is having Christmas with us and we are having dinners on the eve (lutfisk) and the day (turkey and ham). The cat is having a feast of her own, tearing down the colored glass balls from the tree and biting chunks out of the silver threads that Ardyth has put up with great care.

JANUARY 19, 1950

We have been snowed in since January 15. Everything is covered with a silver thaw, ice and snow, and Ardyth has not left the house since the horseback party at Borghild's on January 1.

She had a terrible poisoning of her mouth and gums after using a new toothpaste called Ammonium Ion—or A.M.I.—which is supposed to prevent decay. I brought a sample home from the office thinking it might come in handy in case there was nothing else in the house to clean one's teeth with, and A. went ahead and brushed her teeth with it daily. After a few days she thought she had a sore throat, which I diagnosed as virus pharyngitis and which kept on getting worse by the day. Finally it dawned on me that she had had another such episode about eight months ago, though confined to her gums after using Ipana. Anyway, on January 10 we discarded the A.M.I. paste, gave it a curse, comforted each other—mostly I encouraging poor A.—and slept for the first time in several days without fear. Honestly, for one day I got scared she might have pemphigus!

The evening before yesternight we discovered that some of our books stored in boxes in the servants' quarters had become warped, and I was afraid they might suffer if we left them there until the Literary Guild sends enough money to put up a library which would befit our collection and taste. So we decided to unpack them and put them up on the few shelves that were in the house and on tables and floors in the basement.

Ardyth began to put certain copies on a special table and explained to me that hence, she wants all books divided into those that help in our work and increase our knowledge and learning. All others should be sorted out, kept on separate shelves, or even sold or given away.

The Peaceable Kingdom is 14th on the best seller list in the cities:
Chattanooga, Tenn.
Tulsa, Okla.
San Antonio, Tex.
St. Paul, Minn., reporting. Curiously, Portland, Oregon did not report it—by mistake or omission of the clerk, according to Freddy's information at Gill's.

Whenever I have to talk to someone in matters regarding Ardyth's affairs, I move on touchy ground. I am so overly inclined to speak and reveal—I could often kick myself in my seat—and Ardyth cherishes not to say anything, even thinks it nobody's business to know anything at all about her—so that my indiscretions have given rise to quite unnecessary arguments, tears and heartaches. I am trying hard to be reticent and promise to be still more careful of what I say in the future.

JANUARY 23, 1950

We came across the article "Authors and Psychopaths" by W. Russell Brain, in which the psyches of Swift, Donne and Dr. Johnson are discussed from the psychiatric viewpoint. Particularly interesting to both of us was a paragraph on the "sufferer's attitude to the past. More than most men, the obsessional is in bondage to the past; for what is an obsession but a past idea of which he cannot rid himself? In Johnson's own words, 'an everlasting futurity' is 'determined by the past.' The past is both inescapable and unchangeable: for Johnson, therefore (read Ardyth!), guilt endured, and salvation must ever be in doubt."

We are both gaining in weight since we quit smoking (two months ago). This needs a comment. Ardyth, the much stronger of the two of us, really quit smoking and has not touched a single cigarette. I am not so lucky. I smoke about one or two a day, and each time with feelings of disgust. I feel bad about it not because I am afraid this amount of smoking might hurt me, but because I seem (so far) to lack the willpower to quit and to never as much as think of a cigarette.

Ardyth has her theory about willpower, which sounds interesting enough to me to put it down here. She thinks nothing of willpower as such and believes it never works in regard to anything at all except if and when it is harnessed to either fear or desire. So a man, if he fears death or doom strongly enough, will if need be stop eating or moving, let alone such a trifle as smoking. But if he had to depend only on his willpower, he will fail. Similarly, a girl in love will do almost anything if she believes it will bring her nearer the goal of her desire.

So now that we have checked our smoking habit, we are about to curtail eating. Both of us are about 5–8 lbs. overweight according to my feeling, about 10 lbs. if we believe Ardyth. No desserts and no more butter on my bread.

JANUARY 24, 1950

We have a new schedule. After I come home at night, we have dinner. With the inevitable cup of coffee served afterward, Ardyth reads to me the pages written the day before, which have been gone over during typing them today, and we discuss them. This discussion more often than not consists of my being real enthusiastic and sometimes carried away, and she protesting and repeating it isn't good at all. Then I change my clothes and she cleans up the table, and then each of us goes to his study and we write. Letters to be answered, books to be kept, and entries in this and other books (addresses, memos, or interesting phrases come upon during the day, and so on). This way we keep up our correspondence as well as pay our bills and remember things we might otherwise forget.

I am sorry that Ardyth did not keep a list of books she has read. It would by now (since the time we have known each other) be a catalogue of considerable length. And I can testify that she really reads any book she starts, without skipping. At this moment she is interested in American gypsies, and I am bringing sundry volumes on that subject home from the library or buy them. I cannot tell what the attraction or fascination about the gypsies is, but I am sure it'll come out sometime somewhere.

The Peaceable Kingdom has progressed from the 15th to the 8th rank on the best seller list of the N.Y. Herald Tribune, and curiously enough, Portland—that is, Gill's bookstore—is not among those reporting her. I have to ask Mrs. Bristol why.

After many ways and three rooms had been tried by Ardyth as her work room, starting in the basement and coming up to the dining room and bedroom, she has now chosen the second bedroom facing the west to work in.

She has complained often that after typing or writing longhand for several hours, her neck would hurt and feel like a stiff neck radiating down toward the left shoulder. We talked about it and I advised her to try lying down while writing, like Dorothy Thompson or Proust used to do. (Others had to stand up and write at a high old-fashioned desk-secretary, like Rilke or Thomas Wolfe.) So for the past two weeks she has been lying down on a bed with her legs drawn up and a heating pad on her tummy and found that she did not tire at all and felt no pain in her neck or shoulder. We are as happy about that as a legless man who suddenly got an artificial leg and can walk without crutches, and feel we have licked a very bothersome problem.

In our bedrooms at this time are the following books: *An American Doctor's Odyssey; The Poetical Works of Alice and Phoebe Cary*

(A.'s latest discovery); Eichler's *Customs of Mankind*; and *Moby Dick*. These we discuss vicariously before putting out the light, and we never put out the light before we have agreed on anything we might have started out disagreeing on. It makes me, at least, sleep better.

January 26, 1950

Last Sunday we had Marion, her boys and Mother for dinner. Michael, who is a lanky, tall and very restless though sensitive boy, now 12 years old, behaved, as usual, quite loudly and talked all the time. His grandmother does not approve of him talking so much, and neither do I. As a matter of fact I told him so during the meal, and was at once seconded by Mother. Ardyth sent me a glance which meant her unequivocal disapproval. After several words back and forth Michael left the table, and it took a few minutes to restore the unconcerned feeling which prevailed before that episode.

In the evening after the family had left, their arms as usual being loaded with food and little presents, and many kisses of love and reassurance had been exchanged, Ardyth and I did not talk right away and sat silent in the living room. I immediately sensed that there was something in the air but did not know what. We both took to reading whatever we found on hand, both thinking about that something that was between us. Finally Ardyth said: "Why do you always have to talk? Why do you hurt Michael? I would so much like you not to do that, for I remember how I felt when I was reprimanded when I was his age. Sometimes it seems to still hurt me today. Let me tell that story that happened in Claremont, but I have told you that story many a time . . ."

"No, go ahead," I said, "I can't remember."

"Well, when I was in Claremont I had a little room in the Claremont Inn and had to share the toilet with the rest of the guests living on that wing of the floor. Once I went to the toilet and found that there was no toilet paper there. I was much annoyed and thought, I have to call the maid to bring some paper at once. But on second thought I hesitated, telling myself, if I go back to the room and wait a little, somebody else will have to go to the toilet and be as annoyed with the lack of paper as I am now, and he or she will call the maid and give her hell and then the maid will be mad at him or her. And then I can go and will have the advantage of having paper without the maid being mad at me. And sure enough, exactly that happened within the next ten minutes. Now, you saw Mother calling Michael down. She served the purpose and put him in his place. If you had kept still, he'd never think of you and be mad at you when he remembers that episode. And children do remember."

FEBRUARY 1950

This is the coldest winter we have had since I settled in Oregon in 1925, and according to the papers the coldest winter on record. Our pipes in the basement that feed the washing machine (Bendix) have been frozen for three days and we can't wash. Otherwise the house is in excellent shape, in fact better than we expected. We decided to buy it and wait only for Ardyth's money from the Literary Guild to pay it off. Every morning when I leave, she asks me where I'll be so that in the event the bean pot arrives she can let me know instantly.

The other day a gentleman and his wife came to see me in the office. He was very, very tall and wore a long black, graying beard and bore up with astounding erectness, for I could see he was quite old. Beside him came his very, very little wife, dressed all in black, with a black ribbon around her tiny neck and a black veil covering the upper part of her face. As I got up from my chair and met him halfway to the door, he addressed me, shaking my hand: "Sind Sie der Sohn des Carl?" [Are you Carl's son?] While I was looking at the distinguished stranger, whom I had never seen before, and thinking where to place him and nodding in approval to his question, he quickly added: "Ich bin mit Ihrem Vater in die Schule gegangen, Mariahilfer Gymnasium, 1873–1875." [I went to school with your father at the Mariahilfer Gymnasium in 1873–75.] Twenty-two years before I was born! "Sie schauen aber Ihrem Vater gar nicht aehnlich." [But you don't look at all like your father.] He turned out to be the Chief Surgeon of the Police of Imperial Austria and was born the same year my father was, that is, 1860. So this man was 90 years old and knew my father when he was a child.

Interestingly, it occurred to me that I knew next to nothing about my father during the time of his early youth, and the annals I remember date back no further than about ten years before he married my mother. We talked for a time, he in German and his wife in English, about the old times, of which I knew of course little, since it was his old times and not mine, and then about some present complaints of his wife, and it looked as though the past 15 years or so, with all their upheavals, revolutions and migrations had passed him by completely, or that he did not wish to touch upon them. When I ventured the question of where he was living and how they are making out in New York, he only said: "Gott sei Dank, ich habe mein Geld nach Amerika gebracht vor 20 Jahren als ich noch jung war!" [Thank God, I brought my money to America 20 years ago, when I was still young!] When, before they left, I offered to be of assistance in anything I could do, he took me by the arm and whispered in my ear: "Machen Sie mich juenger!" [Make me younger!]

If I have a chance, I will have Dr. Kien and his wife for dinner and hope to learn a few things I did not know about my own father. He is in Portland on a visit to his only son, Dr. Kien, a dermatologist with the Veterans Administration.

FEBRUARY 13, 1950

Ardyth gave me the following list of book titles to bring home:

>   Tenella F. Armytage: *Old Court Customs*
>   Bayley, Harold: *The Lost Language of Symbolism*
>   Brand, John: *Popular Antiquities*
>   Camden, William: *Ancient and Modern Manners of the Irish*
>   Clodd, Edward: *Magic in Names and Other Things*
>   Hone, William: *The Every Day Book*
>   Mallery, Garrick: *Customs of Courtesy*
>   Marshall, Frederic: *International Vanities*
>   Mitchell, Arthur: *The Past in the Present*
>   Pardoe, Miss: *Louis the Fourteenth*
>   Parsons, Elsie Clews: *Fear and Conventionality*
>   Williamson, George Charles: *Curious Survivals*

I got only the Parsons. But I did buy *The Story of Language* by Pei, which seems to have made up a little, at least, for the missing others. They are not in the Portland Library and I learned many of them are very rare; the most advertised of them all is supposed to be *The Lost Language of Symbolism*.

Although *The Peaceable Kingdom* has become quite popular and reactions come from all over the country—practically all very favorable—the *N.Y. Times*, *Harper's* and *The Atlantic* ignore the book.

The severity of the winter has raised havoc with our garden plants, and we fear the expense of repair. Curiously enough,

Ardyth has developed a veritable love for evergreen plants in the room, which she has never exhibited before. In fact, she several times in the past made the statement that she doesn't care for indoor plants, they bore her. Now, since we got for my birthday several months ago a very common philodendron from my sister, which she allowed to halfway perish because of indifference, her attention was suddenly, during the coldest days of the winter, drawn to the pitiful looks of this plant, and in the past two weeks I noticed her turn to the window every so often and take a look and often report to me with joy: "Look, this poor little thing stretches out" or "Come here and see how it recovers." I had to bring some garden pots and bone meal home, and she reset all of the six potted plants the other day with the help of Mrs. Hauge. When I came home that day, Ardyth reported that she did not allow Mrs. Hauge to handle any part of the plant. She just helped by holding a pot or bringing in some earth from the garden.

FEBRUARY 27, 1950

Both of us had a cold. I started first about a week ago, Ardyth came down with it just 48 hours later. We started with a sore throat and a heavy nose and no fever. Thereafter came those vile hot flashes that felt to me like those of women in the change, although, of course, I never had one of those. But since yesterday I am recovering and beginning to feel like me again, whereas Ardyth keeps it still going.

I am putting all these trivia down here because the continuation of Ardyth's real bad feeling has, as the days go by, more and more the aspect of psychosomatic complaints she has had so much experience with.

Mr. Brooks, the editor of Houghton Mifflin, has written her that the trade edition has sold up to now only 14,000 copies (the Literary Guild we don't know yet), which will bring in some less money than we expected. Now Ardyth does not crave the money, but we have to take care of Marion, her two sons and Mother. And she wants so very, so very bad to settle them and get settled herself in her *own* home that the thought of moving again, I think the thirty-seventh time since we married, makes her sick.

For two days the metacarpal joint of the index finger on her left hand has been swollen up, and I don't like even the thought that she might begin with arthritis deformans or a related form of rheumatism. I am downright worried. (She does not know it.)

Tomorrow I am taking blood of hers to the clinic to have a sedimentation rate taken.

Mr. Brooks also wrote that he and his wife are coming west this fall and he would like to take a big chunk of the manuscript of her next book back home so that no one might be able to ask him on his return, "Was this trip necessary?" Ardyth's reaction was at first a joyous one, as though she were going to meet an old teacher of hers who wants to encourage her. But that night she confessed to me that she does not care for writers or editors or publishers or anybody in person, and she does not think anything can be helped by personal contact. She even said that she could not think of a single subject she would love or enjoy discussing with Mr. Brooks, and moreover that if his wife should be one of the smart-alecky college graduate types, she would feel only antagonistic, with little or nothing gained by the visit. We do not, of course, know Mrs. Brooks, and all this is just a bit of mental gymnastics, and I do hope that Mrs. Brooks will be a naive and unpretending lady whose company will make Ardyth bloom and we can invite them to visit Mt. Hood or some other point of interest and discuss things, as for instance, Why don't we produce any great writers now? Or do we, and we just don't recognize them?

She is holding *Moby Dick* in her hands and on her knees deep into the night and long after I have fallen asleep and keeps on telling me of this wonderful writer, the depth of his feeling and the surprising beauty of his imagery and metaphors. From him through her, I learned some amazing facts about the whale, the sperm whale especially, that I had never heard before. It's all to be read in Melville's *M.D.*, and I won't go into that until we have the money to look it up in scientific terms in a new book on the whale.

Poor me. I have taken to smoking again after a pause (that refreshed) of three months, because I had gained five pounds in that time. But I am afraid as I write that down that that was only an excuse and I was weak and could not resist, and because I was not afraid. I have not yet learned to be afraid, despite our newspapers and commentators, and am glad of it. For how otherwise could I calmly counteract the many fears that beset my sweet wife?

I have to come back once again to Ardyth and her malaise after her cold. She knows herself, only too well, that much of it is the language of her body, over which she has little if any control. She worries her head off about meeting old Mrs. Wallace and telling her that we won't buy her house, which both of us love so dearly, and is even afraid that the old lady, being Irish, might put a curse on her for doing so.

But even so, and moreover, she is just sick about having to interrupt her work for several weeks because the family simply does not allow her to come to a mental rest. Not that they do something actively or disturb her physically. On the contrary, all of them, on her side as well as my own, try to be as discreet as possible, having learned to know her and love her in all these years. But they are steadily on her mind, and she can't dismiss the thought of them any easier than the thought of her work. However, she promises me that the moment we are settled in her own house and Marion and the boys are being taken care of, she too will settle and calm down. Mrs. Wallace's house would have been IT if we could have afforded to keep two houses going. But as things turn out, we have to contract and live in the same house and are now looking for a duplex.

AUGUST 30, 1950

It is almost incomprehensible to understand the speed with which time has whisked us through the past six months. We moved to 2475 NW Northrup, in itself a major undertaking considering the complete overhauling of three floors and the housing of two families with a mother in between, the completing to within three or four chapters of the sequel novel to *The Peaceable Kingdom*, the rewriting of *The Spur* and selling it to Messner (who promises publication in the early spring of '51), and the agonizing meetings with our hospital staff and partners (on my part) in order to dissolve the partnership, which was no longer bearable due to the coming into the open of two of its members as communists.

With all this going on, our spirits are higher than ever, and thanks to the heavens Ardyth's health better than ever. It will take me several weeks to catch up with events, because each in its turn contains elements of drama and suspense worth being remembered, as it were, now that it has become history and regresses into the mist of the past.

As usual when moving, Ardyth went into its every detail with an enthusiasm worthy of a great event, which such moves always are. This time the hope persisted that this will be more than just another move, because there is work to be done and at least the next five books are to be written here, right in the attic, where the studio was established with cobwebs obtained from Florida hung on the wall and a special little platform built in for Violet the "litter-ary" cat to watch Ardyth during the working hours, and because a home was to be given to Marion and her boys, to whom both of us have become very much attached. Therefore a contractor was engaged, Mr. Bruce Jones, the brother-in-law of my previous secretary Eileen, and was asked to rebuild the downstairs, making it one with the basement, where a room was provided for Michael and Timothy because Grandma feared the boys would make her nervous if they were around too much, and by being nervous about the boys, the nervousness would reflect upstairs. So a ladder was built into the basement in order to avoid going out of the house and into it through the back when going to the basement, a conveyance the boys never tire of and slide down many more times a day than their duties call for. The basement was made into a large utility room which contains a shower bath, toilet, and all the machines for washing and ironing the salespeople at Olds and King could talk us into. In a special niche was put Marion's piano, an old-timer of the past century, which has not been in tune since I met it and her, to which she is drawn from time to time as an outlet for her artistic inclinations to compose popular songs and accompany the piano with her voice.

The downstairs was made into a comfortable apartment, all newly decorated with paper and curtains and furnished with what Marion brought into the marriage plus what we gave her from our own possessions and bought new. To top it all off, a very large bottle or glass container built to pickle cucumbers, and gallons of them, was made into an aquarium with sand on the floor and three goldfish in the water and put into the entrance hall for the lasting entertainment of Timothy and his Grandma.

The upstairs, of course, was specially prepared with the unfailing sense of the mistress of the house for colors, dimensions, and odd as well as one-of-a-kind pieces. The color scheme was the red side of the spectrum, or rather both ends of it, omitting the middle; red in all its shades and purple contrasted against the virgin white of the walls and curtains. This makes the flat warm and welcoming throughout most of Oregon's wet year. During the heat season, which never lasts longer than 5–6 weeks, A. puts slipcovers over much of the furniture, white or at least pale, which with the shades drawn and the cooler in the basement going makes it a pleasant oasis even on a very hot day.

A dark red carpet and picture frames, as well as several large lamps, all gilded or of bronze or brass, give it a rich and lush feeling, which would be possibly a little too much if it weren't that something takes all the attention one can muster at once away from the furniture—that is, the books. A library is built all around the back half of the living room, into which the books are arranged NOT by subjects and NOT by alphabetical order so that one could hope to find a volume at once. NO. They are all arranged by color and size in a fashion to impress themselves on the eye rather than the memory. No two books with a black back or with any matching color stand side by side, but the colors and book bindings are chosen by the eye and for the eye, and present that way undoubtedly the prettiest sight a library has ever offered anywhere in the world. If my protestations are heard once, they are offered a hundred times that it is almost impossible to find a book if one wants it, a haunting experience if one is positive that the book IS THERE! But this feeling of uneasiness is at once parried with disarming charm in something like these words: Now if *I* would know exactly where to find a book each time I look for it, I would have to forego the infinite pleasure of letting my eyes wander around and thus discovering many a volume of whose presence I had been unaware, so that I can promise myself to take a new discovery down from the shelves the next time I am looking for something to read.

I confess I have come over to this point of viewing things, although most librarians will disagree with us.

JANUARY 30, 1951

I am making a card catalogue of our library. This I do not at all with an eye to arrive at an evaluation, or to count the volumes, or to assist a potential future purchaser. Only one thought guides me in undertaking this painstaking task, and that is to obtain an overall view of what the library contains. This alone can give an idea of what Ardyth's interests are, for whatever book we incorporate and put on the shelves she has read, is reading, or will read. Sometimes it's just the title of the book or a quotation from it, sometimes a sentimental thought of some incident in which a particular book played a role, or it may only be the time she read it in the past during maybe a trying experience that makes her cherish it or its author, and the very thought of having it available gives her comfort. Then there are the volumes without which "she could not be" or the ones whose authors she names among her teachers and friends, and finally there are quite a few which she quickly takes down from the shelves every time she goes to the little girls' room, for not even there can she stand to be without the solace of words.

This morning I got up a little earlier, having two cataract operations scheduled, the first starting at eight. While I was shaving, Ardyth made my breakfast and put it on the table, as appetizing as if it were breakfast being served to Henry J. Kaiser at the Waldorf Astoria. I love her for it every time. Afterward I saw that I still had about ten minutes and lit a cigarette sitting down opposite her in the library. Suddenly she said: "Never do you look so noble and almost transfigured as when in the morning, before leaving for the hospital, you are waiting to do your chores." (This is the expression we use when going to the toilet.)

The apartment is now finished, with curtains up and every piece in its place. As could be expected, it is all in A.'s color scheme: pink, red, purple, white, all seating modern, everything else antique. It looks and feels like Ardyth all over the place.

JANUARY 31, 1951

Now that the apartment is finished, curtains up, the stairway into A.'s studio completed and cleaned, the smudges on the woodwork rubbed out by Helen, an occasional maid, we discussed last night whether or not to invite some of our friends (most of them wished upon us, as A. likes to say) for a sort of housewarming. At first she made a list of who should be asked, then thought of entertainment, games to play and food to serve, and suddenly began to cry. What's the matter? I asked. "You know," she said "I hate people, I loathe them, all of them. If only they'd leave me alone. Why is it that if I would go to Cuba or England for a year, nobody would think anything of it and take it for granted that I am not here, only because I would have removed myself bodily. But if I want to leave with my mind and imagination, be absent from real life, see no one for a year and work, work hard and at the same time be a good wife to you, they'd think I am crazy, or I think every one of them would take such a thing as a personal insult directed only against him!"

Then I reassured her that the party was off and that no one was more important than her work, and we will do as well without a party. Moreover, I brought forth that in April, when *The Spur* was to come out and my nephew Philip would visit us, we would have to have some company anyhow, and she began to get hold of herself again and smiled. Her migraine went away and she sat on my lap and hugged me. "You know, dear, I knew you would understand me. I am burning to go to work, and every minute that I am delayed is torture to me."

We went to bed and slept wonderfully well.

For the past few weeks, every now and then she speaks of Dorney Leaf and how she will go about the book. I love to hear her talk to me about it because each time she mentions the book, something becomes clear in her mind, until tonight she said: "The book is finished! All I have to do is what a sculptor does. He has the block of marble before him long before he begins his work, which has been enclosed in the marble since all time. All he has to do is chip it out. That's all I have to do."

FEBRUARY 4, 1951

The day before Christmas 1950 (five weeks ago), Marion got married to Claude Massee. I am afraid I have no more luck with this brother-in-law than with any previous of mine, and there were five. Claude and Marion knew each other from school days and he was married twice before. His last wife died about a year ago of sarcoma and left him a little boy, who now is eight years old. Claude makes a living by filling some 800 automats with candies, gum and cigarettes on a daily round in Seattle.

Tomorrow, Michael and Timothy are following their mother to Seattle. Both of us love these two boys. They both are exceptionally well bred, good-looking, and show personality. Ardyth kept away from the children as much as possible because she was afraid of becoming too attached to them, and often used the excuse that they have to study to keep me away from them for the same reason. She adores them, talks to them as if they were grownups and their opinions of great importance, their secrets portentous, at the same time keeping herself their equal playmate. She gave them the run of the house and only reprimanded me if Timothy spilled a glass of water over a new piece of furniture or Michael, throwing his long legs, knocked down a newly bought old cup and saucer and broke it. One other charm unique to her must have engrossed the boys: her way of flitting away like a shadow upon the hillside, a motion not common to other women. In the midst of a wonderful hour of fun or learning, she would fly away at the sound of an intruder and was gone.

I noticed as they grew older that when I took one of the boys on an errand or somewhere, her wit became their unconscious standard of others, while her sweetness was like nothing but that of her own favorite violet flowers, and whenever Michael tried to compare another girl or woman, it was with reference to her. We see them join their mother now with a feeling mixed with a little sadness, although we did not see them very often and left them most of the time with Grandma.

Tomorrow Verne Bright is moving into the basement room which we had especially built for the boys. Ardyth always wanted to do some kind thing for a poet, and I guess she could not have hit upon a better choice. Verne is now past 60, a bachelor who works at the Oregon Historical Society as a librarian for a pittance and lives 25 miles out of town with his foster parents. This way he will have an abode in Portland and be able to work on any of his several projects undisturbed and without having rent to pay.

Kitty Messner wrote that *The Spur* will be published on April 6.

FEBRUARY 9, 1951

Mr. Bramble of Messner had Ardyth out for lunch on Tuesday. He showed her the jacket for *The Spur*. She liked it so well she almost fell over. It is so much better than that of *The Peaceable Kingdom*, done by an artist of great insight. The edge of the jacket is all draped by blood-red heavy curtains. On the front cover Lincoln sits in the box with Mrs. Lincoln lit up brightly, while behind him the assassin looms large, his face turned away from the president, disconsolate if not disgusted, with his gun limply in his hand pointing toward the floor. Behind him is a young woman with a hat and veil looking down toward him. Ella, the prostitute? The spine of the book holds the body of the spur in silver, each end extending toward one side of the cover. The back of the book shows, beneath the red drapery above, in the light of a blue moon, a little scaffold with two of the conspirators hanging from the gallows, beneath them the conspirators talking around a table, and on the bottom Booth having his leg dressed by Dr. Mudd. The whole renders a very impressive panorama of the drama.

Mr. Bramble thinks the book will sell well despite the fact that no book club has taken it. Ardyth must have had a real good time with him and apparently liked the man, because she had never come home so excited and animated as that afternoon. Mrs. Bristol of Gill's asked her to autograph on the day of publication, April 6.

The apartment below is empty for a few days, since Mother took the boys up to Seattle to join their mother. Maybe because of the good mood after meeting Mr. Bramble, or maybe because of a sudden change of mind, she suddenly decided to ask Mother to stay downstairs and on the spur of the moment took me by the hand downtown to Olds and King and bought furniture for the whole apartment. Nothing was to be said about it. It would be the great surprise. After we got home, I asked A. whether she was happy. "I would rather have done that than anything in the world." And that same evening before going to bed she suddenly said, after a long silence while each of us was reading: "I would rather believe in God than have a million dollars." Such remarks, which please me no end, remain unanswered and are received only with an approving smile on my part. The fact that we both believe in God and both of us are deeply religious without having the need of, and often with resentment against, all professional servants of the Lord makes us click so wonderfully.

While I study and worry about some of my patients with cataracts and other ailments, Ardyth reads all she can get on Butch Cassidy, the Robbers Roost and the Wild Bunch, and complains that the writers of these Western accounts cannot write and that she has a very bad time to make out what really happened. It's all so confused, so bewildering in the lack of chronology and so poorly motivated, if at all.

The contractor's bill for the stairway up into Ardyth's studio is $590.00!

FEBRUARY 17, 1951

Ardyth has begun her fourth novel. Working title: *Summer Growth*, from a poem by Thomas Hood. Before writing the first draft, she is organizing the life and adventures of Butch Cassidy, "the last bandit of the West," into a readable story, written in the Rocky Mountain speech which she masters so beautifully, and she reads me each evening after dinner what she has done during the day. She is so swift with research and yet so exact that I am often nonplussed how she gets the stuff organized. Sometimes I take the time to read some of the material she works on (Charles Kelly's *The Outlaw Trail* or Professor Webb's *The Great Plains*) and marvel at what she makes of an otherwise completely unorganized hodgepodge of facts and names. At once most of the neurotic complaints dwindle away and leave her for many days quite free of any pains and aches, which, while she does not work, are as regularly present as the dust in the air. She eats almost nothing during the day. Black coffee and a piece of dry toast for breakfast, three cups of black coffee with one or two pieces of dry toast during the working day until 6 p.m. At that time we have a simple dinner, which she begins cooking as soon as I come home from the office, about 5:30 p.m. BUT, just when I am ready to go to bed, she gets hungry. More than once did I catch her making candies of brown sugar, butter and ground nuts and eating them half a pound at a time between 11 and 1 o'clock at night, crowning this feast with a huge red Hood River apple at about 1:30 at night. And never does she forget afterward, when I am just at the best of my first part of sleep, to warm her fingers, which are ice-cold from the ice-cooled apple, on my cozy body, wherever she happens to catch me first, front or rear, and wake me up to her great delight and say with a kiss (which brings me back to full wakefulness) "Excuse me darling, I just had to get my hands warm before going to sleep."

Much as I resent by reflex such abrupt handling of the sweetness of the beginning of sleep, each time I am disarmed by her charm and fall right into her mood, even though my body recoils at the touch of so much ice coldness.

She still does not want to see any of our friends and will not, I'm afraid, until she is forced to at the time when *The Spur* comes out.

FEBRUARY 22, 1951

Mrs. Stewart Holbrook called up to tell me that Bennett Cerf will be in town March 1 and had asked the Holbrooks whether they could arrange for him to meet Ardyth. She (Mrs. Stewart H.) is having a tea between 2 and 4 for that purpose because Cerf will be here only between trains. Ardyth called, in a subdued voice while I was on the phone, under no circumstances to call her to answer the phone. So I could only thank her for the invitation and tell her I'll call her back.

When I told Ardyth of the content of my conversation with Mrs. H., she looked at me furiously as though I had committed a wrong and at once began drawing her breath as if she were suffocating. She does not want to go and she wants to be left alone. Steinbeck and Hersey don't go to parties either, and when Steinbeck's last book came out he took a yacht and sailed away. She does not look like she would like to and has such a hard time to get herself together. At the same time she wondered whether she would not need a new pair of shoes and a new hat for the occasion. I listened patiently and told her to go down to her mother for a while.

While she was gone I was phoning with the hospital, where I have a patient with an uncontrollable nasal hemorrhage, and gave orders to give him another blood transfusion (the third in two days). Then I called Dr. Virginia Gilliland, our surgical resident, to hold herself ready if and when I would have to go out at night to the hospital to ligate the man's carotic artery.

By the time I had made the necessary arrangements about this patient, Ardyth came up from her mother's and began washing the dishes, a task we nightly do together to the accompaniment of jazz on the phonograph. Suddenly she said I better call Mrs. Holbrook before she (Ardyth) changes her mind. As soon said as done. When we were through with the dishes and I tried to joke or laugh a little, she looked at me earnestly and said, "I feel deep anger against you, as though you were forcing me to do something I don't want to do. You infuriate me!"

I did not answer but went on reading an essay by T. S. Eliot in this month's *Atlantic*. Then after a few minutes she informed me that Dr. O. Chambers of Oregon State had died today of cerebral hemorrhage. We both knew this man well. He was A.'s prof. in psychology while she went to OSC, and I operated on him during that time. [. . .] The reminiscence of Dr. Chambers helped the present situation a great deal, and I left the room with the feeling that our friendship is as close as ever.

FEBRUARY 27, 1951

We are doing well, I mean we are feeling well, work hard and deem ourselves happy. The new novel is underway. Ardyth today read me the first five pages of *Good Morning, Young Lady*. The working title *Summer Growth* did not live long. At my question as to where the new title comes from, she read me these lines from a cowboy ballad of Wyoming:

> *My foot in the stirrup, the reins in my hand,*
> *Good morning, young lady, my horse he won't stand.*

At that time Mrs. Jacobson called A.'s mother and told her that Freddy thinks that we should attend the tea in honor of Bennett Cerf by all means. When A. came back from talking over the phone, she said: I think we won't go to that tea after all. Why did you blab to Freddy that there was any problem about going?

I assured her that a few days ago I did tell Freddy that Cerf had asked the Holbrooks whether they could arrange a meeting with

A., but I never did say that she might possibly not go. But to no avail. With gradually mounting emotion she rationalized her reluctance to accept a perfectly friendly invitation and went on: "Everything we do has a price. Why do I want or should I meet Mr. Cerf? To begin with, I want you to know that I am very much impressed with the man, the way the Greeks must have been impressed with their gods. He is one who moves among the Olympians of today and knows everyone of achievement. There is a definite aura around him that awes me. Of course I should meet him, because a word put in here or a remark dropped about me there would make me known to his many readers and call attention to me or my work. Then, I might be curious how he looks and behaves, and maybe I can learn something from him, either a little anecdote or the way he tells his stories or something interesting about somebody I admire, or loathe. That's on the positive side of the ledger.

"Now think of it: I am at the beginning of a new novel, the most delicate and for me most difficult part, because after the first few chapters I always feel I am sailing along and have no more apprehensions until I approach the end. Of course, you know that the worst time of all is always when I write *finis* to a book and face the void of not writing. But now I need all I can give for the first chapters. Every move, thought and distraction annoys me terribly. All of Thursday will be lost because I have to fix up and think about what I'm going to wear and how I'll look. It's always so when meeting someone of the opposite sex. Friday I might not be able to work because of the impression I took home after meeting the man. Next consider: It won't be me going up there at all. It will be another me over whom I might not have any control, and I shudder to think of what would happen if I'd behave awkwardly, fall or vomit or faint. I think I couldn't write and live in peace for six months thereafter. Now, right this moment when I look at my dear hand who does my work so faithfully for me, I am loath to think it might tremble or my lips might quiver or I would not be able to think of a witty reply. I am in earnest, Egon," she assured me with real and honest tears in her eyes.

I could say little to refute her argument, because I knew that what she said was for her as true as the famous formula was for the Einsteinians. So I shyly but firmly said: "If that's your considered opinion, we will not talk about it anymore and drop the matter. If you work fine during the next few days, you might feel yet in the mood to go, otherwise we will phone that you got suddenly sick with a sore throat. They won't question my word. Am I not a throat specialist?"

Of course they would believe any true-sounding excuse, for who would be so foolish as to miss an opportunity to meet a man like Bennett Cerf?

I changed the subject and told her that Dr. Waknitz, our orthopedist, is leaving for good for Seattle, where he is opening an office of his own, and that he and his wife would so much like to have an opportunity to see her and say goodbye. She smiled and said: "Maybe on Sunday." I timidly broached the subject of asking one or two other couples of the Permanente staff. At first she nodded half absent-mindedly and said: "That reminds me of a letter of Cicero which Oliver Wendell Holmes once read to Longfellow." Oh? said I. "Yes, you want to hear the letter?" "Of course I do."

"Well, Mr. Holmes was at dinner with Senator Sumner at the house of their mutual friends, the Fields, you know the Mrs. Fields to whom Sarah Orne Jewett wrote the letters we have up there on the shelf. When Mrs. Fields called her guests to the table, it turned out that Mr. Holmes and Longfellow were animatedly talking outside the cottage, Mr. Holmes just saying that he had read an amusing letter of Cicero in which Cicero gives an account to his friend of a visit he had just received from the emperor Julius Caesar. He had invited Julius to pass a few days with him, but he came quite unexpectedly with a thousand men! Cicero, seeing them from afar, debated with another friend what he should do with them, but at length managed to encamp them. To feed them was a less easy matter. The emperor took everything quite easily, however, and was very pleasant, but, adds Cicero, he is not the man to whom I should say a second time, 'If you're passing this way, give me a call.'"

So I guess we will have the Waknitzes with their men once, next Sunday.

MARCH 5, 1951

Deep winter since yesterday, with snow two inches high. When I came home at five in the afternoon, A. told me that never does she work as well as when it snows. We remembered that almost all of *The Spur* was written two years ago during the six weeks when Portland was snowed in.

I can hardly believe that we managed after all to go to the Bennett Cerf reception at the Holbrooks'. It took the usual two jiggers of whiskey, of which A. takes each swallow with a grimace, as though it were the strongest paregoric, about an hour before she wants the effect of its weakening some of her inhibitions. Since she was afraid that somebody might smell a whiff of it, she took a tablet of the latest pharmaceutical nuisance, namely, "Nullo," a chlorophyll preparation or something which promises to annul every body odor for about 24 hours.

The reception was boring, Bennett Cerf did not make much of an impression on either of us, and Ardyth was at her best and felt, as she told me on the way home, like a fish in water. But no sooner did we arrive home than she began with her frequent complaints of nausea and ill feeling and kept on complaining right along. After dinner I gave her a new box of See's candies, which I thought would take her mind off herself. She began sampling them, in that she bit first into one and then into another and into a third and fourth, always putting the half or two-thirds of a candy she had bitten off back in the box. As so often before on such an occasion, I told her that that's no way to do, especially as I don't want to eat so many candies, that is, all those she had put back into the box in a defective status. "I have waited for that pleasure 37 years," she said, "that's long enough. Now and for the future I will enjoy that pleasure of 'sampling the candies.'"

We are reading, alternatingly, the letters of Emily Dickinson. I brought the new edition home, which just came out, edited by Mark Van Doren. At first A. thought some of the letters showed signs of a crazy person, to which I could not agree, but soon, maybe after reading another 30 pages, we agreed that this was "a rare bird indeed," in a way one of the greatest delicatesses I have ever tasted in literature. As A. thumbed through the book, she suddenly stopped and read these lines, which fit her as though the writer had thought of her instead of herself: "How strange that I who say NO so often can't stand to be told NO, and I who run so frequently cannot brook when somebody tries to run away from me."

The discomfort that came in the wake of going to the Cerf reception lasted until today! (three days). It makes one think whether A. was not right when she said a few days before that everything has its price.

MARCH 13, 1951

The day before yesterday we saw the jacket of *The Spur* again. Frank Scioscia, the salesman from Gill's, gave it to me and thought we might keep it. His reason was that it has two mistakes in its text. One is that my name is misspelled as "Edgon," and the other that I was working on a biography of the man who "invented" the eardrum. It should, of course, read "discovered" the eardrum. This mistake has now been removed, and only the first so many copies will have that silly error of the editor.

Frank also told me that he has read *The Spur* and was taken by its impact and the beauty of the prose. He thought it should turn out to be the important book of the season. I hope he is right. How is one to tell how the pudding tastes before tasting it? Poor Ardyth is suffering from terrible stage-fright, such as I have never seen her in before, and I am using all the psychology I know on her to persuade her to be patient and unafraid.

Fortunately some news came by telegram this morning from Mary Drayton. Mary has been working on *The Peaceable Kingdom* for many months, making it into a play, and both of us felt sort of sorry for her because we firmly believed that *P.K.* would never go on the stage. We thought that it touched on a taboo (polygamy), and producers of Broadway and Hollywood alike would therefore avoid it. The experience with Preminger, who tried to sell it to Fox Studio, seems to have confirmed this belief. Now this morning this telegram arrived from Mary:

"Kingdom bought by Top Flight Producer. Contract being drawn. Rehearsals to begin August. Production set for September. Yippy. Love, Mary."

Ardyth was pleased. She had her mother call me at the hospital, where the message reached me between two operations. I knew from the tremor of my mother-in-law's voice how this telegram had moved her. "Her" story being played on Broadway. "Her" mother being made into a public hero, Linnea. The writing of the book had never made much of an impression on her, and often I heard Ardyth cry about the utter lack of understanding on the part of her mother. But this, a play, Broadway, New York, got into her head and she sees fame and fortune. I hope she won't be disappointed. She never thought of or knew that out of ten shows on Broadway, no more than one or two survive.

When I came home, Freddy Jacobson called me to verify the news that my mother-in-law had instantly telephoned his mother. I can hear the two ladies chatter over the phone! And interestingly, it impressed Freddy as much. He too saw fame and fortune, and wanted me to convey to A. his best wishes from the bottom of his heart. I felt like laughing into his face when I thought how monotonously indifferent he acted while she wrote, and how often he emphasized that *P.K.* of course was primarily a book for women. As though women were no readers and could not be trusted. And as if to cinch his conviction about Fame and Fortune, he added: "Today is Tuesday. I hope you guys don't go down to the writers' meeting (the local press club to whose meeting we have been going each month for the past two years). All you need is to pay your dues, but you surely don't need to mingle with these people."

Last Sunday we had Verne Bright up for the evening and A. had him read some of his poetry. I am grieved to have been reminded of Pope or Dr. Johnson or whoever is supposed to have said: Better no poet than a poor one. But I guess we are stuck with him in the basement, where he'll probably live out his days. When he moved in a month or so ago, we wished him a long and successful life.

MARCH 18, 1951

Sunday, sunshine, morning, my mother-in-law's birthday, which she celebrates more arduously every year, not this year only, than the nation remembers Washington's. For days ahead she figures who will write her and who ought to write her and when every one of these remembrances should turn up in the mail. The night before, she always dreams of her mother! or professes to it, and every year we believe this to be true. And every year the turnout becomes a little larger, because most of the family is catching on to it and has as much fun with this birthday as the celebrated one.

This is a good time to tell about the family and ALL its members, the more so because Mother's sister Laura (I can't remember her last married name, she had so many and kept each for so short a time) sent for this year's celebration a letter containing what she calls The Genealogy. In studying it, Mother soon became aware that her sister Laura went ahead rather ruthlessly and put down everything, that is, such members, children and offspring which are ordinarily not mentioned, and so slightly marred the birthday commemoration.

Mother had first a son, Jimmy, when she was 18 years old; this is Ardyth's brother. He is twelve years older than Ardyth and was never loved by his mother, which apparently he resented as soon as he could think and still resents, because he studiously keeps away from her, has never contributed as much as a penny to her support since she became a widow, and is very rarely spoken of in our house. His relation with Ardyth is that of a casual acquaintance of olden days, confined to exchanging greetings of the season. He did not even congratulate her on our wedding, not to mention the possibility of a wedding present, and we have seen him only once since we were married, when A. and I visited California during the war and came through Stockton. We stopped at Jimmy's for dinner and I noticed his gaunt, slightly stooped figure with a little wizened face. He is four or five years my junior. I don't know whether he was among this year's congratulants.

Next of Mother's children came Grace, three years younger than Jimmy. Grace was a quiet little girl, always on the plump side and soon, sooner than anyone in the family, acquainted with the boys. She was nine years old when Ardyth was born and was the one who sang cradle songs to her little sister, dressed the first doll for her and told her the first fairy tale. When Ardyth was old enough to be taken for a walk, it was Grace that took her and bought the first lollipop to put in her mouth. But Grace must have been a girl with insufficient thyroid, soon leaning to the chubby side and being very soon attracted to the opposite sex. At barely sixteen she ran away with an Italian barber, who married her and with whom she had two children. She left the barber husband after a few years to seek her happiness with another man and wasn't heard of for many years.

When A. and I had been married about three months, Grace suddenly turned up in Portland and Ardyth took her in, thinking she could do the housework for us and be a sort of help to her, remembering how loving and caring she had been in her youth. Poor Grace, when I met her then for the first time, was a pitiful sight. Without front teeth and her scanty blond hair graying, she was bathing her big feet in the kitchen in the dish pan and, looking at me with a blank look, said softly "hello." She stayed with us about ten days, and on the eleventh day was gone. A. told me later she got a letter from some man in the East and the same day she took off. That is now exactly ten years ago, and no one has ever heard of her. She was not among Mother's congratulants either.

Then came Ardyth, almost ten years later, as a surprise and unwanted. Her story I can't put down now. It is, like all of her, one in a million, for there is a blossom about her of something more distinguished than the generality of mankind, as her friend Boswell has remarked of himself.

Last of the children was Marion. She was expected and wanted, as A. has often told me. She developed to be a pretty girl and married Kenneth Pettibone. His story is by now history. He has never been seen or heard of after he disappeared with $75,000 almost two years ago and left her with her two handsome sons, Timothy and Michael. We are glad that Marion now is happy with Claude Massee and will remain so in Seattle, where with our help she bought a house and is making her home now.

All these sisters and brothers, and of course many more, were diligently put down by Aunt Laura in her genealogy of the family and so brought to mind—on a day which is supposed to remember only the good things—many things which are never mentioned in the family and so mildly beclouded the sunny atmosphere.

Laura is the sister who followed Mother by a year or two in the sequence of children. She is a Walkyrie type of unmistakable Scandinavian descent, with a thin, unmodulated voice which she tries to help along with grimaces and Bible quotations, and so gives soon the impression that she has only one wish, that no one should deprive her of the hope of eternal punishment or maybe eternal reward—no matter which, as long as it is eternal. She lives by herself and among her many friends in Los Angeles and has a job with Metro-Goldwyn-Meyer, where she sews and embellishes the dresses for the Ice follicles or whatever they call them. Occasionally she sends Mother a box full of rags and remnants of silks and taffeta and laces which she collected, and these are here then made much of and used for doilies, doll dresses and other niceties which are unfailingly shown to visitors, never without mentioning that the materials came from Aunt Laura, who got them from the Studio, and so forth.

Thus Mother's conversations steadily rotate around the sisters and brothers and Marion. The children who did not come up to her expectations are never mentioned, and relatives of whom she disapproves have no place in her vocabulary, and I have learned to forget them in her presence.

MARCH 21, 1951

The Spur is available in bookstores, a little ahead of the publication date, set for April 6th, a week preceding Lincoln's death. We both are a bit shaky about the reception, even though Freddy and Frank Scioscia did what they could to reassure Ardyth.

Curiously enough, now after more than a year and a half since the galleys of *Peaceable Kingdom* made the rounds in Hollywood, a letter from Preminger arrived saying that one of the large producer-directors is interested in the motion picture rights. In the meantime, we are still waiting to hear about the contract that Mary Drayton's agent is making with Houghton Mifflin about the stage play of *P.K.*

In order to get our minds off the doings of the entertainment world, A. decided to take up some study. She was encouraged in this by Arnold Bennett's little essay "How to Live on 24 Hours a Day." Bennett advises about one to two hours' daily study of any subject of serious interest, no matter what. But to be pursued in a way we have to do in school. If only we keep it up for, say, one term, or about three months, we are bound to learn enough to make things worthwhile. We figured out how much time we waste during an ordinary week just to rest up. Amazing how much time is being killed. So we went right ahead, and A. chose FAUST.

APRIL 2, 1951

The Spur is on the bookstalls, one week prior to publication date. We are waiting for the reviews, although A. will not have it to learn their contents. If they are bad she'd get boiling mad, if they are good she'd be afraid they'd make her conscious of whatever it may be, so she won't listen. But I, of course, want to read them. Unfortunately, last night Freddy called and read the first review to come his way, by one Mary Jane Campbell of the *Oregon Journal*. It was one of those damning by faint praise, too short and missing the point of the book altogether. A. overheard part of my conversation with Freddy and half guessed the content, half drew me out. "May she die of the mange" was her first reaction, with a flushing of her lovely face. "We are moving to California" was the next, with a widening of her pupils. Then, after a while: "I guess that girl was right. I *did* write 'thick' in the chapter where Lincoln dies. We won't talk about it anymore. I have come all the way through, *up* from pride to humility."

APRIL 3, 1951

In the morning I was at the funeral of my optician Ed Salzer, who had died three days ago so suddenly as to stun all of us. It was "a wonderful funeral," as I heard some of the attendants say afterward. I hate funerals and wish I never would have to attend one, although I approve of them.

In the afternoon I did a cataract operation on an old lady. She should see with a ROUND pupil. I was satisfied.

After dinner, well prepared by Ardyth in the way of fried liver and avocado salad, she read me the last chapter she had written on her new book and we both were happy that she had hit it off. Tears were running down her cheeks and I felt a lump in my throat, though I am not sure whether because of the story or because of A. being so moved by it. But we both cried when Dorney said goodbye to Rock Springs, Wyoming, after her sister died.

Afterward A. confessed to me a dream she had had some time ago. She felt herself lying on another person, a dead person and a woman whose long, lustrous black hair fell by her side and with which Ardyth's hands played. While she told me of this dream, she held the first volume of *The Letters and Literary Correspondence of the Countess of Blessington* in her hand, which I got for her a few days ago from the Beauchamp Bookshop in London.

An hour or so later we retired, and while I turned to my right so as to avoid the light from A.'s lamp, she was reading the Blessington memoirs. Some time later, just when I had sunk into the depth of the first sweet sleep, she woke me suddenly and exclaimed "That's the raft!" shaking me softly by the arm. I turned around and saw her as excited as I have ever seen her. "Now I can write my fourth book," she began. "I never thought I could do it, because I never will write directly about me. But now I can use Countess Blessington and her story as the raft that will hold all I have to say about the thirties, can use every one of the characters here in Portland and need not omit one single thing. I must have felt it when I told you of my dream this evening. I did not know it then, but I must have somehow thought of it, or else how could I have thought of that odd dream?" And she went on to tell me at great length how the story of the fourth book will have to build itself around the Countess and how closely her character approaches her own. In fact, that was the only person she could have found in all literature who would lend herself and her experiences to what she was trying to do. We talked in bed til early morning and smoked a good many cigarettes. But we were happy.

The last thing I remember her saying was: "Please don't count *The Spur*. It was and is not one of my real books. It was only an artificial insemination. I can never be real fond of it."

Egon's Journal

MAY 1, 1951

Ardyth's mother is gone to Salt Lake City for a visit with her sister Tekla. Her brother George and his wife Anna asked her to join them on the trip, which will take about two weeks. When we said goodbye to Mother at the bus station and walked back to the car, Ardyth smiled and softly but beamingly said, "I am soo happy."

The relationship between the two becomes more and more difficult despite, or even probably because of, the fact that both avoid with the greatest care ever to speak their minds to each other, forever smile and say sweet words about everything, thus carrying the smoldering resentment as an ever-increasing burden. Many times I see A. return from downstairs fighting for breath with pain in her chest while her features reveal the held-back hatred. The old lady, I suspect, does know little of her daughter's true feeling for her, but she tyrannizes A. by her very presence. Never does A. buy something without buying something for her mother, too. If I buy a dozen heavy bath towels, I discover that within a week or so we only have eight left. The rest went to Mother. If I bring home a case of beer, I discover two weeks later that I could not have possibly drunk all that beer myself, because it is only once in a while that I drink beer at all. But the missing cans or bottles went downstairs. As far as I am concerned, I don't mind, God knows. But poor A. can't do anything, go anywhere or buy a dress or ware of any kind without being tyrannized by the thought of having her mother participate in it, and never without afterward suffering or complaining.

It is too bad that we have in our acquaintance several of these mother-fixed "poor Jerusalems," to use Mark Twain. Freddy Jacobson who leads a most miserable existence with his mother in a tiny little apartment, my cousin Marietta who has to support her parents out of her rather meager earnings, Howard the mother-fixed artist who A. tries to tell me has never slept with a woman except once (and did not like it), and so on. Why should I go on enumerating these cases, which are as numerous as the stars? To support one's parent or parents is one thing, to become their slave is another.

In yesterday's Sunday magazine section, A. saw a picture of Dr. Steiner and his wife Deborah entertaining guests by exhibiting their collection of records of classical music, and right below the Steiners she found the Everetts (her dentist). These pictures made her furious—yes, furious—and she exclaimed with genuine wrath,

Journal pages with a back-and-forth between Egon and Ardyth:

80

April 2nd 1951

The Spur is on the bookstalls, one week prior to publication date. We are waiting for the reviews although A. will not have it to learn there statements. If they are bad she'd get boiling mad, if they are good she is afraid they make her conscious of whatever it maybe, so she won't listen. But I of course, want to read them. Unfortunately last night Freddy called and read the first review to come his way by one Marty Jane Campbell of the Oregon Journal. It was one of those damning by praising criticism, too short and missing the point of the Book alltogether. A. overheard part of my conversation with Freddy and half guessed the content half drew me out. "May she die of the mange" was her first reaction and a flushing of her lovely face. "We are moving to California" was the next with widening of her pupils. Then, after a while: " I guessed that girl was right. I did ~~right~~ "thick" in the chapter where Lincoln dies. We won't talk about it anymore. I have $$$$$ come all the way through up from pride to humility."

/write

April third

In the morning I was at the funeral of my optician Ed Salzer who had died three days ago so suddenly as to stunn all of us. It was "a wonderful funeral" as I heard some of the attendants say afterward. I hate funerals and wish I never would have to attend one although I approve of them.
In the afternoon I did a cataract operation on an old lady. She should see with A ROUND pupil. I was satisfied.
After dinner, well prepared by Ardyth in the way of fried liver and avocado salad, she read me the last chapter she had written on her new book and we both were happy that she hit it off. Tears were running down her cheeks and I felt a lump in my throat though I am not sure whether because of the story or because of A. being so moved by it, but we both cried when Dorney said good by to Rock Springs Wy. after her sister died.

Afterward A. confessed to me a dream she had had some time ago. She felt herself lying on another person, a dead person and a woman whose long lustrous black hair fell by her side and with which Ardyth hands played. While she told me of this dream she held the first vloume of the Letters and Literary Correspondence of the Countess of Blessington in her hand which I got for her a few days ago From the Beauchamp Bookshop in London.
An hour or so later we retired and while I turned to my right so as to avoid the light from A.'s lamp she was reading the Blessington memoirs. Some time later, just when I had sunk into the depth of th first sweet slepp she woke me sudienly and exclaimed "That's the raft! " shaking me softly by the arm. I turned around and saw her as excited as I have ever seen her. "Now I can write my fourth book" she began. I never thought I could do it because I never will right directly about me. But now I can use Countess Blessington and her story as the raft that will hold all I have to say about the thirties, can use every one of the characters here in Portland and need not omit one single thing. I must have felt it when I told you of my dream this evening. I did not know it then but I must have somehow thought of it or else how could I have thought of that odd dream?" And she went on to tell at great length how the story of the fourth book will have to built itself around the Countess and how closely her character approaches her own. In fact that was the only person she could have found in all literature who would lend herself and her experiences to what she was trying to do.
We talked in bed til early morning and smoked a good many cigarettes. But we were happy.
The last I remember her saying was: Please don't count THE SPUR. It was and is not one of my real books. It only was an artificial insemination. I can never be real fond of it."

Egon: So many of your statements about me are NOT TRUE — especially when love!

You say I have said something. I never ONCE have said what you said I said — it's all LIES. If I should die before you, don't ever publish a word of your "Boswellian" rambling (my God, was he as inaccurate as you? it scares me) about me, because if you do, I'll haunt you. Boo!

Love & Kisses
Ardyth Kennelly

Oct. 26, 1953

Ardyth:
Maybe I can't remember every word. But I could almost tell what words passed, if not quite. Yet I have not put onto these pages, Ardyth, a single thing that I have not actually, whole and real, in my memory. What remains there must be the essential truth for me, no matter how slight it may turn out to be. Don't you think that all that was not ours finally escapes us? I do. I always mistrust, in written or recounted memories, those long, interesting conversations that we sometimes enjoy very much. Because talk, real talk between people, is so unexpected and surprising to those us it is uttered in any moment in nature. It flows through one like wind. One simply cannot remember one's own real talk. One cannot remember the quick, evanescent, exact movements of one's own independent soul. The most one can do is to recall the general feeling or mood of a long conversation in after years. Love and more kisses

Egon.

June 18, 1992 — I take this note all back — he didn't really lie — this is how it was — Now I'm 80 and still after 30 years can hardly bear it without him.

"I hate these people." I asked her why she hates them, for surely they have not done her any harm. "I hate them like I hate my blood vessels, which by their refusal to dilate keep my hands and my feet cold when I urgently need them to feel warm. My blood vessels do not *want* to do me harm, either."

A few months ago I bought a lot of books from an English book dealer, among them the letters of Jane Carlyle. When the books arrived, A. asked "Why did you buy these? I'll never read them." For the past two weeks she has lost herself in them and we talk much about Jane. Never did A. find a woman so much like herself as Jane was, and rarely did anyone enchant her more by her very being, thinking, style, and manner. Last night after she finished the first volume at one in the morning, she softly woke me out of the first deep sleep of the night with one of her inimitable kisses and said, "Thank you for buying these books for me."

The new novel is coming steadily along. The first part is finished, as the door closed on Dorney's childhood with tears in both A.'s and my eyes. But she works very hard, every day from nine in the morning til four in the afternoon. Naturally she neglects cooking and washing a bit, so that every morning when I open the drawer for some socks, I carefully count how many are left. Today I saw to my dismay that there were only two pairs left, and I decided that tomorrow on my afternoon off I'll go and buy another half a dozen. I have, as it is, about two dozen in the house, but they are all worn and dirty. Now the simplest thing, of course, would be to wash them myself. Were I to do that, however, I would invite almost disaster, because naturally A. would discover me either in the act (of washing them) or when the socks were hung up for drying, since I can find no way of drying them in hiding.

Tonight I complimented her on the dinner, not because it was so good, but to cheer her and make her feel good. But she is so smart. Reading my thoughts, she said: "I cannot cook anymore. It tastes like health food. Everything. Just like in one of the places you go to for your health and tell yourself that it's good for you and force it down against your very being." Now, that's exaggerated. It isn't really bad. But, both of us knowing how wonderful a cook she is when her heart is in it, she made that remark to show me how she disapproves of her attitude toward daily life.

Yet I don't know what we could do about it, because she refuses with finality to hire a housekeeper or any sort of help. This is because her mother never had help in the house and A. would not dare to avail herself of help in the house if Mother would not have someone too. Since we would have to pay such help, naturally, A. goes without it and tries to do the best under the circumstances. But how long she can do it, working like a soldier on the march to battle and keeping house the way she wants it to be kept, I don't know. As far as I am concerned, everything is wonderful as long as we are in good health and she is working contentedly. But the poor girl every once in a while gets wild with grief that she does not do her part and fails in her relationship with people, and so feels an utter failure. Those are the hours which need my utmost tact and understanding to bring her back to reality and make her understand that she cannot serve two masters at the same time.

Today, the first day Mother is gone, she is happy and calm, breathes like other people do, without drawing every other breath, and can smile. At the bus depot last night, we bought the pocketbook edition of Kathleen Winsor's *Star Money*, and A. has been reading it ever since in her time off. It will help her to be a better woman, a better writer. She does not need such stuff to improve herself. But it makes her apparently feel better when she sees how dismally wretched, or wicked, or miserable others are. I think that the Winsor girl is an example for any writer how NOT TO BE.

We are looking forward to the visit of my nephew Philip, whom I have not seen for 21 years and who will spend two or three weeks with us before going to Canada, where he will settle in Vancouver, B.C. (Although I have a feeling that Ardyth dreads the responsibilities connected with being his hostess.)

MAY 10, 1951

Sunday night my nephew Philip is coming for a visit and will stay with us for some two or three weeks. I haven't seen him for 21 years and am more than curious how a boy whose ears I lanced on Christmas Day of 1930 at the age of 10 looks in May 1951, after having spent the last thirteen years on the Malayan peninsula. From letters, pictures and testimonials, I assume that he is the best-looking specimen of our clan, even though he can only claim half belonging to it.

About a year after Philip was born, my sister Lilly, his mother, got a divorce from Philip's father, Walter Skrein, who was the son of the owner of one of Vienna's leading newspapers. She became engaged while the divorce proceedings were still in process, to a captain of the Austrian Army, one Rudolph von Flesch, whose escutcheon I later discovered on a specimen of his underwear. This Mr. von Flesch demanded of her as a condition of marriage that she should not bring her son into their marriage, to which she gave her youthful but unwise consent. Philip was given into the care of my mother, together with the maid who had carried him in her arms almost from his birth on and whose name I can only remember to have been Paula.

After a few weeks' stay in my parental home, Paula one day consulted me while I was doing locum tenens practice for my father, the first time I was on my own, entirely, with a private practice. Paula, with a small but marked blush and after several hesitations, confessed to being pregnant (she said a little pregnant, which meant not very long) and implied with her eyes only the wish that maybe I would relieve her. I told her I'll think the matter over, trying to gain time until my father returned. A week or so later, when Father came back to the practice and I told him of Paula's plight, we decided to help her, mainly because we thought her services to Philip indispensable.

The child throve with her and she loved him for all of us to see, while his mother was busy getting married and located in Berlin. Flesch, with the help of my father, was going into business there, I believe selling some things; I can't remember what. But I do remember that my father soon lost his investment in that business.

To come back to Paula: We performed the operation in my father's office, which was, like all or most medical offices in Vienna, right in the residence, and all went well. This was the first and only time in my life that I performed an abortion, and it will therefore always remain an essential reminiscence in my life.

Not long afterward Paula married a Herr La Croix, who was a clerk or bookkeeper in a government office. At first my mother was quite disconcerted with the idea of losing Paula, and Paula hated to leave Philip, and Philip became a matter of grave concern to all concerned except his parents. Paula, apparently after discussing the affair with her fiancé, soon came to my mother and asked her for permission to take Philip along into her new marriage, and I remember the many hours of debate and arguing this brought about between my parents. But, feeling that a young woman who loved the child like her own would possibly be a better mother than a loving, almost doting, but aging grandmother, it was finally decided to give Philip to Paula with the understanding that my parents would contribute to his maintenance an amount deemed sufficient and thus preserve the right that under normal circumstances was the mother's. Paula thus became the Mammi to the child and later boy.

Walter Skrein soon married again, the secretary of the famous Professor Wenckebach, the heart specialist, and as far as I remember never cared much about Philip's well-being, first because he never had any money to care with, and second because he soon became the father of another boy. But later Philip became acquainted with his stepmother, and she became Mama. As he grew up my sister, who had soon after her second marriage given birth to a daughter, Nanny, met Philip occasionally at my parents' home and possibly even at Paula's. I don't know. She was called Mutti.

In 1938 Philip, in danger of being trapped by the Nazis, was whisked out of the country and given a position in Singapore with Tels & Co., a rubber- and tin-buying concern or corporation which was in the hands of Walter Skrein's sister, who had married a Mr. Tels. And so it happened that Philip was out of reach until now, when he comes back after all these years because he did not want to spend all his life in the tropics. It was decided that he would take leave from Tels & Co. and, travelling around the world, come to the Pacific coast, where he intends to settle in Vancouver, B.C. This would involve no difficulties with immigration because in 1945 he became a British subject after serving with the Australian armed forces during the world war.

During the war I once wrote to him on the occasion of his birthday, to some army camp in Australia, expressing the hope that his mother was well. I thought, of course, of my sister Lilly, who had remained behind in Vienna and cared for my parents until their death, and was later rewarded for it by being put into a concentration camp to be killed by the Nazis. Fortunately the war was over and American troops liberated the victims of the camp before the Nazis' scheme could be completed. But Philip answered my letter then with the anguished remark that he could not answer how his mother was because he did not know which one I meant, since he had three.

In two more days we shall welcome him and find out what a nephew looks like.

Last evening was delightful. A. and I were sitting, as so often, in the library, each of us reading a book. As happens on such occasions when two congenial people are reading at the same time, we interrupted each other several times by calling the other's attention to a passage that sounded as if it would be particularly attractive or interesting to the other. I often do. But Ardyth does it in her own way, which is to suddenly exclaim over a remarkable passage or quote some arresting observation. I cannot remember what she was reading, but suddenly I heard her say: "So the Brownings never saw each other naked." Of course I looked up from my book and wanted to hear more. No. No further comment was forthcoming. When my efforts to elicit some details from her were in vain, I began reading again Montaigne's essay "On Friendship." Suddenly I heard, "When Howard does not want any visitors to come, he puts an orange in the window." This too, of course, intrigued me. But I could get no further than with the remark about the Brownings.

She kept on reading, lost to the world to all appearances, when the bell rang and I smilingly asked why she hadn't put an orange in the window. I heard her say "And what if I had, whoever it is would hardly know the sign," and saw her run into her attic studio.

After I paid the newsboy, who had come to collect for the paper, and called that the coast was clear, she came down and after a while said with all the quiet charm she is capable of: "You know, when someone comes to the door unexpectedly, like now, I sometimes wish we were kangaroos." "Why?" I inquired. "Because in that case we could jump into each other's pouches and disappear." We laughed til the tears were running down our cheeks.

We resumed our reading and read for another hour or so, I guess, at any rate long enough to get another bit of information worthwhile to remember. "Listen to that," she interrupted me, "Dr. Johnson's first teacher was one Tom Brown. He wrote a little book called 'On Spelling' and published it with 'dedicated to the Universe'." After discussing this tidbit, we decided to have a bite before going to bed, and A. made some lovely peanut butter sandwiches for her and some with baloney for me. Delightful. They never taste as good when I make them.

JULY 1, 1951

I have made no notes for almost a month. There is no special reason to account for it. That I did not want to write down anything would be a lie. I simply didn't. And now I am sorry, because there are always things worth being remembered.

I am keeping the books of the family. Keeping books is in these days as necessary as it is to have a degree or a license to carry on a profession or business; otherwise, a tax collector would get *better* than even with you. That, nobody can afford. So while I was going over bills and receipts in my desk I find this note:

"December 29th 1950 11 PM. Ardyth thought of the idea to bring Butch Cassidy in as protagonist to Dorney Leaf."

At first it was to be the story of a teen-aged girl, using some material her mother had told her of her youth. This was just right for what A. had promised Paul Brooks to do in her next book. But it was to be the story of a poor girl, without any idea of having an outlaw as a hero.

Last night I asked her what had given her the thought of Butch Cassidy. She could not answer that question. But after a moment of silence she looked at me, blowing out the smoke of a cigarette, and said: "I love to think of things past and forgotten (but not by me) and remember little episodes or lines I have written, sometimes on the inside of book covers, which made me love things of the days now gone. This makes me feel as though I receive them again as a gift, for of the past nothing belongs to us except what we love, and I desire to possess everything I ever experienced."

JULY 25, 1951

Somewhere in my desk I found this note, dated Dec. 29th, 1950, 11 PM: Ardyth thought of the idea for Dorney Leaf to be coupled in the next book with the story of Butch Cassidy.

Now, about seven months later, the story is well on its way, about halfway through, and Dorney as well as Butch have become real persons. A. is reading to me her daily output after it is typed, and so has made me familiar with these characters to such an extent that I find myself thinking of them more often than of my sister and her children, and catch myself being concerned about their future more than I was ever concerned about mine.

I hate to see her work so hard; up by the alarm clock at ten minutes to seven AM. A cup of coffee with one piece of toast and she smokes a Parliament cigarette. Then I get up, and while I shave she makes my breakfast: 2 med. boiled eggs, 2 pieces of toast, and a cup of coffee. While I sit down for this best-tasting meal, she makes the bed, picks up loose ends in the house, and prepares her "tray" for upstairs: 2 hard-boiled eggs, a pint of black coffee in a thermos bottle to last her all day, and 2 pieces of dry toast. Then comes another cigarette, with me smoking a Lucky, while we settle on what I am to bring home or whom I should call or what letters have to be mailed and so on, and off she goes to her studio, carrying her tray carefully up the narrow stairway (designed by herself and built by Bruce Jones). Within a few minutes I hear her on the typewriter, as fast as my best secretary ever was, obviously oblivious to all the rest of us—and the only time she succeeds in being unaware of herself.

I finish tying my tie, put a new handkerchief in my pocket, take a last look in the mirror—being happy that my hair is still black with my 57th birthday no more than two months away—and announce my leaving with a whistling. Swiftly I climb the stairs and we kiss—long, true, looking at each other's eyes, and when I want to turn she hugs me once more and says "Please be careful, won't you darling—you're all I've got!" After reassuring her and with another glance at her (already typing), I leave. It's about 8:30.

When I come home at 5:30 PM she is sitting on the salmon-colored couch, dressed, all fixed up with a book in her hands. It's always a whistling that announces my coming as I enter the house, answered by her with "Hello, darling." I never sit down at once after kissing her, but dispose first of the things I brought home, such as groceries, books or whatever she had wanted me to bring, and rush into the kitchen to fill the icebox, then into the bedroom to shed my clothes (in a hurry) and then look at the mail, especially if there is news from a publisher, agent or the tax office. At this point she shows impatience with me and calls me down: "Why don't you sit down and smoke a cigarette and leave these crummy letters for later. I've written nine pages, but they aren't good. I am afraid I won't be able to use four of them tomorrow. It's no good."

"Would you let me hear something?" I beg.

"It's no good, and it's not finished, and you won't like it. But if you don't mind"—and she gets up and brings the pages she had written the day before and corrected today—3 or 4 or 6 or 9, whatever it is—and begins to read. And every time, every day, she makes me smile—or cry or sigh with delight as she reads and the story develops, like a mother does with her little son reading him a story. And never can I tell at first whether it is the story and the writing or the incomparable art of her reading that gets me so. Only later, after hours or days, do I see the great artistry and skill of the style, especially when I can read the pages after Miss Arnsberg has transcribed them.

JULY 7, 1952

Back from vacationing at Virginia City, Montana, and Yellowstone Park, with Michael and Timothy as youthful guests. *Good Morning, Young Lady* on the way. Ardyth full of plans for fifth book.

Tomorrow morning I'm resuming work again. A. wants me to take out a license in California to practice because she feels in Portland either an exile or a prisoner. A sudden meeting with almost anyone is a torment to her (like meeting Stewart Holbrook tonight while shopping at Fred Meyer's). Stewart didn't say a word except "Just back from my vacation," which I parried with "same with us," and Ardyth, I felt, was shaking inside and thinking one thing only—how she could get away fastest. She would feel freer in California, she thinks, best of all places, she says, in Santa Monica. Tomorrow the work routine for her, too, will begin again. She has not written a word since February.

But she is writing schedules—like budgeting in old days:

how often to eat—and what each time;
how many hours' work;
how many hours to devote to scholarship (reading poetry, writing down quotations, sources or interesting topics);
how much time for relationship with other people;
how much time for housework.

She made a similar plan for me and means to enforce them for both of us. "The best commander lies in ourselves," she told me a little while ago.

With only a new brassiere (without shoulder straps) on and a wide bright iridescent green skirt, she looks terribly tempting tonight.

After dinner I took her shopping to Fred Meyer's. There, amid the anonymity of a 5 & 10 cent store, she feels well, purchasing sundry nothings, and can spend an hour or so in complete happiness. Many a worthless article will later on, endowed with her imagination, be sent to mother, sister, sister-in-law or friends, all of whom will cherish it not for its own sake, but for her thoughts, words or wishes which accompany it.

To her mother she loves to send dolls—if possible, big ones.

JULY 20, 1952

Ardyth, while ironing a tablecloth, just told me the title of her next book: *The Unwilling Hyacinth*. She always likes to have a working title before starting to write. It makes her feel that now she is in business.

I am engaged in answering the tax collector's annoying inquisition and preparing the answers to his queries for a meeting with him in Mr. Forsyth's office next Thursday.

AUGUST 8, 1952

We have to pay back taxes for 1949 and 1950 of $2,494.76 plus 6% interest. On top of it Mr. Forsyth's fee. This makes a total for the two years of $17,060.00.

Ardyth has been for the past three days in Seattle to inspect her new niece, today six days old. Name: Ardyth Linnea.

But I heard over the telephone from her that Marion's marriage with Claude might break up.

APRIL 3, 1954

[*letter to Egon's cousin Claire Bunzell in Los Angeles*:]

Dear Claire,

Do I hear a rumor that you and Emil might come to Portland? Within the last two days I had two calls asking "when you are coming" and I didn't know a thing about it. George Kien and Paul Eisinger asked me. I wish you would elaborate on this matter.

I have not written so long because it seems that Ardyth is doing all the writing now possible in this house. It's noon now, Sunday the 16th of May, and Ardyth is sound asleep while the sun shines and the cat is enjoying it on the balcony. About three weeks ago she changed her schedule and went on graveyard shift. She starts to work after what she now calls her breakfast at ten at night and works until the early morning hours. Gets to bed at four and sleeps late. She says she does it because this way she can combine living with working and possibly better capture the mood of a burning city at night, but I suspect her of doing it because graveyard shift pays better. What do you think? Anyway, in a few weeks she hopes to be done with what I am sure is her best so far.

At the same time she is housecleaning, which in itself is no mean task, considering that it looked here like the castle where there was hay on the floor and they threw the bones under the table. "It had to be sweetened."

As to myself, I have little to tell. I am so surrounded by patients that I hardly notice the world outside. They swarm about me in ever increasing numbers—I have a waiting list of appointments until July—and instead of curbing the practice, I see it growing. Politics are so invariably depressing, with the antics of men who take advantage of a hero who cannot make up his mind and looks in vain for regulations within which to give orders, that I prefer not to read the papers and keep the radio silent. Instead we enjoy steadily our ever increasing long-playing record collection. While I am writing you, Othello loves Desdemona in Verdi's best tunes, which probably accounts for my poor typing.

I would much like to hear from you, doings and plannings and the news you have of Marietta. When do they start on their trip around the world? How long will Emil continue to work?

Do you see Lilli sometimes? The poor thing wears herself out, I fear, having her job now plus Nany's business. She writes encouragingly, though, about the latter, but is rather distressed about Nany's affairs of the heart and being lonesome. She would like us to come for a visit to L.A., but neither of us can afford it at this time. You know we want to go East in August and I cannot take the time off, since I have no interest now in L.A. except family. I love, though, to know that all of you are doing well and are in good health.

We think of you both much more often than you would give us credit for and wish *frequently* to have you here for an evening. Too bad we have the lower apartment rented and would have to forego the pleasure of having you in the house while you visit. Where will you stay? With the Newtons? Tell me all about it. If I can do something, I would like to know it. Paul Eisinger has left the hospital today with a damaged but still seeing eye. He won't be able to work for several more months.

That is all of my learning that I can recall.

With love for each from each.
  Egon

OCTOBER 13, 1954

Back from New York with more appreciation of home. I feel that this excursion will work out as a turning point in Ardyth's life. She was, at the time of leaving Portland, in a depressed and extremely labile mood, insecure and beset by doubts of ever being able to work again. The lack of warmth and understanding on the part of Paul Brooks of Houghton Mifflin has unquestionably contributed to making her feel bad.

But within two weeks after our arrival in New York, the weather turned around. She saw Andrew Salter, who succeeded in reassuring her about her work and her ability to deliver irrespective of mood and feeling insecure, and he at once got her in touch with Naomi Burton of Curtis Brown to act as her agent. As a psychologist he failed utterly in her case, so that after six sessions she suddenly asked me to call his office and deliver this message: "I wish to terminate treatment at this time." (The day before, she had forgotten in his office a beautiful pair of long gloves bought the previous afternoon, and she never went back to get them.) From that moment on, I knew she would find the balance of her fighting emotion by herself and go on on her own.

Naomi Burton got in touch with Paul Brooks and was able to reassure Ardyth, and to produce within two days a telegram from Brooks that he accepts the new book and that he will negotiate everything through her agent. This in turn led to sufficient positive feelings that we bought a number of exquisite porcelain pieces, among others the famous Affen Kapelle (monkey music band), consisting of 11 pieces of enchanting monkey musicians.

On September 22 Georg and Martha had us for dinner to celebrate my 60th birthday. It is easier to write this number, 60, than to reconcile oneself with being 60 while one does not feel like it. Only stronger glasses are necessary.

After four weeks in New York we left for Amherst to investigate the grounds, trees and house of Emily Dickinson, then for three days to Indiana to visit J. W. Riley's place in Greenfield and back home.

First thing Ardyth did was to bring the color of her hair back to natural. She looks sweeter than ever and should be less self-conscious. Next was a conference with the slow-speaking contractor Rimer, who is to remodel the house. He'll start to work in one week and we will have to move to an apartment.

JANUARY 18, 1955

We are back home again and the house takes on shape again. It is interesting to watch Ardyth arranging things. A shade, a nuance unnoticeable to most people makes her worry. That's spotty, she would say, or No—a simple no, and a table, lamp shade or costly vase is discarded and sometimes replaced with a cheap piece if it fits the color she wants or the shape she visualizes. The end effect is invariably surprisingly pleasant. And so, although I often object at the time she moves and arranges and samples, I invariably in the end agree.

We have now something like 57 drawers in the house. She has filled every one in perfect order—she can find everything in time—but I am afraid I have to make a sort of telephone book to find the number of the drawer.

I have never had it so good—we often say, looking smilingly at each other.

Up Home has been purchased by the *Ladies' Home Journal*. Houghton Mifflin had the manuscript for over three years and sent it back just when A. was working without sleep on her last chapters of *The Sky Is Not Cloudy All Day*. Now H. M. wants to publish it at all cost and effort. Things always become more desirable when someone else wants them too. Once they are tucked away, like a book (a rare one) in a library or a painting in a museum, they lose much, if not all, their attraction. Any good thing, no matter how expensive, is more desirable—or desirable at all—if I know that one can purchase it. Then, and then only, am I really interested. Museums and libraries have their use.

We have succumbed to the lure of TV. Ardyth and her mother listen together for the first time to Ronald Colman and Red Skelton, and I feel antagonistic toward it—as though I am in mortal danger of being deprived of *time*. As though my time were so valuable. No one would pay me a penny for my time, yet when I think of sitting in front of the screen and following the nonsense interrupted only by the greater nonsense of advertisements, I can't help feeling like being robbed, and the worst of it is that I fear I, too, will succumb to the dope in due time.

JANUARY 26, 1955

I have performed thousands of operations in my life. But there is one which, no matter how often I am called to perform it, causes in me what I call, in lieu of a better word, "stage fright." When I am to operate on a patient fighting for his life, I am never ruffled. But when I operate on an *eye*, the thought that "to see or not to see is the question" makes me feel nervous the evening before and often keeps me from sleeping well. This operation is the cataract extraction, the most difficult but also the most beautiful and, when well performed, the most satisfying in the whole realm of surgery. I have never known a patient who was displeased or dissatisfied after a successful cataract extraction.

While we are still working on the house, I am often asked how it will look and what, if any, the plan is. I can never find the right words to describe it and refer my inquirers to be patient until Ardyth's description is published in a magazine. She alone will describe it with the charm it really has. I am usually pretty good in conveying an impression—and that is all anyone can give with spoken words—but I recalled the note of Heine at the death of Byron: "The departure of Byron touched me deeply. He was the only person to whom I felt akin. We were much alike in a good many respects. Joke about it as much as you want. I have read little of him, and that not frequently. But I always felt on an equal footing with Byron, as though I had sat in school beside him. But with Shakespeare I am never easy; I feel forever that I am not of his kind. He is forever the omnipotent powerful chief, and I only a civil servant, and I always imagine he could fire me at any moment."

Ardyth consented to be painted—painted as a fortune teller. Charlotte Mish, who wears her poached-eggs eyes with dignity and conviction, will do the picture.

There is an anecdote that is told of Marlowe. He was advised once by a friend to have as many people as possible die in his tragedies. I always remember it and sometimes wish I could write tragedies myself so as to let all my ill-wishers die there.

Ardyth is anxious to get back to work, she tells me, and I love to see her putter around the house and cherish pink.

It is easy to work
When the soul is at play.

FEBRUARY 7, 1955

Charlotte Mish has begun painting Ardyth.

FEBRUARY 9, 1955

Charlotte Mish and Graziella Boucher have been known to us since the 1930s, when Ardyth worked for a while on the Public Works Program. We knew they were two spinsters who loved animals (their dog Blackie is still alive, who helped the war bond drive and collected $1,000 so that in 1944 the Mayor decorated him and gave him a lifelong dog license) and whom the town suspected to be a little more or less on the Lesbian side. Since they always flattered everyone, they were considered harmless.

Ardyth suddenly thought this would be a good time for a portrait, especially since there was an opening for a picture on the wall opposite Odette, and it so happened that around New Year's Graziella, the blond sixtyish little female, ran into us or vice versa, and at once proposed the portrait by Charlotte, emphasizing that Charlotte had wanted to paint Ardyth ever since she had known her. Today when I came home I found Charlotte at the easel, and as I watched her as she was—small, very thin and sickly looking, with enormous proptotic eyes emphasized with thick black and green mascara, curls around the forehead dipped in henna and a sharply bent nose—I said to myself: My God, this poor thing is a weak but striking replica of James McNeill Whistler.

Would that I can say that again when the painting is done.

Up Home has been bought by the *Ladies' Home Journal*, which will serialize it beginning April through July. In August it is to come out as a book with Houghton Mifflin.

FEBRUARY 20, 1955

We are at a stalemate. The painters have not finished on time and we have to spend the weekend among the clothes, boxes, books, sundry disjointed tables and hundreds of loose pieces which lie scattered around on the floor of the rooms. There are only two chairs in the house to sit on, and Ardyth is very impatient. Whenever she feels frustrated, she eats—mainly bagels—peanut butter and honey and assorted sweets. Everything she had foresworn at a previous period of high activity. There she sits, bemoans her gain of weight, says she feels sorry for me because she looks so terrible, and sometimes fights tears.

Then suddenly she shows me a note she made a little while ago from George Moore's letters to Mr. Dujardin. I read (while she smiles): Literature is an indiscreet art.

FEBRUARY 27, 1955

Ardyth is housecleaning, the first time since the house was rebuilt. Our floor is finished, and the work above no longer interferes. While she was puttering around singing fragments from the music of *Gone with the Wind*, I read Richard Chase's *Emily Dickinson*. What perceptive, lovely interpretation! I never tire of her, in whatever disguise, book or poem, I meet her.

Then we listened to N.Y.'s Philharmonic with Menuhin playing the violin concerto of Brahms. I remembered hearing him in San Francisco in the twenties when he was about fourteen years old and appeared with his teacher Louis Persinger. They played Beethoven sonatas for piano and violin, and the melody of the Frühling sonata still rings in my ears.

Menuhin has a wonderful voice over the radio, and I listened spellbound as he reminisced about playing under the conductorship of men like Weingartner, Muck and Furtwaengler—all dead now. He and Heifetz hold now the violin for our ears—Ysaÿe and Jan Kubelik, who enchanted me in Europe, are forgotten.

As the applause died down at the end of the Brahms, I remembered the limerick:

> "There should be more screwing,"
> Said Mrs. Menuhin.
> "One little goody
> Gave us Yehudi."

ON MARCH 5, 1955:

Margarete Ullman, with whom I was married once upon a time, got married again to one Elwood Ullman, thus ending my bondage of alimony of almost 16 years. I hear that she chose to get wedded one day after her ancient mother died in the bathroom. For that purpose the Ullmans flew to Las Vegas and flew right back to attend the corpse's funeral. Danse macabre.

MARCH 19, 1955

Up Home is appearing in the *Ladies' Home Journal* beginning next issue (April). It will be serialized for five months, then published by Houghton Mifflin in book form beginning in August. *Ladies' Home Journal* paid $20,000 and H. M. advanced $2,500. The reprints of *Albrecht von Graefe: The Man in His Time* came a few days ago and are being sent out now to 800 ophthalmologists.

The house building progresses fast now, and we should be done by the end of the month and not later than the first week of April.

My sister Lilly and her daughter Nany will visit us during the week of April 21. The first time in three and a half years. Family get-together. Has to be.

MARCH 23, 1955

When the essay on von Graefe came out,

[*note handwritten by Ardyth and taped onto the journal page:*] A timely quotation from Kipling—copied for Egon:
> *If you stop to consider the work you have done*
> *And to boast what your labor is worth, dear,*
> *Angels may come for you, Willie, my son,*
> *But you'll never be wanted on earth, dear!*

APRIL 4, 1955

Marion got a court decree for divorce from Claude Massee. She retains her home and he is to pay 75 dollars a month. The family feels relieved of a nightmare.

We listen more often to television. It did what I never expected it to do: it gets me in touch with the contemporary world much more than sitting in my office and listening to the complaints of my patients. These have not changed much since I went to school. But somehow the jokes of the comedians and the technical performers have improved—only the politicians are the same.

Charles Darwin to my and everybody's nephews [*clipping taped onto the journal page*]:

SCIENTIST

> On Page 1, you can read what our critic thinks about Mr. Darwin & Co. We ourselves were looking at the book with a fascinated eye and were taken by Mr. Darwin's approach to marriage. Darwin jotted down a series of notes a year before he did marry and, it seems, without any lady in mind.
>
> The scientist listed among the advantages of matrimony: "children (if it please God)—constant companion (& friend in old age)—charms of music & female chit-chat." Among the disadvantages: "terrible loss of time, if many children forced to gain one's bread."
>
> Then he sums up Euclidian-fashion: "What is the use of working without sympathy from near and dear friends? Who are near and dear friends to the old, except relatives? My God, it is intolerable to

think of spending one's whole life like a neuter bee working, working, and nothing after all.— No, no won't do— Imagine living all one's days solitarily in smoky, dirty London house— Only picture to yourself a nice soft wife on a sofa, with good fire and books and music perhaps— Marry, marry, marry, Q.E.D."

April 14, 1955

The eve of Ardyth's 43rd birthday. We are celebrating quietly by hanging pictures and talking of books.

She handed me Virginia Woolf's diary and said: "Please read it, I mean, only the passages I have marked, and my notes. You'll see how much alike we are." "If two do the same, it never is the same," said I. Besides, she is the one woman writer whose looks I cannot stand. Just look at the picture of her on the back of the wrapper. She looks like a long-faced dog who is silently and sadly waiting for his master's feeding him or giving him a withdrawn toy.

Yet as I went on reading, I could see the similarity of emotions, reactions and ambitions.

April 15, 1955

Ardyth's birthday.

We indulged in enjoying—by taking possession of—our remodelled home, meandering through the drawers, shelves and boxes, sorting, discussing and ordering the sundry little papers we had gathered on the way—a picture of Sarah Bernhardt in her casket taken while she was still young, with a note from her hand laid by its side, grass from the grave of Emily Dickinson put in the volume of the first edition of her poems, a letter of Kipling and a picture, "Hands Up," put up by the Pinkerton detectives in 1888 in Spokane, Wash.

In between, saw Judge Medina on television tell us that he reads five or six books at the same time—Hazlitt, Ruskin, Stendhal and Virginia Woolf! The Curious Reader. Comme chez nous.

Last week we took Michael and Timothy for a stroll in the Grotto. On the way out, we passed one of the priests talking to a young couple. He was enormously big, red-faced, and waved his hand, which was dirty. All of us looked at him for a moment, for he reminded of one of the clerics in Chaucer. And suddenly I remembered a patient, also big and red-faced, whom I took care of some time ago. When I saw him (I told the boys), I remarked, sort of on the side: "My, your hands are dirty." To which he replied: "You should see my feet!"

I love to remember this because of Ardyth's laughter, which was Byronesque.

April 20, 1955

Ardyth is reading me passages of Virginia Woolf's diary. She underlined many lines that sound as though Ardyth had put them down regarding herself.

I am receiving dozens and dozens of fan letters on the Graefe and enjoy every one of them. Ardyth received less for any of her novels than this little essay brought, and just as well, because she hardly ever looks at them and rarely reads one. If it's good, as usual, she says "Oh—she or he does not really mean anything" or "How unimportant," but if it says but one single adverse word, she gets furious. She never likes to read about her writing. How different from Virginia Woolf.

May 7, 1955

Yesterday during the visit of the Goldsboroughs, who had come to photograph the house, I experienced my first AGONY, or fear of death. Just before he was leaving at midnight, I was suddenly gripped by severe pain in my chest, which I was sure was a coronary heart attack.

Goldsborough had examined me routinely two days earlier at the clinic and found, as was known to me, that I am mildly hypertensive with beginning changes in my electrocardiogram. I thought I took this message—which was confirmed by Saward—philosophically. After all, few become sixty years old without showing somewhere some sign of deterioration. But come night that day—about midnight—a pain in my chest gripped me. Goldsborough was in the next room taking pictures. I called him and he tried to appease me. He soon left with his wife Hazel, and left me in a terrible mess. I began to shake like I had a chill, and shake with my hips! and knees. I could not lie still in bed and could think of one thing only—morphine. If I have to go, I might as well be unaware of it. So I had Ardyth call Goldsborough, who refused to come out (and right he was) and told her that morphine was contraindicated. She was to give another sedative (Seconal) and I would soon fall asleep. That's exactly what happened. I slept soundly until 7:15 AM and woke up sleepy and weak, but—how wonderful—without pain.

Ardyth was so good to me that I find no words to describe it. She even brought a beautiful vase of cut glass to the bed for me to let water, so as not to have to get to the bathroom, explaining that it'll make the next flowers she puts in it only bloom longer.

Ardyth, for about six or seven years now, has been pursuing the color pink. Her upholstering is pink, the basic color of the apartment is pink, she is nuts about pink satin glass (Bristol) and, finally, she goes wild over paintings that have a base of pink. Like some of Matisse and Gauguin. I often teased her as being possessed by pink, or color-crazy. But she persisted.

The following note appears in today's *Time* [*clipping labeled "Time, May 9, 1955," taped onto the journal page*]:

> THE ECONOMY
>
> In the Pink
>
> Noting that pink has become the U.S. color of 1955, in house furnishings as well as in clothing for both men and women, Chicago's H. W. Gossard Co. (girdles) last week announced a change of policy. Instead of emphasizing its recently popular blacks, blues and reds, Gossard will feature a new line of foundations in pink. Psychological research, said Gossard, had shown the reason for the U.S. color trend: "Pink represents a mood of sentimentality, good times and luxury."
>
> There was evidence to support that conclusion. Last week the U.S. economy was producing more goods and services than man has ever enjoyed anywhere.

I intend to incorporate some of the pictures John Goldsborough took in these pages.

How I wish that some of the loved or respected personages of the past would have left us some pictorial records of their habitations, possessions and surroundings.

MAY 15, 1955

Opening of the Pacific Coast Meeting of Oto-Ophthalmologists, at 5 PM in the Multnomah Hotel. I'll attend the opening session and probably a few of the lectures. I don't know what to think of, but I do lose all interest in following the scientific pursuit of Medicine. While Literature becomes more alive for me than ever, Medicine only shows that man still must die, that though he dies in the hospital and mostly painlessly, he still dies. And from the riddles of life—cancer, the origin of life, and arteriosclerosis, death of life—we are as far away as we always were. All speculation.

This morning at breakfast Ardyth volunteered a most cheerful message, more welcome to me than anything this convention of eye specialists could possibly reveal: her suddenly discovered love for the Pacific North West. She never liked it—never felt at home here and never could become interested in its history. The state was one into which she was thrown through the accidental death of her father. Her youthful reminiscences were all contained—so she thought—in the Mormon Country of Utah. The Willamette Valley was the locale of her poverty and humiliation, and Portland only the Portland of the Depression in the thirties, which had rejected her and made her feel all that the ones who do not belong complain of.

Last August, after finishing the novel *Marry Me, Carry Me* just before we left for New York, she suddenly began praying that she might learn how to like—even love—Portland, Oregon, the North West. Before, she had played with the idea of my getting a license to practice in California and moving to San Francisco. But after she finished writing about the S.F. earthquake (in this last book), or maybe just accidentally around that time, she began seeing a future for her and us here in Portland. The plans for the house took shape—how to remodel it and how to furnish it, and suddenly one day, around the end of September 1954, on 44th Street—it was in New York near the Astor Hotel—the idea of Dr. Gaudio came, and the part of his life he spent in Oregon and the way he died. The title came a few days later so she could mention it to her agent before we left N.Y.: "When in Disgrace . . ."

This morning she told me in detail the story of "The Peacock and the Bride," which she thinks to have done and in the mail by the end of this month, and spoke of two more Oregon! stories she was going to write.

I am now bringing home the best things I can find on Oregon—McLoughlin, Whitman and the Indians.

While I am writing this page, Ardyth is proofreading *Up Home*. I feel better than I have been during the past two weeks.

JUNE 15, 1955

Ardyth finished "The Peacock and the Bride" today. When she told me when I came home tonight, she was all smiles. I know she sat up last night until the early morning hours and was back to work again at 8:00 AM today when I left for the hospital.

I feel better than I have for some time.

JUNE 20, 1955

Ardyth read to me out of Simone de Beauvoir's *The Other Sex* the chapter on creative women. We especially discussed the writer. The stimulus for this was given by Dr. Frank Baxter's discussion of Dorothy Wordsworth on his TV show on Sunday noon, when I made a gesture as though I were trying to dispose of Dorothy as a "flower poet." (I really wasn't, and probably just wiped my nose.) But if I did, it was worthwhile, because it got Ardyth started on this subject. Beauvoir is no doubt the greatest living woman thinker and writer.

JULY 3, 1955

Spent the day with Ardyth driving to the coast at Ocean Lake. Peaceful, heavenly—holding hands.

She spoke of buying a home on the coast when I *want* to quit working, which I never will want, and living at the coast.

Thought of the fact that almost all famous woman authors remained unmarried. Brontë, Emily Dickinson, Selma Lagerlöf, Ellen Key, Louisa Alcott, Jane Austen, Eudora Welty, Edna Ferber, and so on. Simone de Beauvoir explains it all.

Ardyth sent "The Peacock and the Bride" and the pictures of our apartment home to Naomi Burton. Today she answered that she loves every part of it.

I am pleased that Ardyth has learned to love the North West and become absorbed in its history. With all the fifty or more writers here, there is not one who could do what she can, and how my hopes did get up when, while we were discussing her work and the story of the Mormons, she softly said:

> *Not what the stars have done*
> *But what they yet might do*
> *Holds up the sky . . .*

And then she added: "You know, today for the first time I really thought that I will (not that I might) be one day the grand old lady of literature in this part of the world."

JULY 20, 1955

After ten days in the hospital I have returned home, and am now allowed to sit up in a chair four to five hours a day. I have no pain, just a little earache once in a while in the left ear. My spirits are as high as were those of Marie Antoinette when she milked her cow into costly Sèvres vases. I am sitting in one of our pink armchairs dressed in silken mot mot–colored pyjamas which Ardyth bought for me in one of her tender moods. And while I listen to the high fidelity, I am startled how wondrous it feels to listen to Pogner giving his daughter away into marriage to the best singer, right here in my home in Portland, Oregon.

AUGUST 13, 1955

Read during my illness. August–September 1955.

The Tattooed Countess	Carl Van Vechten (I remembered what M. D. Luhan wrote about his "outstanding" teeth in her *Movers and Shakers*.)
Oblomov	Gontchareff
Moment in Peking	Lin Yu Tang
Children of God	Vardis Fisher
Lorenzo in Taos	Mabel Dodge Luhan
Movers and Shakers	Mabel Dodge Luhan
Background	Mabel Dodge Luhan
Shaw on Music	G. B. S.
Peace of Mind	Liebman
Letters	Santayana
Mozart's biography	Turner
Sons and Lovers	D. H. Lawrence (did not get through)
The Magic Mountain	Thomas Mann
Cybernetics, or the "Use of Humans by Humans"	Norbert Wiener
Haunting Music	Theodor Reik
Self Search	Theodor Reik
Gustav Mahler	Alma Mahler (in German)

AUGUST 26, 1955

I am recovering and feel like I am on a prolonged vacation. This gives me time to observe Ardyth (besides my own twinges and allusions of pain in shoulder, tongue, ear and jaw on my left, which alarmed me at first but which have by now become my companions who tell me every so often: You've got to remember also things you don't want to remember).

Ardyth and I have become still closer, if such was possible. She knows that I don't like to be idle and sit and eat and read and talk and sleep. So she comforts me by telling me that I helped her to become what she is (as though I really did!). She says: "You always try to get things done even though often you don't make an effort to do anything yourself. You seem to use all your power upon delegates to carry out the work. This way—perhaps a compensation for that barren feeling of having nothing to do!—you achieve a sense of fruitfulness and activity vicariously. You have the power to do things but haven't learned how to use it. Our need of achievement in our competitive world is so desperate, our wish to return to the universe all we have taken out of it is so great, that when we haven't learned just how to do it ourselves, we try to make someone else do it for us if we can."

My driver's license has been withdrawn. First came a warning to me from the license office that I have to appear before an officer to explain my too many traffic violations! Probably I didn't come to a complete stop or took a wrong left turn or overparked once too often. Anyhow, this letter came just when I was in the hospital. Ardyth did not want to upset me and didn't tell me about it. When I didn't appear for that hearing, another letter came a few days later notifying me that my license number 829705 had been suspended pursuant to the provisions of Sec. 482.240 and 482.260. This Ardyth also withheld from me, in order not to upset my blood pressure, and called the license office. There she told the officer that I did not appear because I was ill in the hospital. To this the man answered that he will base his action upon "present physical condition."

When I came home, she began talking of taking driving lessons and made this appear very urgent to me. I did not know up to that moment one thing about my license having been suspended. But when she began repeating to me that people who had more than one traffic violation were going to be called before a board to review their driving peccadillos, I became impatient and flared up to *please* leave me alone with such trifles and that I don't care to drive anyhow, and not now, and why is that suddenly so important? Well, finally she came clean and showed me the letters and the statement of the suspension of my license and the *two* reasons given: failure to appear for or pass required tests, and present physical condition. She explained it all so sweetly and so tactfully that she made me shed a skyful of tears.

Meanwhile, she had been taking lessons at $5.00 an hour, several hours a day, with the "Easy Driving Method School" and in the evening with Bill, the next-door neighbor. When she wasn't feeding me or tending to one of my needs she was driving, burning gasoline at 36 cents a gallon. But one day about last week she told me that Alice Iltz would take her out to Gresham, where it is easier to get a license, because the driving around Gresham is easier than around Portland. And so she went the following day to the police station and reported at Gresham for the test. She promptly flunked and said the officer never looked at her. But after a little while he told her that she should practice driving for another six months and then try again.

Well, undismayed by failure, she made another appointment with the Portland bureau for 8 AM the following morning and, sure to flunk again, reported for the test drive. An hour later she was home and had a license! I never, never saw her as flushed with success as at that moment.

Two Literary Guild awards, five novels, the most enchanting house in Portland and being the sweetest woman and the most adored one in the world did not make her feel like anything. But to have a driver's license was some accomplishment. You may laugh, but for me that was not very strange. For I always knew that Ardyth was keeping her writing level, in her mind, with other acts of living, like cooking, scrubbing the floor (like D. H. Lawrence) and keeping house. It was not *writing*, something separate from life. It was the speech and the song, for her, of her own voice, and the writing of it never seems as important to her as the living behind the pen. That is why she *never* thinks of herself as *literary — never as a writer*.

And now that she can drive, she has a feeling of liberation and can't get enough of it. Every time she goes out, it's an experience. For Ardyth never lets the little things pass. Everything is significant and symbolic and becomes to her fateful in one way or another. Perhaps that is why she makes life so thrilling for one, makes the house alive for everyone who enters and makes life always intense *for me.*

August 31, 1955

We went to the airport to get Aunt Laura (one of the restless Olsen sisters), who quit Los Angeles to "settle" in Eugene. On the way she is stopping with Mother a few days. As we watched the planes coming and leaving, Timothy said: "Aunt Ardyth, wouldn't you like to go on a plane trip?" At first she didn't say anything. Then, after a while, she said to me: "Never, unless I am compelled by circumstances." Timothy: "But think how fast you'd arrive." Ardyth: "The going is the fun, never the arriving." And in an aside to me, "I don't even want to get famous in a hurry."

I have had a number of dreams lately which were quite extraordinary and, as I told them to Ardyth, amused and puzzled her as much as they did me.

The other day we had some people for dinner and Mother had made a meat pie. All of us *had* to praise it, although it was obvious that none of us liked it. That night I dreamed (toward morning, as my dreams usually come) that I went into the garden with Vinnie Dickinson. When I asked her how Emily was, she said that Emily had just died, and she showed me the corpse. It was all wrapped up in a meat pie. I never saw one scrap of Emily, yet woke up and was convinced that in the pie crust was Emily dead.

A few days earlier, I dreamed that Ardyth asked me to put some of her new manuscript away in a safe. Suddenly it dawned on me that I carried the best safe thinkable with me. In boring my finger into my right big toe just under the toenail, I found that the big toe was undermined and I could introduce my finger way into the toe and bottom of the foot. I was astonished at the absence of all blood, and after examining my finger several times for blood and finding none, I moved the finger several times back and forth into and out of the toe. Then I put the rolled-up pages of Ardyth's manuscript in that space of my toe and closed the toenail, which formed the perfect lid to the safe.

September 23, 1955

I went through my heartache all over again following President Eisenhower's attack. But I am recovered and have made arrangements to go to work (without doing surgery) beginning on October 3rd.

Last week Marietta and Robert Spencer were our houseguests for three days. All intellectual, strictly following the prescribed ways of today's University life, getting one grant after another. I never realized how much she looks like her father.

Marion sold her house in Seattle and moved lock, stock and barrel to the Grace apartments, two blocks down the street from us, where Ardyth and I lived for about a year before the war. Michael stayed in Seattle because he is just going good with his theatrical talents and thinks he might get some sort of scholarship from there. He is a senior in high school.

SEPTEMBER 30, 1955

Up Home is not doing as well as we expected as a book. Strange, because all of us thought that it would be selling, being so closely related to *The Peaceable Kingdom*.

Just had a little talk with Ardyth while she took a bath. The subject was her future plans with writing. A novel? Some short stories? What? Of course she knows exactly what, because a writer cannot or does not deliberately pick a theme or subject to write on if he isn't ready for it and hasn't carried the idea with him for some time, even though he never talked about it or even thought of writing about it until a sudden thought, word, or bit of news struck him and brought the thing to a focus. So she told me: "If I don't succeed with short stories, it is just as well. I'll do well with novels, as in the past. Of course, I see on your face that all YOU want is money, acclaim and being talked about. But I assure you, I would like it best if no one knew me or of me and I could just work. In fact, I shall put up as my motto a placard in my studio:

> *Live, Learn and Labor.*
> *For Fame and Fortune I don't give a fart —*

You mesomorphs stick to the ideals of youths forever. All you want until you die is money and sex and don't ever see the futility of it all."

OCTOBER 15, 1955

During the days I did not feel well, Ardyth had a tendency to make me "confess" and tell her what was on my mind, of course with the conviction that much of what I suffered from was a "nervous breakdown," a word I detest and a disease which I firmly believe has no place in my body. (For about ten days, I have been feeling my old self again and have no complaints whatsoever. I am back to work again but take, at the advice of Dr. Morton Goodman, Saturday off so that I have a two-day weekend.)

Coming back to confessing and self-analysis, I must say that as to myself, I never believed it would do anything for me if I was in a bad mood or physically upset. As a healing method, I never appreciated psychoanalysis. I am sure that my life remains a secret even to my best friends and I live generally unconsciously, that is, without analyzing myself and without much self-observation. Michel Corday reports in *Anatole France: D'après ses confidences* (Paris 1927, p. 58): "Far from knowing myself, I always took trouble to ignore myself. I consider knowledge of oneself a source of worry, unrest and tortures. I came as little as possible to myself . . . As a small boy and as an adult, young and old, I have always lived as far away from myself as possible. Ignore yourself: this is the first prescription of wisdom."

Goethe spoke to Eckermann in April 1829 about the claim to know oneself: "This is a strange demand which until now nobody has fulfilled and which in reality no one can realize. Man is with all his senses and drives directed toward the outer world, and he has much trouble recognizing it as such and making it serve his purposes and needs. He knows about himself only when he enjoys himself or suffers. He learns thus merely through pain and pleasure what he must seek and what to avoid. After all, man is a dark being; he does not know whence he comes or whither he goes. He knows little of the world and less of himself. I do NOT know myself, and God forbid I should." "How can one learn to know oneself?" Goethe asked. "Never by observation, but by activity."

We are getting acquainted with our library of records of classical music, and I enjoy how Ardyth becomes familiar with, and ever more enthusiastic about, the different composers. Now, when we put on a Schumann or Schubert trio or what have you, she takes pleasure in quizzing me, and of course most of the time I don't know straight up. But it's fun and a new source of joy for her.

She just finished a short story, "Beauty Is Only," and will send it to Curtis Brown next week. Now she has to interrupt work and prepare the house again for the photographer from the *Ladies' Home Journal*, who is coming in two weeks to stay here three or four days.

My cousin Ernesto Rosenthal from Buenos Aires writes me quite regularly, and long letters. Lately there was more news from him, first because Olly, his wife, had to have an eye removed in Vienna because of a tumor, and then because Peron and the Peronistas have been overthrown and the Rosenthals are quite excited about it.

NOVEMBER 7, 1955

Ardyth is restless because the *Ladies' Home Journal* postponed the photographing of our home for two weeks, and thus everything is being held up for the time. But—since she brought it all upon herself, and since we really need the money (to pay taxes with), and since she wants the seal of approval of the *Journal* on her decorating—we don't talk much about it, or if we do, we nod our heads. Yet she can't breathe—is anxious about her heart and has at this time an attack of palindromatic periarthritis on her right (beloved by me) forefinger.

Never mind all this—we were washing dishes after dinner tonight and [. . .] I tried to put down our conversation.

She said, "No one in the twenties could have written as brilliantly as James Baldwin (*Me and My House*), Brinnin (his reminiscences of Dylan Thomas), or Dylan Thomas himself write today. Why, the twenties were child's play."

"Who do you think were the pathfinders?"

"Proust—I am sure—and probably Gertrude Stein."

"What did she do?"

"What do you call it? She let light in."

"What?"

"Well—help me—honestly, sometimes I think I am losing my mind if I can't think of a word . . ."

"Oh, no, you're not—that happens to me all the time."

"That makes me mad. It's an architectural term and you know it. It lets the light in. What is light?"

"Photos . . . ?!"

"No—fenestration operation!" she exclaimed.

"But that pertains to otosclerosis—to sound, not to light."

"What is fenestration?"

"Comes from *fenestra*—a window—light."

"Well, that's what I mean when I speak of Gertrude Stein. By the way, last night I took Machiavelli's *The Prince* to the toilet."

"Did you?"

"Yes. Every time you read just a sentence or two of one of the real great ones—he gets you."

"Just what of Machiavelli got you?" I asked.

"What was it again? Yes, where he says—'just try to imitate the great ones of the past. The mere trying, even if you can't even approach them, will make you appear a better man and a man more charming!' This thought just enchanted me, and I had to think of it again."

This made the time while we were washing dishes and cleaning up the kitchen pass so fast that we did not even notice what we were doing, and we went back into the library room in an enchanted mood—nothing of heartache—both our hearts had ached when we began—and no anxiety.

Spiritus flat ubi vult. [The spirit blows where it will.]

[Undated notes, apparently Egon's reminders of what he intended to write about:]

Invitation to the boys
How they declined and why
    and our next plans as to home life with Mother and a maid. Possibly trip to Europe.

Emily Dickinson's letters seen after reading Beauvoir.

Ardyth's income so far.

For the first time she no longer feels that her foremost wish and thought is to get rich and have money so she can show these SOB's, but to work and to develop and accomplish, because for once she knew that she is a better writer than she ever thought she'd be.

Freud's epigram about money not bringing happiness ever.

Then followed the humorous visit at Kosher Sam's grocery store.

Thereafter Michael's triumph.

NOVEMBER 12, 1955

Michael came home from Seattle for the Armistice weekend. Yesternight he stormed up the steps of the apartment flushed with his triumph of having won his (Franklin) high school's contest for the best essay on "Why I Love America." We listened—glad, sympathetic and really interested, especially when he elaborated on the chances opening up to him if he should make it through the

State—a trip to Wash., D.C. and their National competition and possibly a four-year scholarship to any school in the U.S. We were tickled. I thought the essay was real good and he had a true chance. His face was half flushed, half ultraviolet burnt, he had a stiff knee from a displaced meniscus and a store of stories, hopes and plans.

After he left, I talked with A. for some time about our reaction to his success, and found to my surprise that it left her with much less joy and satisfaction than I had anticipated. "I cannot help it, but I have no sympathy with the artist—he pains me too much. I have to turn away from him because he reminds me too much of myself. I am sympathetic only with the dead artist—oh yes, I love them all, because I can learn from them, how they overcame this situation, developed this plan or facet of their personality, and how they succeeded or failed. But the living ones—leave me alone!"

Freddy Jacobson brought us Brinnin's *Dylan Thomas in America*. I think it is the most devastating and most violent dying of any man I know, because Dylan *and* his wife Caitlin revolted only against themselves. At this phase of the 20th century, there is almost no other death as significant for the aesthetic man as that of Dylan Thomas. From Poe and Baudelaire to Van Gogh, Verlaine, Rimbaud and Hart Crane—Thomas beat them all.

Also I have read vol. II of Jones' biography of Freud. There is the photograph of the famous couch. To think I sat on it at the age of 12 or 13! And never knew, of course, that I was sitting on "The Couch." Who could in 1906 or 7?

December 16, 1955

Ten days ago I had an attack of auricular fibrillation. It took me about a week to recover from it. During this time I thought of doing a pictorial history of Medicine of the 19th century—staying away from the pompous conventional pictures and portraits reproduced in the "Histories of Medicine." I should like to collect as many private photographs and daguerreotypes as possible of family life, of daily activities, vacationing, lovemaking and illness (up to death), in which situations and activities all of the famous have been involved. I think there should also be room for photographs of physicians who sought fame and fortune outside of Medicine. Whatever will come of it, it should keep me busy and interested for a long time.

Ardyth began working on "Uncle Sam." Enchanting story. Told me tonight at dinner that she might possibly write several stories on Virginia City, Nevada. She thought she was through with historical material and would do only contemporary stuff. But the past is no package one can lay away and forget all about it. Especially for two such history-conscious and history-loving people as we are.

During one evening talk she changed the title to "When the Wind Blows..."

December 28, 1955

This morning I saw a Mr. Brewsterhouse, who complained of itching eyes. I examined him carefully and wrote him a prescription for drops to be used twice a day. He was pleased he did not suffer from something serious and thanked me.

I asked him to come back next year and see me again. "Next year? No, Doc, I'll come back next week." I twinkled my eyes and he, looking at the large calendar in my office, understood.

As he left, he turned at the door and said with a finger pointed at me: "I knew you were a fine fellow, Doc."

"What makes you think so?" I asked.

"My brother-in-law—he has said so many a time!"

"What made him say that?"

"Oh, ever since you took out his eye, he thinks you're a swell guy."

[*From a newspaper article by William Moyes:*]

For the second time in two months a Portland home . . . this time that of Ardyth Kennelly, author . . . will be written up in a national magazine.

The *Ladies' Home Journal* for April, which will be on the stands March 20, will carry story and pictures of Miss Kennelly's house which she remodeled last year. The title of the article (which may be changed before publication) is "An Author Remodels Her Home."

Work on the feature was done by Cynthia McAdoo Wheatland, an editor of the *Ladies' Home Journal*. She is a granddaughter of the late Senator McAdoo.

She came to Portland in November and spent a week on the piece. With her was one of the magazine's top photographers.

JANUARY 4, 1956

The only programs Ardyth and I *really* enjoy are boxing and wrestling. This astounds everyone I tell about it because everybody expects that both of us, being of a sedate and sort of scholarly type, would take to this body-bouncing last of all. But each Monday, Wednesday and Friday evening, here we sit—almost holding hands with the pleasure in seeing von Poppenheim and the great Yamato judo each other out of action, or watching Rocky Marciano knock the life out of some other fellow. Yes, that Ardyth and me, who would not be able to survive a good push with the little finger of any one of these gladiators.

APRIL 3, 1956

Olly Rosenthal died of sarcomatosis and I have been comforting Ernesto across 5,000 miles to Buenos Aires. His last letter said, "Write me much and long and soon. Your letters are my medicine."

My sister Marianne is going through the last stages of cancer of the breast and wants me to send her medicine to Hungary!

In the case of Olly R., she and her sister died in their fifties from sarcoma, one beginning in the eye, the other in the genital sphere. In the case of the relatives on my mother's side, Mother and her sister Hedwig both died of cancer of the breast and Marianne is following them, only about 12 years younger than her elders.

Tomorrow I will finally find out the amount we have to pay in taxes. It's too high, I know, but at least we will know. With Ardyth rebuilding the house, I can't figure it out myself.

Ardyth has been working out a new time schedule with diet, work and seeing people. This time it's THE THING, and she gave me a timetable which takes care of things until the end of the year. I am charmed by it even though I doubt very much whether she can adhere to it for long.

We have never known each other more than we did at the beginning, for it was then complete and immediate in our first days together. I wonder if this is not generally true. We do not know people by experience. Experience, through the passing of time, merely ratifies the first full realization we received. With some people it is a thin surface one penetrates, and bottom is soon reached. It's pleasant to know shallow people and find them always the same. But of course there is a deep knowing when there is depth to sound. In some people one finds a whole universe, finding in them all time and all space, with what the past has won and everything that has bloomed and withered on earth. There are not many such people. I have only met one the end of whom I have never reached: Ardyth.

I am having fun collecting photographs for a pictorial review of Medicine's last hundred years. After I have gone through several hundred biographies and essays, I shall ponder about what a man who has done so should be able profitably to tell others. There are plenty of eccentrics among the good doctors of the past.

What began as "Uncle Sam" is now called "When the Wind Blows," and was finished on February 16, 1957, under the definite title *Wild West Wind*.

April 17, 1956

We went to see Paul Petri last Sunday. He is very old now, but apparently well. Walks a bit stooped, is snow white and still tells the same old stories I heard 30 years ago. He talks a great deal of Lillian, yet I am not sure whether he really misses her.

Ardyth talked about books with him, and he lifted a volume of Costain and said: "I read that lately and I was glad. There is one book that does not contain sex!" On the way home she remarked that that remark gave him away, since it indicates that they were not half as close as it might have seemed. And after he emphasized that Lillian almost never went to bed before three or four in the morning, A. thought that that showed they might never even have slept together. Although I think one cannot judge only by such remarks.

A new little German book arrived on the diseases of Beethoven which I am to review for the *Bulletin of the History of Medicine*. I am reading aloud from it every evening to Ardyth. What we never realized is that Beethoven, since he was 27 years old, suffered almost more from an intestinal disease that gave him diarrhea (typhoid?) and made him miserable all his life than from his deafness, which might have been but the consequence of this abdominal trouble. (So, at least, thought my teacher Haschel Neumann.) And when I read that Beethoven's favorite dish was macaroni with cheese and that he drank coffee made with 60 beans to a cup, Ardyth could hardly believe it.

As everything, yes EVERYTHING in Beethoven's life, not only his music, was uniquely interesting, so were his adventures after

Egon's Journal

death. I don't think that the story of his body, his diaries, and his ears (the specimen of) and of his biographer Thayer can be surpassed as to surprises. Thayer couldn't finish writing the biography after he had devoted all his long life to the collecting of material and travelling all over Europe to interview every being still alive that had known or might have known the composer. He wrote two volumes in English, which were first published in German. Thereafter he could not touch the material without getting such violent headaches that he reeled. He stopped work on it altogether and turned to writing plays and poetry while he was stationed as American consul in Trieste. He died there on duty without having completed writing Beethoven's biography. Yet the Thayer *is* the definitive biography, since nobody else had the testimonials, notebooks and interviews at his disposal. So every single future biographer cannot but point at Thayer as *the* biographer. So it is that the German Viennese Beethoven found his biographer in an American from South Natick, Massachusetts.

END OF JOURNAL

DECEMBER 28, 1946

[*Ardyth*:] Silly lists we once made.

My Battle (Egon)

Against	For
Formalized religion	Tolerance
Music	Good life
Doughnuts	Roast lamb
Noise	Cool bed
Dirt	Soft shirts
Chaos	Ardyth
Fishing	Good books
Cataracts	A new car
Dentists	Friends
White bread	Swiss cheese
Travel	Money in the bank
Children	New anesthetics
Relatives	More science
Lanudymon	Psychoneurotics
Heat	Sterilization
Missionaries	Gargoyles
Nightgowns	
Receptions	
Corned beef & cabbage	
Kafka	

My Battle (Ardyth)

Against	For
Cold	Poetry
Heat	Coffee
Work	The moon
Idleness	Snow (far off)
Science	The ocean
German music (Wagner)	Artifice
French literature	Love
Cigarettes	Petulance
Skiing	Clothes
Mexican art	French painting
Indian art	American painting
African art	Second-hand stores

South America	Horses
Vivien Leigh	Dogs
Modern lighting	Cats
Streetcars	Wagons
Movies	Boats
Doctors	Egon
Nature	Me
Healthy people	Ireland
Sick people	England
All writers	Long-haired furs
Most food	T-bone steaks
Automobiles	Pleasure
Conscience spectacles	Fame

Ardyth in 1942

Ardyth autographing *The Peaceable Kingdom*, with Marion and Egon, Nov. 9, 1949

Ardyth's writing studio from 1950, upstairs at 2475 NW Northrup St., Portland

The duplex on Northrup St.

Marion Kennelly

Egon and Ardyth in their library

Ardyth's Memoir, Part 2

AS HE SAYS, HE ASKED Dr. Goldsborough for morphine but he didn't have any, so he took Seconal. It calmed him down and he slept that night. Seconal and Demerol are hardly ever prescribed now, I understand, as they are so addictive, but thirty years ago they were everywhere and doctors had them in their desks, carried them in their bags and handed them out right and left. Soon Egon couldn't get through a day or a night without either one or the other or both, and maybe he took morphine sometimes too. I was such a blind, self-centered thing, I didn't, couldn't, wouldn't see any of this. I knew he was more devastated by his attack than one would have thought possible, considering that Dr. Goldsborough told me it wasn't so much an attack as a warning. Though after Egon died, I learned he had had an episode of heart failure (which he didn't tell me about) during his last months in the army, when the war was over and I had come on home to Portland ahead of him. That first attack he may have blamed on coffee, cigarettes and anxiety about getting out of the army and starting life again at almost fifty, but ten years later *this* attack, when he drank decaf and scarcely smoked and life was just peaches and cream, must have seemed to him for *no reason*, so he couldn't defend himself.

I didn't know about what he describes, how he shook all over uncontrollably, I didn't know that, he was always the one who could handle anything, relatives, overdrafts, mortgages, moving, our cat up a tree and not able to get down, calm and soothing when I would be carrying on like a wild woman. And now here he was gone all to pieces, shaking (oh, God), even his hips. I think I was the one who really killed him in the long run. He speaks so kindly of me in his journal, but I was really what Francis Bacon would have called a "discipline of humanity," kind of a penitential scourge, not tender or sympathetic as I should have been. When he was shaken to the fundaments like that, in mortal terror, crying, reaching out, what did I do? I was like the South American general in the movie *The In-Laws* who orders the frantic target before the firing squad to "Stand up! I'm busy, I've got work to do, be a man!"

I remember one night to my everlasting shame when he was carrying on—he realized I think in not too many weeks that he had become an addict, and on this particular occasion may have been trying to get through the night without the pills or the injection—my patience wore thin, and instead of holding him on my lap and kissing him and loving him as I would do now, I just left him flat. "You'll just have to live or die!" I said and went upstairs to the attic, locking the stairway door behind me. How I have grieved over the callousness, the heartlessness of that. But it seemed like I had to test *God*. "What do you want to do, torture and torment me? Well, look, right here is where we lay it on the line."

Right up until his attack I was working, we had irons in the fire. He loved everything to do with a book coming out, negotiations with the publisher, fan letters, reviews if any, all that. But this particular book (*Marry Me, Carry Me*) had been very hard to write, on manuscript page 507 I came up against a writer's block I have never really got over to this day, though I did finish it like crawling on my bare knees over miles of broken glass.

I say "writer's block," but what I really think happened, whatever talent I had just petered out like a vein of ore. Because of all the help and babying I had from both Egon and Mother—and the *input* from both too, actual data and programs, as you might say, into my circuits—it seemed like a lot richer vein than it ever really was. *Marry Me, Carry Me* wasn't snapped right up, and so the trip we took to New York in 1954 to celebrate finishing it wasn't a big success.

There was a medical convention being held, Egon had a display of old medical photographs, manuscripts and autographs that I was supposed to help him display but didn't, he also was being honored for a study he had done of a man named von Graefe, a scientist who discovered something totally new about the human cochlea but I couldn't tell you what, he was supposed to sit two seats over from Helen Keller at a banquet for her, and other such marks of high regard. I should have been at his side, his proud wife, I wasn't, I wouldn't do anything, I was having sessions with Andrew Salter, the psychologist, renowned at that time for his book *Conditioned Reflex Therapy*, to try to get over feeling so terrible and sad, and fearful of people, and like I would never work again, which last to all intents and purposes did come true.

I went to Mr. Salter because his book made me feel as if I could change, but he and I didn't hit it off, and, "more dull and baffled than before," after a few appointments I stopped seeing him, leaving a pair of lovely new gloves behind in his office, as Egon mentions in his journal. Egon couldn't have had a worse companion. I was horrible, hysterical, probably right then was when his loyal loving heart got the crack in it that would kill him. One day it rained when we were out wandering around, I went into a second-hand store and bought an old second-hand umbrella that probably belonged to Judge Crater, and in trying to open it somehow cut my finger. It didn't bleed much, but the next day started itching so much I could have clawed my finger off, and a couple of days after that I had a red streak running up my arm, blood poisoning. I still have the thermometer he ran out and bought, and he gave me tetramycin. I lived, more's the pity for him.

We started out in New York at the Waldorf Hotel, going to do this (our one and only trip and holiday together) up brown, but thanks to my seeing an ad in the *Times* we moved to the Iroquois, where I seemed to remember reading that Jed Harris, the great impresario, had lived his last years in poverty and more or less disgrace—maybe we had his very two-room suite, it was dismal enough—right next door to the hallowed ground of the Algonquin. Only once would I venture into the Algonquin lobby, though, and once we ate dinner where we could look right over and see the famous Round Table itself, famous as King Arthur and his knights'. But I didn't enjoy it, the waiter greeting us with *bonsoir*, the evening wear I saw, and edgy and tearful when we got back to the Iroquois, I berated Egon for not tipping enough. That visit, the only one we ever made to New York and the only one to any place except the Oregon coast after the war, lasted nearly two months (Egon had saved up vacations), and maybe during the last half I started gradually not being such a pain in the ass, I hope so. But in Boston no decision had been made about *Marry Me, Carry Me*, whether the publisher was going to take it, and I kept on feeling nervous and at loose ends.

We started home by way of a trip to Amherst. Emily Dickinson's house was a private dwelling then, lived in by an elderly couple with a famous pharmaceutical name like Merck or one of the other ones. Egon had such savoir faire, he could meet people, go anywhere and do anything, and he just knocked at the front door, a maid dressed like a maid in a movie answered it, and then the lady of the house came. Egon told her about his Emily Dickinson collection, quite wonderful by this time, and though they were having Sunday dinner and had guests, the maid was allowed to take us up to Emily's actual room where she wrote the poems and let the basket down with cookies in it for the children. The room. The very *windowsill*. And that was the only time on the whole trip when for a few hours I wasn't cold or hot or sick or mean or scared or anything, but just transported. We saw the pantry where she used to run and hide, like I have done and do, and where she rolled out pie crust on a floured board like an ordinary person. And the maid let us go out the back door, and there was the path between trees and bushes to Emily's brother Austin's house, "just wide enough for two who love," and we took it, and then there was the graveyard with Emily's grave where I was actually standing.

Cremation is all very well, but if the person is *there* it makes all the difference.

ANYWAY, THE BOOK WAS finally accepted, I got paid and turned my attention to fixing up the house. Then I bought some clothes and thought we should try to have a social life. But that didn't work very well.

Then Egon had his attack or warning or whatever it was.

We got a television. The West Coast was slow in getting a line out here across the Rockies for some reason, so it was years before Oregonians were hooked up. After an evening with ours, he was absolutely stricken. "Our lives will have passed and we won't know we ever lived." But then he began to like some of the programs, such as *Omnibus*. I don't seem to remember paying much attention to the TV at the time and never have since, and always thought there could be no worse torture than to have to watch it flat on your back in a hospital, for instance, all day long.

THAT SONG "I Enjoy Being a Girl" is cute, and I think girls really feel like that (I did), but I can't say I ever felt comfortable with a lot of what went with the territory, such as discharging the menses, a simply terrible thing to have to do, it used to seem to me. But I think one reason for that attitude was because sixty or seventy years ago in farm country and small backward towns, what we had to use (torn strips of old sheets, dishtowels and pillowcases, folded and pinned onto our undervests) was no different from the menstrual clouts of 1000 B.C. These were not thrown away when soaked through but on washday could be seen soaking in a tub of bloody water in the cellar like somebody had been murdered. What a wonderful invention Kotex seemed to me the first time I ever used one, and a great luxury too.

I never was that excited about reproducing, either, and must confess it appeared to me more of a hardship than a privilege, the price you were supposed to pay for mortality, as if you had run up a big bill with God before you were even born. I couldn't imagine having happy children, Mother always said she would feel sorry for them, I would feed them too much and keep them too bundled up. But anyway, Egon and I decided we would be each other's baby, and he kept his part of the bargain but I didn't. To him, as to my books and to many other things in this world, I was a raven mother.

Menopause, another female perk, is either a hasty or a long-drawn-out process, according to who it is. Some women make it last until old age, needing fans, collars and windows that can be opened wide until age 75 or older. It becomes a source of power. With others, such as beautiful actresses pretending to be ten years younger than they are and not wanting to remind people of time passing, the "change" comes and goes like a thief in the night.

We had windows that would open wide and French doors. While Egon was convalescing, he would sit out on our balcony and meditate or read, and I would sit out there too sometimes. We would talk about how I was going to write a book that would be snapped up (the current one had flopped) and we would get rich and—but we never seemed to know what we were going to do *then*, such as travel or buy first editions. We would go that far and then everything would just stop, an awful feeling.

Eventually Egon went back to work, but things had changed for him at Kaiser Permanente. He was still head of the EENT department but worked fewer hours, got less pay and finally, after a few months, wasn't a partner anymore, or whatever the arrangement was that those first doctors (after the war and after the shipyards closed) had with the Kaiser organization. I said not to worry, we could get along on less money, and it was really better for him. But I think he felt he had lost prestige, was out of the group, wasn't one of the guys anymore. Then a new H. L. Mencken–type assistant ophthalmologist was hired for the EENT department who I think did *something*, because Egon would come home just killed from being around him. Eventually that doctor left, but not before a lot of real psychological harm had been done.

Egon kept working, but his addiction must have been getting worse, although nobody could tell that by looking at him. But he never seemed to enjoy himself anymore, he napped a lot or sat staring into space. That didn't scare me then, I knew his heart flurry had been a worry to him and also that things weren't as they had been at the hospital, and I thought that if he was calmed down, that was better than to be stirred up. I also thought that he was just blue and would get over it. I didn't dare think how he had changed, especially his ability to know how to *handle* anything that might arise. That, as I found out on one occasion that really scared me to the fundaments, was just *gone*.

This must have happened on a weekend because he was at home, it was early afternoon. And I don't know what happened, but I was crying and carrying on. Probably I had been up in my so-called work room confronting the typewriter and looking at the big desk I had had built in, and drawers and shelves and everything just perfect for Edna Ferber or Pearl Buck, reams of paper till hell wouldn't have it, the complete Oxford dictionary, the great huge edition that cost hundreds of dollars. Maybe I had been standing there looking around and all of a sudden started to sweat and get sick to my stomach. I wouldn't, on account of Egon's health, have run downstairs screaming and in hysterics sobbing I can't do it anymore, *I just can't do it*—but I'd have sniffled and said I was blue and the Magic of Believing didn't work or something like that, I just don't recall what. But to him it must have seemed like a crisis, and what I do remember is that instead of putting his arms around me and soothingly talking the way he usually did, he just kind of stood off to himself and looked at me, and then all of a sudden he was holding out his hand and in his palm I saw these pills, quite a few, I can't remember if they were different colors but they were capsules, not flat pills like aspirin. And he said, "Here, darling, take some of these—and you will—" His voice kind of trailed off and then he said, "And I'll take some too—and we will—" I don't know whether he was going to say "kill ourselves" or "sleep" or "take a nap." But whatever it was, I know I said no, no, no. I was simply horrified to think of the two of us piled up on the bed, dead or sleeping or napping through the afternoon and waking up groggy to find it was night! Anything was better than *that*, pain, agony, the torment of the damned. Oh, Egon, no.

And that snapped me right out of it. I don't remember anything else about that day, whether Egon took the pills himself or not—I don't think he would have, because he saw my absolute horror. I knew we had come to some kind of a turning point, but I didn't say to myself, what made him do that? I saw that his nerve had failed before my eyes, and I knew that neither he nor I would ever be the same again. Now I know I shouldn't have let it go with that, put the whole thing out of my mind, but that's what I did. I think I thought that all that was the matter was that I was having a hard time writing, and that if I could fix *that*, then everything else would get better too, his heart, his moods, his eyes would sparkle again, he would be funny and cute and *everything would be all right*.

So that's what I resolved to do—write, if it killed me.

"Up betimes," as Pepys used to say. I would keep regular hours. Maybe write something all through, dash it off, "first fine careless rapture" and all that, *then* correct. Or no, write a page and correct and polish right then, get it absolutely perfect and then go on to the next page. No, that wouldn't work either. I was like the centipede that never thought of his hundred legs before, but now here he was "considering how to run." Considering from morning till night. Trying this, starting that, reading, "the problem is I don't *know* anything," "I read but I do not retain," "if I could just learn…" But I couldn't, and the funny part was that after writing five books, big books too, I didn't seem to know then, or now, how a person really does it.

I was like one of those old anchorites out in the desert on a regime of torture. I had to stay in that attic so many hours a day, "if it rains, if it snows, if it stinks." I would write a History of Dieting, wouldn't that be interesting? go clear back to the Egyptians, Lord Byron was the first Englishman to diet for his looks, not on account of gout. Egon when he was at home downstairs by himself got very lonesome, but he didn't say so. He wanted so much for me to "do it again"—not for the money, writing isn't very lucrative (even book-club money isn't all that good) if there's no sale to the movies and it doesn't get on the charts. You might as well kick yourself tired, as my grandma used to say. Of course I'm talking about a half century ago, it might be different now. But Egon loved the transaction, the letters, the possibilities, when the proofs came and then the book itself. What I should really have done, if I had had sense enough to come in out of the rain, was to write books *for him* (to have written), with him laying all the material out in front of me, I know I could have persuaded him to let me, and maybe some dim reason like that in his subconscious was why

> *He had decided undismayed*
> *This was the place for Chance, and I*
> *The [one] for him; and so he stayed.*

He learned English as a child, but to come over here to America and write English and jump right into belles lettres, as I know he longed to do, he just couldn't have done it. Nabokov is the only one I can think of who really pulled that off, and even then I can hear a faint accent. Joseph Conrad is always given as an example, but his English is like a car that's been totaled, fixed up so it looks okay, but when you ride in it you know by the seat of your pants that there's something wrong, some kind of an underlying shakiness.

I hated autographing, couldn't stand to talk about the books, hated to answer questions or letters. But Egon loved all that. Before writing turned into such heavy weather, I liked writing, getting done and then my conscience not bothering me till the next day. He liked me to read the day's output, I thought because he liked the stuff or was interested, but maybe just to have proof that I wasn't upstairs just goofing off.

About minor things I used to be quite sharp with him, such as if we had company and somebody took a book off the shelf and started to look at it, in about a minute Egon would go over and take it away from him and put it back in its place. Or how no one could set a wet glass down any place with any comfort. Not much else for me to complain about, he was an angel to live with, sweetness and goodness itself, and put up with crap from me and my family that you wouldn't believe.

But one time I got absolutely *furious* at him, and I remember with regret that I said I hated him, I was going to leave him, that I wished I had never laid eyes on him! What did he do? Gamble our house payments away? Kick my grandmother in the stomach? He sat at the breakfast table one morning after my first book came out, cheerful as he always was when he was himself, sweet and smiling, and told me the dream he had had the night before. This was quite unusual, as I was the one who usually told the dreams. In this dream, he said, he was back home in Vienna, in the lab of the clinic where he used to work. At first he was alone there, but then his Chief came in. They talked awhile and then this doctor said something like, By the way, I hear your wife writes books, she's a wonderful writer, is that so? And Egon said—this dream conversation was in German, he just translated for me— Why, no, sir—that is, she does write, but it's just really women's-magazine stuff—

Well, poor Egon. He kept saying, But it was just a *dream*. And I kept saying, You wanted to *say* that, you wanted to put that into *words*, you wanted me to *know* what you really think, you wanted to *say* the book doesn't really amount to anything! You wanted to *tell me*, and you hide behind a dream.

I was simply livid, the more so because in my heart I knew that what he had said in German to his old Chief was true, it *was* just women's-magazine stuff. Well, of course he protested, begged my pardon a thousand times, had no idea I'd take it that way, maybe he got down on his knees. Anyway, pretty soon I forgave him, as I hate people going around sulking for days on end. Scream, holler, throw things, then get over it, that's what I always say. And I never mentioned it again.

That happened, as I say, after the first book came out. But at the time I'm speaking about now, I had written five books and was desperately seeking to write a sixth but had forgotten how. For hours every day I was upstairs trying to remember, and as winter had arrived, Egon came home to a cold, dark house . . . And the crazy part was, I was trying to do it for him. He was trying to do things for me too, and the upshot was, we were like the couple in O. Henry's *Gift of the Magi*, the story about the husband selling his watch to buy a comb for his wife's hair and the wife selling her hair to buy a chain for her husband's watch!

The best thing would have been to give up, throw in the sponge. And had his health been good the way it used to be, I could have done that, but now it seemed as if my work was like some kind of a life-support system for him, and I didn't dare pull the plug. And besides, one real success and he'd be cured, he wouldn't have heart trouble, he'd be just like he used to be, a hundred percent. Of course I didn't say any of this out loud, but I know I thought it.

All those wasted hours! hundreds, thousands.

HE TOOK PIANO lessons for years when he was a boy, and once at a friend's house I heard him play for about five minutes and I just couldn't believe it. A native-born American who played that well would be doing it and showing off constantly. But the damn Viennese, all those critics and connoisseurs, if you're not good enough to be a professional, then don't do whatever it is. I shouldn't have paid any attention to his protests, should have got him a piano, made him play for me, he'd have enjoyed playing, would have loved the praise, it would have passed the time, maybe he could have joined a chamber music group.

He had his heart set on getting a checkered suit, a black and white shepherd's check I think was what he meant, but we would shop at Sichel's or somewhere else and we never could find one. Now I see just what he wanted all the time. What was the matter with me? I should have taken him to a tailor, picked out a piece of material and had the damn suit he wanted *made*. Why didn't I do that?

Once he said he wished he could have been a magician, and he used to buy little tricks at the novelty store and try to do them. Succeeded, too. But he needed encouragement, and an audience, and I (I guess it was my fault) kept him so isolated. When I think of it now, it was just so sad, he was like a little crippled boy that can't get out but sits by the window and watches the other kids outside running and playing.

He should have had a dog. We had a cat, Violet, for seventeen years, but she mostly collaborated with me. He needed a garden. We had three window boxes and a kind of brick trough with greenery in it, but a floral outfit took care of these. Otherwise not one inch of real ground, it was all cemented over. I don't say he would have *gardened* necessarily, but he'd have loved to oversee somebody else doing it. Toys, too, automatons like in the movie *Sleuth*, he'd have kept them in perfect running order. An African Grey parrot. Company. He needed company, needed to be a center, needed to play, needed to put on his checkered suit and do his tricks and have everyone applaud, needed to sit down and play some big showy concerto *loud*. But instead of that, what did he have? a cold dark house, rows and stacks of books, and a tired and irritable bat up in our belfry.

Well, I'm exaggerating a little, I never let the house get cold and clammy, and I always turned the lights all on. And his life wasn't *terrible* like David Copperfield in the blacking factory, he did lots of things he liked, such as hanging out at the Old Oregon Bookstore and buying antiquarian stuff, gradually through the years he learned to cook several dishes, even Linzer torte (without salt, I noticed but didn't say), we played records, musical comedies and the swing stuff I persuaded him he liked, not the operas I now could play from morning till night. Sometimes we would have a picnic in the Rose Garden, I wasn't *always* a pain in the ass, and he enjoyed working at Kaiser. We liked our evenings of reading and gabbling. But the middle of the nights were terrible, he would wake up frightened, his heart pounding, covered with sweat, and just that one time did I lose patience with him and leave him and run upstairs.

Looking back, I see I got used to him being changed, being subdued and his eyes seldom sparkling, and never connected that to him taking something or shooting up, as they say. If he had suddenly got animated and kind of hysterical (the way we kids used to get sometimes when Mother would step in and say to quit it, we'd be crying in about a minute), I probably would have. But he was just quiet and kind of muffled, and such a thing as Seconal or Demerol wouldn't enter my mind, I'd just think he was tired and resting and everything was okay. Well, God forgive me.

Forgive me for how I treated his things as if they were mine. Not money, he handled whatever money there was, I never paid any attention to that. (He gave me an allowance, the girls nowadays think that's terrible, and maybe I would have thought that too if he had been penurious, but he was just the opposite, so I always felt like the lucky girls I used to envy at school with the cashmere sweaters and the alligator shoes and their own roadster.) No, what I treated as if they were mine was anything of his I wanted to throw out when I cleaned house or made order—papers, letters, stuff that the drug companies give to doctors and they take home to clutter up the medicine chest. I jumbled up his magic tricks and gave away his clothes.

Forgive me for the riding boots. Because they were so much more than just *boots*. And I think when I gave them away, it was like I was giving away part of *him*, part of his actual body, it really was. I tried to say earlier that Vienna was full of anti-semitism (long before Hitler) and that while a lot of Jews *tried* to assimilate with the Gentiles, not many succeeded. Though out of the ghetto and not practicing their religion, once a Jew always a Jew, which must have been brought home to Egon every day of his assimilated youth. Two populations in one city, Jew and Gentile, and never the twain shall meet. They hardly ever did in the real sense of the word, although in the elegant waiting room Egon's father provided for his aristocratic clientele, Egon often passed the time of day with one Gentile patient or another. The Jews, even rich ones, may have had to wait in the common people's waiting room, I don't know, as I never asked. Anyway, one of these aristocratic Gentiles was a Baron Mautner, who took a liking to Egon and was always glad to find him available for conversation if he had a few minutes to wait.

Then came the assassination at Sarajevo and World War I. Of course it wasn't called World War I in 1914, but just "this mess," which would be over by Christmas. Egon, 19 and in medical school, was soon called up. Because of his medical training, little though that was at the time, he was put in the medical corps and sent to the Eastern front. About two days later his whole outfit was put out of commission, captured by the Russians and taken to a prison camp deep in Byelorussia. Egon was not one to reminisce, but once he told me that when they were captured, it was like in slow motion. There was all this shooting and fireworks, pinwheels like the end of the world, then everything got perfectly quiet and the smoke started drifting lazily away. Then here came these Russian horsemen galloping towards them with swords flashing, and the funny part was, the horses were little and short-legged, almost like Shetland ponies, and the Russians—Tatars—were little too! It was like it was all just in miniature and you shouldn't be scared.

IN THE PRISON CAMP, I guess Egon set up as a doctor.

The Russian Revolution took place *during* the war, and as soon as the Czar was overthrown, the Russian soldiers opened up all the prisons and set the war prisoners free. That is, they tried to, but the snow was clear up to the windows and falling, so nobody would leave the barracks. "Thank you!" they said, in that particular case meaning *no, thank you*. But when spring came and the snow melted, out everybody rushed into the chill spring air and started for home. Walking, of course. Egon hiked all the way to Turkey, and the Red Cross sent him home from there to Vienna. As the war was still on, he thought he was going to have to go right back to the front, wherever that might have been. But Baron Mautner, his father's old patient, had decided to set up a small hospital for convalescing officers on his estate, and as doctors were in short supply and Egon had had medical training and experience, the Baron pulled strings to get him on his hospital staff.

Baron Mautner had a huge estate, a racing stable and even a racetrack. He also had a beautiful wife who had been on the stage, in light opera, but by this time she was middle-aged and in the secondary stage (affections of the skin and mucous membranes) of the syphilis her husband had given her long before, so she was hardly ever seen. The hospital was in one of the outbuildings, set up with every convenience for seven or eight patients, two doctors and one assistant (Egon), and two or three young ladies to do the nursing. It goes without saying that the recovering officers were titled persons, Vons, Excellencies and so on, not of the common run, and of course they were Gentiles. As a prisoner of war Egon really mixed for the first time in his life with Gentiles, but they were from the lower orders. The ones he was meeting now on a daily basis he could never have had anything to do with in a million years. But they would have liked him, he was awfully well educated even then, he'd had enough medical experience in a prison barracks to seem to know what he was doing. And he was good company, full of jokes, could play chess and bridge, and with a war on and nobody knowing how it was going to end, the old distinctions (at least for a while) didn't apply as they once had.

The first batch of patients started to get better, more came in, one of the doctors was called back to the front but it was decided he wouldn't need to be replaced, that the remaining doctor and Egon could handle things. I can imagine that Egon was very proud and kind of cocky, and that when he was asked if he would like to ride with some of the officers now riding every day on some of the Baron's beautiful horses, he would say yes, and climb up in the saddle as if he knew all about it. Apparently he did turn out to have a good "seat" and an aptitude, although he had never ridden before, and soon he was racing and taking hurdles and everything—at first in boots and riding clothes furnished to him by the Baron, but then in his own outfit, for his father was as proud of him excelling in this new activity as Egon was proud of himself, and paid for custom-made boots and a whole riding outfit, all of the best quality.

Of course when the war was over and Baron Mautner's little hospital closed and patients and staff went back to their usual lives, there wasn't much use for riding clothes anymore. Baron Mautner, helped along by Egon's father's X-ray machine, died of a paresis brought on by his old syphilis not long after the Armistice, and none of the Gentile friendships ever came to anything.

But those months on the Mautner estate were a high point, I can well imagine, in Egon's life. Called Herr Doktor although he wasn't one yet, waited on by servants, in wonderful surroundings, good food, wine, pretty girls, aristocrats to go riding with, riding, jumping, racing and playing polo! It must have been hard to go back to the real world, a bleak place in Vienna after the lost war, tough studies at the medical school—and the meanness encountered in the streets every day as conditions got worse and anti-semites sprang up like an Invasion of the Body Snatchers. But Egon had his riding outfit and his boots, and to assure himself that it hadn't all been a dream, all he had to do was open his wardrobe door and look.

The riding outfit came to America with him, of course. In no time he was riding with the cavalry officers of the Oregon State College ROTC. And as a patient in the Corvallis hospital, I *saw* him making his rounds on that one occasion dressed like a gentleman rider, and I nearly swooned with the glamour of it. That the day would ever come that I would have the boots and everything to contend with from a housekeeping, order-making standpoint, I naturally never imagined. But there the boots were, falling off the rack, down on the floor and gathering dust. And the rest of the outfit using up hangers and closet space, and when would he ever wear any of it again? Never. As a bride, and in fact for some years, I would ask about throwing things away. How about—? What do you say—?

And each time the outfit was in danger, he would tell me a little more about the hospital at Baron Mautner's estate and why it couldn't be thrown away, and that's why I know what I have written here concerning it. And I would say okay. But then we would move, or I would houseclean, and here I would be confronted with this same bothersome stuff again that just took up room, that he never used. Finally, not only because it wouldn't do any good to ask him but also because by now my attitude was, what's his is mine, so what's the difference? I took it on myself to keep pushing the jacket and pants and vest further and further back into the shadows and then gave them to the Salvation Army, all but the boots. And then as time went on and he didn't miss the clothes, I gave the boots away too, to my nephew. He was about 13 and I must have had him try them on, but if they ever fit it was just for that one day, because in about a week his mother called and said he couldn't even get his big toe into them, and what should she do with them? Bring them back, I should have said but didn't, and so somewhere in the Willamette Valley they disappeared. And when Egon found out, it was like I had *killed* him.

Of course as time went on and I heard the entire story of the boots, I realized what a brutal, really brutal, thing I had done. As it dawned on me about Jews and Gentiles and the hierarchical classes of Europe, and what a thing it was for a Jewish boy to be out on that rich estate riding horses with young aristocratic Gentile officers, realized all the stuff that those riding boots *meant*, then it just about killed *me*, too, that I had given them away. They were never mentioned again, because Egon wasn't one to nag and be quarrelsome, but I am sure he grieved for them for the whole rest of his life—not for the actual boots, of course, but for the memories the sight of them brought back.

Most things I jettisoned were never really missed. I had a certain technique—I would just push clothes and so on farther and farther back in the closet and then finally throw them out. Books the same, a book at a time would be dropped into a hidden carton and when it got full, out they'd go. It was painless for him. I saw to that after wounding him so grievously with getting rid of the boots.

But one day Mother availed herself of a chance to ride up from Albany with a neighbor (she had moved back down there a few months before), spend the day with me and tell me all the news, as a consequence of which something else of his disappeared. One bit of news was that she had started to go to church—Mormon, of course, she having been born into it and thus getting a head start. So much of one that she never had to look over the doctrine, go to church, pay tithing or anything. In her mind the whole matter of salvation had been taken care of before she was born, she was one of the saved and "there's an end on't." It was quite nice having her be like that, not like "religious" Methodist or Presbyterian mothers who made their children's lives miserable. She was tolerant, always had an excuse for human failings, prayed to God when she wanted something, knew all the Mormon hymns, which she would sing while doing housework, and "asked the blessing" before our Thanksgiving or Christmas dinners. There was no Mormon church in Albany in the 1920s and early 1930s, and if the few members wanted to attend Sunday school, they had to go to Salem or Portland.

But by this time Albany had a lovely meeting house, Mother said, a lovely congregation and a lovely Bishop. Because Mormon church officials (except the high-ups in Salt Lake City) are all lay persons who have regular jobs in the real world and only have the church job on the side, they don't get paid. So the Bishop wasn't getting paid, and the sad part was that he was also out of a job at the present time, so he and his lovely wife were having a rough hustle—the poor man didn't even have a decent suit to conduct services in on Sunday. He was about Egon's size, so what Mother wondered was, why couldn't he have one of Egon's nice suits?

Well, of course. The navy blue double-breasted silk suit (that was when men were wearing that slubby silk). I had been meaning to start sliding it back into the shadows anyway. I hadn't done it so far, but that didn't matter, I was sure he wouldn't notice it was gone. Mother was overjoyed, took a few shirts and ties to go with the suit, and called me the next day to tell me she delivered the stuff and it would do your heart good to see how happy the Bishop was, and his wife too, just nearly jumping for joy.

When Egon saw the suit was missing, which he noticed almost immediately (the shirts and ties too), he came out to the kitchen where I was doing something and asked me if I had been out for a while that day, because he thought a burglar must have got in and taken his blue silk suit. Of course he didn't really think that, but just said it to heap coals of fire on my head. I don't know, real Europeans seem to have a different attitude towards their private possessions than indigenous inhabitants over here, and I could tell Egon hated what Mother and I had done. He almost cried. But then he got over it.

And two weeks later the Bishop of the Albany Mormon church dropped dead. Of course he was buried in Egon's suit.

It was just the perfect outfit, Mother said when she called me. He looked just beautiful lying in state and at the funeral. They had an open casket, which Mother liked best and which she said they might not even have had if it hadn't been for the suit.

That time Egon was different from when I gave away his riding clothes. He was almost boisterous, like some kind of village jester, he laughed and joked sardonically, shrugged, acted philosophical, like a rabbi—or no, like a little Talmud scholar *imitating* a rabbi, or a little Jewish boy imitating a wise old sorrowful grandfather. Looking back now at the inscrutable past, I know who that grandfather was, too. He was Egon's mother's father, a banker who in

1899, when Egon was five, lost all his money in some kind of financial collapse and killed himself by jumping out the window of his apartment. "I have struggled so much all my life and now I have lost the meaning of all this struggle. There is a vast emptiness around me, an emptiness which with all my efforts I am unable to fill—" Egon was a sardonic Jewish child for two or three days, then got over that. He turned the fact of his suit being buried in the ground on a Mormon Bishop into a very funny story (hic *jacket* and so on), but I think it bothered him, I think he was superstitious and that he thought there was a terribly ill omen of some kind in what I had done. And now that I think of it, I think so too.

AN ILL OMEN OR something seemed to permeate my attic room for me. As I said, I got so furious at Egon when he told me his dream about seeing his old chief and saying I wasn't much of a writer, just wrote "women's-magazine" stuff. Now, ten years and five books later, I couldn't even do *that*. But I couldn't quit, I had to keep pretending. The History of Dieting, a children's story called "The Peacock and the Bride," different ideas, my agent dropped me, Houghton Mifflin too, an unusable manuscript or two and that'sallfolks. In *The Water Babies*, the poor little sooty chimney sweep runs to the river crying "I must be clean! I must be clean!" And I ran upstairs every morning the same desperate way, "I must be good! I must be smart! I must be interesting so that tonight when I read him what I wrote today, he won't be bored."

I tried to be Susan Sontag and people like that. But of course I didn't have the brains or talent, so I was just gasping for air all the time. Once I was so tired up in the attic working and getting nowhere, the stuff was DOA, that I just sneaked downstairs for two hours while he was at work and cleaned house, scrubbed the kitchen floor and cleaned a cupboard shelf, then hurried back upstairs so as to be working when he came home. Then Mother moved back to Portland and I spent one day a week with her. We would have lunch, go to the thrift stores or for a ride, and that was as healing as potato pancakes after a big diet. And the relatives came. Wherever she was, they were attracted, she was like flypaper to flies.

He never found fault with me, our kin or customs, but took everything in stride, the educated way an anthropologist from *National Geographic* would pass through Vanuatu. That was just the way we did things. Threw stuff away. Glommed on to other people's stuff. Wasted. Cleaned house before the housecleaners came. He never questioned. When we first came home after the war I bought a second-hand washing machine, the old-fashioned kind that turned, tumbled and agitated the clothes in a round open tub before your eyes, and the first time I did a washing, he came down to the basement to watch. As I filled the tub, I was talking to him and not paying attention and I poured in about half a big package of Rinso. The soapsuds started to rise, more and more. He never said, What are you doing? I saw what I had done but acted like I *wanted* the soapsuds to pile up like that, higher and higher and starting to spill over onto the floor, as I figured out what to do. So then I said, as if what was happening was normal procedure, "Well, we'll have to carry some of these outside and throw them away in the alley." So we got a big dishpan and buckets and scooped up the soapsuds, and he carried them out and dumped them, dishpan after dishpan, bucket after bucket. Never once did he say, Isn't this crazy? I said to him, "Where are you dumping these?" The houses along that street were quite close together. "Between our house and the people's next door," he said. "You should come and see. It looks beautiful! Like a snowbank." Well, I ran to see, and sure enough the suds were piled nearly up to the neighbor's windows, they were peeping out from behind their curtains like they were watching crazy people (we had just moved in) and they would never have a thing to do with us. I acted quite cross to Egon. "I thought I told you the alley!" But he never questioned. Soapsuds or whatever. It was just our wild and woolly ways.

The first time I ever saw Egon was when the Oregon State College doctor, a woman general practitioner, brought him to the school infirmary (where I was in bed on her orders) to see me because a student had recently died of a mastoid infection too far advanced to operate, and she was taking extra care. It was five o'clock in the afternoon. I was flat on my back and very sick, and I turned my head and looked through the half-open door, and there he was coming up the stairs with this school doctor. So they came over to my bed, and she said who I was and who this great foreign specialist was, and he half sat on the bed beside me and pushed my hair back from my forehead and said, "Well."

The next time he saw me was the next morning, when I'd been moved to the Corvallis General Hospital and again was in bed and going to be taken to the operating room, where he was going to chisel a piece out of my cheekbone so that the pus could exude and wouldn't go to my brain and kill me. In those days they kept everybody in the hospital for ten days or two weeks, no matter what you had, it wasn't very expensive, so I was there several days. And you *stayed in bed*, there was no such thing as wandering around the halls in your bathrobe. I mention this being in bed in detail because that was where I had been every time this foreign specialist, who I thought was very glamorous, saw me, I had never been standing up. And as the time drew near to be discharged and go home, I became more and more nervous, because for some reason I did not want him to know how tall I was.

I wanted to just slip away and never see him again and have him always think I was about five feet five, which I imagined I looked like in bed. So I made arrangements with Mother on the phone (Corvallis to Albany, my first long-distance call) for her and my dear stepfather to come and get me on a Sunday morning. I said that was when the hospital wanted me to leave, but I had really picked the time because this glamorous foreign specialist made his rounds quite late on Sunday, and I wanted to be out of there. I said the folks should come by 8:30 or 9:00, and Mother said all right. So I was up and dressed, packed and ready, and wild with nervousness that they'd be late or he'd be early making his rounds, and I was just sitting on the bed waiting when one of the nurses came by and stuck her head in the door. "Well, so you're going home today?" "Yes, my folks are coming to get me." "Well, listen, why don't you come down the hall with me to the nursery to see the babies? We had two more last night!" So I went with her, and we were in this sort of darkened room looking at the babies when all of a sudden I felt a hand on my sleeve and I turned to look, and who should it be but the glamorous foreign specialist.

And he saw how tall I was.

Four years after this we were great and good friends, not in Albany or Corvallis, but Portland, where he had opened a practice. Six more years and we were married. Eight more years and Egon had "dammed the ditches and the floods restrained," and I was writing a book. The time we had stretching away before us then! no end to it, more time than the Somali warlords have teeth. A century was nothing.

HE CHANGED SO MUCH after he got sick, which he might not have (I realize now) if he hadn't got started on Seconal and Demerol.

And maybe he wouldn't have if I had done what I should have—really looked at him when he was terrified the way he says in his journal he was. Which I didn't do that first night, because Dr. Goldsborough said it was not so much an attack as a warning. I just said well, it was hypochondria, but as time went on and he became a really sick, feeble person before my eyes, I felt a clutch of fear every time I looked at him. And as I say, the first thing I thought of was that it depended on me, that if I could write another book like the first one, and he could negotiate with the publishers and have fun and all that, why, he would be miraculously cured, like he had gone to Lourdes.

But I couldn't do it, and so through the months and years it was awful. He never was the same again. It was as if great cracks and fissures had opened in his psyche, and because they had, I would catch glimpses such as I had never seen before of him at other stages of his life, how he had been in school, in the family, on Sunday, or going up the Burggasse in the snow to the University, always so nervous, so tense and nervous, the whites showing all around his eyes. And the self I saw most was the child, the little boy whose privileges, when I heard about them, I was as jealous of (shameful as that is to admit) as a person will be of another *person*.

As he got quieter and sat around staring into space more and I was struggling with my demons, why, he began to talk more, talk about the past. And he would tell me about going to gymnasium, as it was called, which meant grammar school, not a place where you exercise. The schoolboys didn't play in the schoolyard the way they do in this country, or in the streets, but the minute school was out they would run right home. And that is what Egon would do, and make a beeline up the stairs to his mother's boudoir. He called it by that name, her boudoir. It was a large room with pretty windows looking south, everything in it was pretty, including his mother, who was only twenty-one when he was born. In the winter the beautiful tile stove would be giving off heat, the lamps were lit, his mother would be sitting there in a pretty dress with pompadoured hair, doing needlepoint. Wasn't it nearly suppertime? I said. Wasn't she peeling potatoes? She never peeled potatoes, because they had a cook. So he would come home, run to her for a kiss and a hug, then sit close and they would talk. Didn't you get something to eat? Because we grabbed something the minute we got in, like starving Armenians. No, because they'd be having *jause* at five, an occasion like an English tea except that coffee was served. Also Egon said he didn't like food when he was a child, they had a hard time making him eat. They had five meals a day, breakfast, second breakfast, the main meal, which all the family gathered to eat at one o'clock, *jause* or afternoon coffee at five, then supper at eight, so he was sick of food and was a skinny little boy. Didn't you have to change your good school clothes? I had seen pictures of his tight little English suit, starched collar, polished laced-up shoes. *We* did, when we came home from school we had to change at once into absolute rags. Oh, no, he said, he just kept his same clothes on, why would he change?

And so he would talk and I would actually feel *mad*, as if he were a rich little boy with all the privileges and I were a poor little girl just seething. But he didn't realize they *were* privileges. That's what poor kids don't understand about rich kids, that their lives are just natural to them, like ours are to us. Poor kids think the rich kids *know*, and that makes it all the worse. Of course it's all relative, "rich" and "poor." Maybe I was jealous, too, of all the attention he got from his pretty mother, who didn't have to peel potatoes and cook supper and holler at you, but could just lay her handwork by and pay total attention. I would sit cold and disapproving and not realize he was telling me what would have healed him better than ten best-sellers—*that* love, that warm, tender Jewish mother's love. "Wrap me in father and mother," said the poet, but *mother* would have cured Egon of all his ailments, his heart would have got better, he could have thrown away all the dope. But all he had was mean Mrs. Danvers disappearing up the stairs.

ONCE, TRYING TO KEEP himself occupied, he went to something like an antiques auction and brought a collector home. And leaving him downstairs, he came up to my torture chamber and told me the man wanted to buy our Meissen monkey band. Well, sell it to him, I said. I can still remember how shocked and hurt he looked. For of course the purpose of bringing the man home was to show off what we had, not make a sale. "Don't you want anything anymore? Our things?" He was almost crying. But he went downstairs and sold the monkey band. He was so sad afterwards. It was like he thought our house was brick but it was really straw, and now here was the wolf huffing and puffing and going to blow it down. I had so little sense, sometimes we'd be lying in bed, it would be raining, we could hear it on the roof, and I would recite from someone's poem in Untermeyer's anthology,

> *One day it will be raining as it rains tonight; the same wind blow—*
> *Raining and blowing on this house wherein we lie: but you and I—*
> *We shall not hear, we shall not ever know.*
> *O love, I had forgot that we must die.*

But *he* hadn't forgot and didn't forget, and on Groundhog Day in 1962 he died.

It was a long time before I saw my shadow again.

I was forty-nine years old. Today was the first day of the rest of my life, which I thought was going to last just long enough for me to get everything tidied up. I gave things away right and left, stacks of rare medical books Egon had collected to some of his colleagues, whom I invited to come with their wives and take their pick. One wife, as I once heard, had been to finishing school in France or Belgium, and she sat on the edge of the couch with her back so straight it made me nervous. Don't you want to sit back and be comfortable? It was really silly to sit up like a ramrod like that. But no. Absolutely perpendicular, they teach them that, I guess.

I actually accepted an invitation to dinner at one of these doctors' houses, actually drove out into winding golf-course-looking suburbia (for the first and only time). The house had a lot of bathrooms, an atrium, two steps down to the dining room. Around the table the guests talked movies, all about *Last Year at Marienbad*, the significance of it, the symbols. I sat mute, cold, terrified. We hadn't been to a movie for a long time. But it wasn't just the talk about the movie that sounded like gibberish, everything did. I was like Hans Castorp thrown off the Magic Mountain and sitting up rubbing his eyes. Where am I? What happened? What shall I do?

One of my first reasoned acts of those first days of the rest of my life was to have Egon dug up. I know it would sound better to say exhumed or disinterred, but that harsher term seems to better express how wild and crazy doing a thing like that was. Of course during the move he was only above ground for a few minutes and then was immediately buried in the grave next to his original grave, and I think if he'd known about the transaction, he would have just taken it without question, as he did the dishpans full of soapsuds to be thrown in the alley. That was just one of the incomprehensible customs of his aborigine wife, and so was this changing my mind about his grave.

It was really quite logical, or seemed so to me at the time. When he died, I bought three grave plots in a row up at the Skyline cemetery. The first in line was his, the next mine, the third would be Mother's. Fine. He died on February 2, and that whole month was rainy, dark, cold and miserable. I would drive up there and park the car and walk on the wet grass to his grave and stand there crying like a newborn that has been left in a trash bin. And with the wind whipping my hair and my coat, for it's quite a high hill up there, I would just look around, the place was completely deserted, I would look in the different directions. And all of a sudden it came to me that he was lying so that if he sat up and then stood up, he would be facing west, and this seemed like the most terrible thing.

We had a picture at home, lots of people had it and you would see it in stores, too, both new and second-hand: "The End of the Trail." Ours was an already colored lithograph, but Aunt Laura had also hand-tinted it (she took that up at one time). Everyone has seen it, the picture of that Indian sagging in the saddle on this horse that was about to go down in a heap. They were facing west. And all of a sudden I realized that Egon (I would always see him as if he sat up and then stood up and came out of the grave) would be facing west, and facing that terrible sunset in "The End of the Trail." And that seemed to me so hopeless and awful that I couldn't stand it. He had to be turned around so that when I imagined him like that, sitting up and then standing up, he would be facing *east*, pale and beautiful and with some clear little stars and a transparent moon.

If I were religious and had been thinking about the Resurrection or something, there might be some excuse, but I wasn't, I hadn't, I just saw "The End of the Trail" in my mind, and what I did was, I went right down to the cemetery offices. And pretty soon here I was in a hushed room sitting across the desk from — Somebody must have been sitting there for me to talk to, and I must not have looked or sounded so much like a crazy person that they would have to send for somebody to come after me when I explained that I wanted my husband brought up and turned around because I couldn't bear to have him facing the way he was "like an Indian," because the official said all right, no problem, but there would be the same charge as for the original interment. Actually it turned out to be much more expensive than that, but cost was no object, as I had insurance money and wouldn't be around long.

It was more expensive because as we talked, I realized that here were these three plots in a row, Egon was in the end or outside one. If he were turned around in his original grave, then I would be on his right side instead of on his left, and I couldn't have that, because I always slept on his left. So that meant the middle grave (mine) had to be what the cemetery man called "opened." Egon had to be transferred to it and I would have to occupy his original grave, which would have to be filled in in the meanwhile, as they couldn't allow a yawning hole up there waiting for me to die. It would also have to be re-seeded with grass. Mother's plot could stay undisturbed. I don't think I acted hysterical, I just remember quietly crying and saying I couldn't have him lying there "like an Indian," and then we got into the business part of how much all this was going to cost and when it was going to be attended to, and I wrote out a check. And really when I went to the car, the rain had stopped and the sun came out and I felt I had taken care of business.

Michael Caine, the English actor, wrote an autobiography lately, and one thing he said on a talk show was that he was just amazed at the things that came back to him as he wrote, things he hadn't thought of for years. I mention this because not until I wrote all that craziness (that nevertheless seemed so logical to me at the time) about switching Egon around did I realize that it wasn't just "The End of the Trail" that was haunting me (I always hated that picture) but something else, too, that I didn't even remember I had seen, and that was, about forty years earlier, when I was a young girl, our neighbor Clyde Peacock's corner field being turned into an archaeological dig.

When the spring flood receded that year, it carried off the dirt over an old, old Indian burial ground, and when Clyde started plowing his field, he ran into these artifacts scattered around, bones and skulls and so on. We gathered from near and far, neighbors, men from the *Albany Democrat-Herald* and the Corvallis paper, and interested persons from the university, the state college and also Albany College, to handle the thing the way it should be done. The weather was awful, dark, cold and rainy, sheets of rain blowing, the field was muddy and soft, you sank down in it, and at first you couldn't see much, muddy boulder-looking things and muddy bones. But the scholars hammered stakes in around the site and strung clothesline, students came to help, and before long, in spite of the weather, "it was all very tidy"—you could get some idea of how the place had been laid out by the Indians, they carefully excavated new graves and tried to assemble what they found alongside, the skeleton and his stuff, his bowls or whatever, muddy and sort of sprouting.

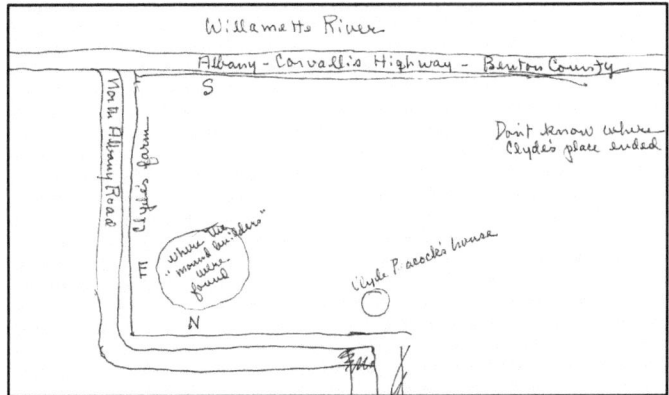

I borrowed rubber boots from someone and the minute school was out, down I would go to Clyde's field no matter the weather, and the scholars would be digging, writing in notebooks and tying on tags. There's a word *horripilation*, meaning the hairs on your skin bristling because of the contraction of the subcutaneous muscles caused by cold or fear and your flesh creeping. So I would stand there and watch, and the day would darken and twilight fall and here would be these dead people thousands of years old lying around covered with tarps for the night, and horripilation would just go all over me. As time passed there wasn't as big an audience anymore, people had other things to do, but I kept borrowing the boots and going and standing right up to the clothesline stretched around close to the ground. And one late afternoon they uncovered a skeleton they said must be a king because of all the bowls stacked on his head, horizontally, and other possessions too, I can't remember what. But oh, the horripilation then. This ancient *king*! these relics of a time so long ago you couldn't even believe the sun shone or the moon rose or the rain fell.

This should be a footnote, but I'll put it here, what the heck. Clyde Peacock was understandably very proud of the burial ground discovered on his property, and he let the archaeologists come and do what they wanted, although it held up the plowing till it got to where he didn't even plant that spring. He and his wife's pictures were in the *Democrat-Herald* and other papers too, and pictures of the dig. In those days, there were no particular standards for archaeological digs and no technologies such as gamma-ray imaging and laser-light examination of ancient relics. But the scholars on the scene were real professionals and did the best they could, carefully laying out the bones and artifacts on Clyde's basement floor and in his garage. Maybe Clyde said that if they did the digging and the work, their schools could have what was discovered, or maybe the schools made offers, I don't know what the arrangement was, if any. But when the work was done and the field put back to rights, Clyde wouldn't part with *even one* bone, tooth or arrowhead. He hung onto all of it like grim Death, and of course the archaeologists were fit to be tied.

What happened, apparently, was that a carnival had made Clyde an offer. But he was no fool, he had been to school, so he thought if a *carnival* could make money off his dead Indians and bowls and pestles, why couldn't *he*? So he made big wooden trays, bought a truck, and he and his wife started off to make the rounds of fairs and festivals up and down the West Coast. But their "Ancient Moundbuilder" sideshow didn't make much money, and after a while the Peacocks came home with their stuff all cracked and broken, as if they'd been hauling around a lot of eggshell china and got in a wreck. Everything was all mixed up, the archaeologists' labels had all come off, you couldn't tell the great king from the fellow that dumped the garbage, it was a fair old mess, and Clyde finally just shoveled all the shards into the basement and there they stayed for years and years, till he and his wife died. And I don't know what happened after that.

But that wet, muddy dig, of course, was why in the dark cold early spring when I was standing there in the Skyline cemetery on the soft soaked ground around Egon's grave, why, "like an Indian" flashed through my mind and I just couldn't bear it.

IF ONLY THAT move from one grave to the other had been the last disturbance for him! But it wasn't. For, just as I acted as if his clothes or anything he had was mine to give away or throw away as I wished, so I did the same with his dear beloved *self*. So he had one more move in store, this time not just from one grave to another but seventy-five miles south, to a cemetery in Albany. For many years there was just one cemetery right *in* Albany and a small one on the outskirts. But after World War II my clever stepsister Ruby, who had a real-estate company and was progressive and looked ahead, sold a farm to some business people who had come to town for the express purpose of laying out a graveyard and building a crematorium, office complex, and for the urns a chapel or oratory.

What seems like kind of a coincidence to *me*, considering that Egon and Mother are in that cemetery and that I will be there too, I'm sure before the coming of the Cocqcigrues, is that the farm it's located on used to belong to this woman, our old friend Mrs. Gregory, who as I mentioned before said that I was the most spoiled girl she ever saw. Mr. and Mrs. Gregory and their five children lived on this farm for many years, we kids used to visit back and forth, and I crawled around picking up potatoes on the very spot where I am going to lie. It's not a big world.

And how Egon ended up down there in Albany, ten miles from the first home he ever had in America, after being buried two different times at the Portland Skyline cemetery, was because when I came back from New York after taking a notion to live there for two years, Mother was 83. So the first thing she told me was that she didn't want to be buried in the grave I had bought for her in Portland next to me and Egon but preferred to be down in Albany, where more was going on, in Ruby's cemetery. That is what the family calls it, Ruby having sold the farm the cemetery is laid out on. Ruby herself lies there, dead at 56, a dear beloved sister. Also in Ruby's cemetery, even while Mother was still alive, were many friends and relatives. And her younger and favorite brother George Olsen would eventually lie there too, dead at the age of 88 on the eve of his fifth wedding.

Mother didn't want to be stuck up in the Portland cemetery where she didn't know anybody, all by herself with just Egon and me. She wanted us all to be buried in Albany. After all, who did we know in the Portland cemetery? A few nodding acquaintances, no relations or close friends, and what fun was that? So when Mother died, which she did at the age of 84, and Ruby's only son and the only millionaire in the family presented Marion and me with not only a grave plot for Mother but five other plots stretching down from it, and Mother was buried, I thought, why not? So up came Egon again and down he went, to the prettiest spot imaginable, trees, shrubs, I'll bet it looks just like the Prater in Vienna.

A cemetery won't buy any grave plots *back*. "We don't need them," they say, "we've got all the graves we want." So, long after Egon was moved, a friend of mine put an ad in the paper and sold my three plots for me. And you know what we found out? You can't get half as much as you paid, and if a grave has been *used*, forget it. So, as Egon had occupied *two* of the three graves, one for about a week and one for four years, and as I gave this friend half for the trouble, I'd have done almost as well to have just let them lie. People should have been honored to get to buy where he had been, like when Beethoven was moved. The ones who loved Beethoven went to his *empty* grave and stood there with head bowed, just like they did above the plot where he really lies, merely because he had once lain there.

Egon traveled alone to his third grave. And that day, I thought of him all day and imagined to myself that he would *like* my having done this, that he would love the surprise so much of not having to stay in the same place forever but to get to move and do something different. The ride down there, seventy-five miles from Portland to Albany, familiar miles, I thought he would welcome. He knew that stretch of highway so well, and the roads around Albany and Corvallis when he practiced as the only ophthalmologist in the valley and specialists made housecalls just like everybody else, even in the middle of the night. And anything going on in Portland—a road show, symphony concert, the Fanchon and Marco Girls at the Paramount—the "kultur" contingent he ran with in Corvallis would drive up to it. He was used to moving. I had to think he'd be pleased. I called Uncle George, and he and his third wife, Alvilda, went to the Albany cemetery so as to be there when the hearse, or whatever kind of vehicle they brought Egon in, arrived from Portland. I didn't see the open grave, that third one, or the second, or the first.

Milton says the Devil never was ashamed but once, but then he was *so* ashamed that he rolled on the ground and bit himself and cried scalding tears. And that's about how I feel as I go to write what I have to write now. I was quick to tell Egon, when he was scared and shaking, to stand up and be a man, though maybe not in those exact words. And when they came and got me and took me out to the Kaiser hospital where he had just died, I did the same with the sick scared shaking quaking thing inside myself. Stand up, behave, be decent, don't be a coward, *don't you dare.*

Two doctors sat with me in one of their offices. We carried on a polite conversation, as when paying an afternoon call on someone who has just moved into the neighborhood. I don't know how I happened to have black suede hand-stitched gloves on, but I did,

I kept seeing myself gesticulating with them and wishing I would stop. I saw that the office windows needed dusting and the light was very bright. Once or twice I thought the doctors were talking German. Then a nurse came in, possibly Egon's office nurse. She asked me if I wanted to see him and said he was lying on a couch and that he looked peaceful, something like that. I said no. Because if I saw him it would be true, while if I didn't it wouldn't, and where would my "Blackfoot bravade" be if it was true? Where would anything be? Our schedule, supper, I had been to the library and got us a batch of books, he would want to see them, and some—magazines had come, *Time* and *Life*— The last checks he ever wrote were for *Time* and *Life*, and he must have renewed them for a long time, because they kept coming for years.

MY FATHER DIED TWO weeks after my ninth birthday. He was a lineman for the Utah Power & Light Company and had just gone back to work again after a strike by the newly started Union. The company and the Mormons (everybody but the Union members and their families) just hated the men for striking. The strike lasted all winter, and I remember us not having coal and piling up in bed to keep warm. And once Daddy cut pictures of food out of some old magazines and propped them up on the table and called us kids to come and eat, he was an awful kidder, and I cried but Marion laughed, and Mother said that showed the difference in our dispositions. We didn't go hungry that day, though, or any day, because there was always flour to bake bread with, and potatoes. And coffee. The company had hired scab labor, so when the real guys got back to work, everything was all screwed up. They couldn't find stuff they needed like pliers, and some safety belts were missing. Daddy had only about a week's wages coming when he was electrocuted on one of the poles on South Temple and State Street, across the street from the Eagle Gate, and he fell thirty feet or forty feet or whatever it was to the ground.

In those days, the body in its casket used to lie in state at home for a few hours in the parlor and then be taken to the meeting house for the funeral, and that is what was done with my father. It's such a cliché, the child not wanting to look at the first dead body he or she will have ever seen that also happens to be the one person they love best in the world, how he or she refuses to "view" that body, screams and cries and gets hysterical and has to be dragged, but an aunt or the grandmother drags her and, kicking and screaming, she is forced to look, and after that there's all the psychological damage, and Joanne Woodward wins an Academy Award for *The Three Faces of Eve*.

I remember how ghastly he looked, they didn't put makeup on them then, and how he had what must have been like powder burns, his pores seemed to be peppered with this dark blue hard glinting powder, from the terrible jolt of electricity. I don't know about the psychological damage, I'd have probably been the same kind of linthead anyway. I've seen several dead bodies since then, Marion's little schoolmate Mabel Wilson, Goldie Crocker, aged only 15 when she drowned in the Santiam River, my stepsister Ruby's uncle George Small, who fell out of a tree while shooting fish and broke his leg and got gangrene and died, my stepfather's mother Mary Catherine Parker, aged 90, who crossed the Plains in a covered wagon in 1853, my stepfather Hiram Parker, who married my mother when I was eleven and to whom I owe anything good about myself, such as always being punctual ("the courtesy of kings") and if I start a job finish it, get up in the morning, pay your debts, vote Democrat. I loved daddies so much, I guess I was fated to love them. Now there aren't any anymore, no matter that you supposedly see them on TV or in person with little kids on their shoulders, driving Little Leaguers in pickup trucks and all that, they're not real, it's just advertising.

I said no to Egon's nurse. I don't want to see him. A few years ago I saw this German movie called *Sugar Baby*. It's about this fat, middle-aged woman who works in a mortuary and the reason I mention it, she's talking to her lover and she says she can't understand why people shun her because of what she does. She says the dead need you to be tender with them and do all you can for them in their last hours above ground. They *need* you. She speaks German, but when I read the captions of her saying that, I felt like a knife went through my heart. Then in *Prime Suspect 2*, just the other night, this black boy had killed himself in jail, was laid out, and his father came and was so loving, knelt down and took the boy's head in his hands and kissed him, and the knife went through my heart again, because that was what I should have done.

But what did I do instead? I didn't go near. Didn't see his face, didn't see if his bowtie was tied that he could tie without looking in the glass, didn't see his hands that always looked like a clever boy's of about fifteen. He needed me to come to him and do like the woman in *Sugar Baby* and the boy's father, and kneel and kiss him and love him and say goodbye. Even the psychiatrists and psychologists say you not only have to say goodbye, but you have to know you're saying it. But I didn't. I never did see him again. The mortuary called, and Mother (this would have been that evening or the next day) said that they said he was ready for viewing, supposedly in his best clothes that I had sent down there. I didn't see him. No, no. At the funeral were just a few invited people. His closed casket was there with beautiful flowers, he was supposed to be in it, and I went over and touched it, briefly laid my cheek on the lid. I don't know if it was him in the casket, how would I know?

It's not very usual, I don't think, for people to act like that. Even the Neanderthals were tender and gathered flowers and tucked their dead in with furs, as though they'd keep them warm, and placed their things around them and cried, and the ones that loved them best probably sat by them a long time and held their hand. Savages, too, anywhere in the world. Even elephants. And beavers. I do know one person, though, who acted like me. She said she could not. No. In her case, the one who had died wasn't her husband, it was her daughter. And I will tell about it not for the fact of saying, See, there *was* one other person! but because something so very strange happened subsequently in regard to her that it almost makes you think there's someone or something, some force, that watches and tries to make things balance. I have changed the names but it's all true, and if this were a story, I would call it "The Angel on the Roof."

When a little girl is born to a mother who always has the jump on her in every way one woman can have the jump on another woman, looks, brains, ability of every sort, there's not much that child can do—try to beat her, say Okay, you win, wait for time to wreak some havoc, go crazy, move far away, jump out a window.

Florence's only daughter, Kitsa, nearly as beautiful as Florence but not quite, nearly as smart and nearly as capable but not quite, when her marriage to Allen didn't work out and she got a good job in Hawaii, moved there, far away. But maybe she expected too much from relocating. So one day, with her hair and nails freshly done and in a lovely outfit, Balenciaga brown, and with her makeup perfect, because her mother would be coming and sizing up every little detail, she shot herself.

But Florence didn't size up anything. As Kitsa knew they

would, mother, father and brother rushed over. But when they got there and took a suite in the Royal Hawaiian Hotel in which to freshen up, Florence's religion, which was Christian Science and never had *not* sustained her before, suddenly gave way. Father and brother had to go alone to the mortuary, "view" Kitsa, choose an urn for her ashes, a niche for her urn, a plaque to be affixed above her niche, and then follow her casket to the crematorium.

All this took quite a while, but that gave Florence time to sit up, put her feet on the floor and gradually rise from the couch. Her religion, like the electricity temporarily cut off, came on again, and by the time Andy, her husband, and Glover, her son, got back, she had taken off her old makeup, brushed her teeth, had a shower, put on new makeup, recombed her hair and was out on the balcony looking at the view.

Glover started to tell her how Kitsa had looked, pretty as a picture, like an angel, kind of a half smile on her lips, and so peaceful it would really have been a comfort. But Andy, who worshipped Florence and was always aware of every little reaction, saw she was somehow balking and shook his head at Glover, so he shut up.

Nothing more about the matter was ever said.

Kitsa might as well have killed herself in her old grubbies with cold cream on and her hair in curlers! But now, of course, she didn't care. To the dead, it's always six of one and half a dozen of the other. Or is it?

Florence was an inspiration, she really was. Some women, losing their only daughter that they had been such chums with and looking so much alike, tall, slender, blonde, blue-eyed, almost like twin sisters—except when you saw them together and saw how completely Florence's looks put Kitsa's in the shade—would have nearly been done in. But not her.

And beauty wasn't all she had, but business sense and every other kind of sense, too. Andy by himself, with just that government job, could never have bought a house like they lived in, cars like they drove, trips like they took, and the apartment houses— how many did they own now? And how about the jewelry? The sable coat? And some women *time* made a big detour around, it was just incredible. Kitsa would have had one hell of a wait.

How old *was* Florence? Well, let's see, she was about thirty when Kitsa was born, and as Kitsa was twenty-four when she died, that would make Florence— But you started out to say— Oh, yes. The angel on the roof. Not the roof to Florence's *dwelling place* on the heights, but the flat roof on her last acquisition, a downtown apartment house, four stories, bay windows, fireplaces, lovely entrance, Florence was prepared to spend quite a bit of money on it. At the back was a ladder that went from the ground to the roof, maybe not such a good idea in some places, but in Portland not to worry. You could go along the street and look right at it there against the back of the building, shaded by a tree, and never see it.

But one clear cold winter night, with the snow thick on the ground and on the trees and roofs, a girl climbed that ladder, up to the roof of Florence's favorite apartment house. Once up there, she walked around a little, looking at the city. Then she lay down in the snow, "made an angel," brought a gun up to her temple and, still supine, pulled the trigger. Nobody heard a sound. The next morning when the news helicopter flew over, surveying the winter wonderland, the cameraman spotted her, made the pilot dip down close and took some pictures.

"An unidentified young woman climbed to the roof of a downtown apartment house sometime during Tuesday night," the story about her in the paper next morning said. "She lay on her back, made a pair of so-called 'angel wings' in the snow by stretching her arms out and moving them up and down, then apparently took her own life by shooting. No one heard the shot. She carried no identification, and attempts Wednesday to identify her were unsuccessful, Capt. LeRoy Street, spokesman for the Portland Department of Public Safety, said. He said she was in her early twenties, about five feet eight inches in height, slender build. She had dark blonde hair, blue eyes and was wearing a brown dress. Anyone with information please call—"

There must be *ten thousand* apartment houses in Portland. Maybe more. But she chose that one.

Chaos mathematics? Some electrical dimension formed by the global networking of electronic machines? A dimension where if disembodied hackers can roam, why not a girl, or anyone?

A photograph accompanied the story in the paper. It almost won a prize a few months later. What it was of was this half-smiling dead girl standing—which it looked like because the picture was taken from above looking down—against this white square that Florence's flat roof appeared to be, covered with snow, with her angel wings going out to either side as though flying in the white radiance of heaven.

That was the first thing Florence saw on the front page when

she took the paper in to read with her morning coffee.
Hello, Mother.
You know you owed me one.

EGON'S FUNERAL wasn't a proper one, there should have been speeches about his life, for it had been very eventful, attention should have been paid. He had tutors clear up until he graduated from medical school, his father spared no expense. If he just would have, he could have played the piano as well as the pianists on the Lawrence Welk show. He could have been a wonderful magician. People liked him a lot. He knew almost everything.

He was the most terrible driver ever to get behind a wheel, but he never really had an accident. He must have read nearly as many books as were in the library at Carthage. His hands were dry and warm and his handshake firm up until the very last. He was cute, when he was young he looked like a cross between a young George Jessel and a young Al Pacino.

He fought in both wars, on the German side in World War I and on our side in World War II. When we were separated from time to time during the war, he may have carried on some flirtations or had an affair. After the war was over, he got a few letters from nurses or whatever they were (also in the army), they sent him pictures of themselves, at least one did. And funny, I was so jealous of him as a boy hurrying home from school to his mother's "boudoir," jealous of the privileges and the love and comfort, but to these girls in the army I paid no attention whatsoever, didn't ask, didn't look, I couldn't even *imagine* anyone getting him away from me, it just wasn't possible.

Egon wrote medical papers that even now are in the archives, could read six languages, talk four. He was a good doctor. He was such a kind, loving, indulgent husband that it was ridiculous. He loved Roosevelt and Truman, also H. L. Mencken, and I am thankful he died without finding out what an anti-semite Mencken was.

Our cat Violet ate pork kidneys, and if company made a comment about her, he would say gravely, "Yes, a large pig has to be sacrificed every day for Violet."

What else, before the colors fade?

He did try to "keep up" till the very end, to work, and I'm sure he must have tried desperately to quit his dependency. But too many things happened through the years, then more stuff all at once till, being of a nervous temperament anyway, he caved in.

Violet died, and like a cheap no-good word processor, his "writer" up in the attic malfunctioned, couldn't be fixed, and the whole situation just got to be too much.

He had passed the tough exams and had licenses to practice ophthalmology and otolaryngology in Washington, Oregon and California. He had— He was— But never a word of any of this was breathed at his funeral, I didn't sketch out for anybody any details for a eulogy or ask anybody to give one. He could have been just some poor person found dead on the street with no identification. So there's a wife for you.

My stepfather wasn't much for organized religion, he was totally good and honest but not religious. Egon's father was a scientist, all for scientific progress, no churches, no more trouble. Egon, for his part, thought that no matter how brilliant everybody becomes, nobody is ever going to know one thing more about the Big Mystery than the first human who ever lived. And Mother, being born into the Mormon church, thought she never had to think about Mormonism or any other religion ever again, because she was already saved. My own father was a lapsed Catholic. So religion didn't play much of a role in my upbringing or in later life. And why I would think I had to have a minister conduct Egon's funeral I do not know. But I did. Some atavistic thing made me hire one at the last moment. He didn't have to do anything except read two of Shakespeare's sonnets, the one that starts "When to the sessions of sweet silent thought / I summon up remembrance of things past" and the one beginning "When in disgrace with fortune and men's eyes / I all alone beweep my outcast state," and he read them very badly.

I sat there in hat and gloves, the words thudded softly, like summer apples dropping onto grass. The minister also had the job of going up to the cemetery with Egon and "dedicating" the grave he would only occupy a week. I seemed to think that that ritual had to be gone through, and by a man of the cloth, and I believe and imagine he did go. But I wasn't checking on anything.

I didn't see my dear one dead, I didn't see him lying in state (if he *did* "lie in state," I had given orders no one was to see him), I didn't see him at the funeral, I didn't see his casket lowered into the ground, I didn't see it come up and be buried next door a week later, I didn't see it brought up again four years later, I didn't see it buried again in Albany. I never saw him, you see, anywhere along the line. The casket could have been empty, somebody else could have been in there, an impostor, a total stranger, you read things like that in the paper all the time. God only knows where he could be. Nobody saw him, there was no kindness and tenderness such as *Sugar Baby* says the dead have to have, no kiss, no snipping off of a lock of his hair (silky and dark and slightly wavy and hadn't started to go gray yet), no note put in his hand signed "meine frau." Once we read that Heinrich Heine had a stupid mistress (not German, she was an Alsatian or something like that) who, having heard Heine introduce her to his friends as "meine frau," thought that was her *title*. So when she introduced *herself*, she always said "I am meine frau" — "I am my wife." I used to sign my notes to him that way. But no note from me went with him to leaden death. No death knell, no passing-bell, nobody looked upon his face, which, as I say, might not even have *been* his face but a perfect stranger's.

FAMILY PHOTOGRAPHS used to be in great style, we had lots of them standing and hanging around when I was a girl, but when I got my own place, I kept them out of sight. In those days they were from professional photographers' studios, large sized, we didn't seem to have many snapshots. I didn't look at any pictures of Egon, didn't have occasion to, and quite soon after he died I just couldn't shut my eyes and *see* him anymore. But lately I can. He looks just like he used to look before he got sick and before life in general and me in particular finally got to be too much. His eyes twinkle like they used to, he gives that little Viennese shrug. If he thought that what he took part in with me so long ago, and living with me, was like a play by Schnitzler or Nestroy, what would he think of dying with me, I wonder? Of his three different graves? None of which *he* might even have been in? Be brave, I used to tell him sternly. Be brave, I barked at myself. And I *was* brave, but only because I wouldn't face up to any of it, not one single solitary part of his death, and what kind of bravery was that?

I HAVE OFTEN wished I were a Catholic so I could go and confess all I have said here to a priest and have him tell me what to do to try to make amends. One time I even had a long conversation with a priest out at the Grotto. He said how lovely it would be if I joined the church, I would find the peace that passeth understanding, and he said I would be given a new name, too. Mary, he said. Well, that ended it for me. Mary. So here I stand, unshriven and unabsolved.

After Dylan Thomas died, his wife wrote a book called *Leftover Life to Kill*, and that's a lot the way my life has been in the thirty years since Egon died, a leftover life. I never got back on track with the writing, though for several years I kept trying, then quit. At first, when I didn't know what kind of an income I was going to have, if any, my smart businesswoman sister Ruby, taking charge for me, said, "I don't know, hon. Maybe you should go back and finish college and get a teacher's certificate, because you might have to go to work." Work? I looked at her like she was crazy. Me? I wish I could say I thought at that juncture of going down and jumping off the bridge, but I didn't, what I actually thought was that I might have to get married.*

As it happened, I didn't have to do either one, commit suicide or get married, Egon is still taking care of me to this day. Not lavishly, but not so modestly either as when I lived in a ten-dollar-a-month furnished room that looked like a set for *Mademoiselle Modiste*.

His darling corpus may very well have been lost in the shell game I have described here. I fear for that more every day as my own end approaches and burial in his arms, or at least snuggled up close, seems such a wonderful end to everything. Dr. Samuel Johnson once said, when the talk with Boswell veered to sightseeing, that pretty views and beautiful scenery were all very well, but that to him there was no prospect but what was "improved by a good inn in the foreground." And that is what Egon is and always was to me, the good inn in the foreground, where I could go and never have another care.

How many times have I moved in the meanwhile? Only six? Three moves is as good as a fire, they say. Six moves! so two big, raging fires. Hardly anything is left of the things we had, pictures, china, books, all are scattered to the four winds. I look around—no, nothing left. But what I have dragged in I think he would like. I made thirteen collages, not small, he would like those. He would like the lamps and tell me whose last words were "More light" (Goethe). The few romances I had here and in New York when I was back there for two years—for after all, it was the time of the soi-disant Sexual Revolution—I don't think he'd be as jealous of as I was of his privileged childhood. They would be to him like story plots that didn't show much promise.

---

* I didn't look then as I do now, I used to dress up, and was also considered by some people to have money and to be able to make more of same.

The time I wasted.

The money I spent.

Age withered me and custom spoiled the infinite variety every human being's got that lives. It is rather indelicate to mention one physical change I have become aware of lately. But it is so curious (at least to me) that I think I must. And that is, my bosoms seem to have parted and fallen carelessly away to either side, bulging into my underarms, while at the same time my two posteriors seem to have fallen together, pressing so closely one to the other that I think I could keep a folded piece of paper there and it wouldn't fall out. Doesn't that seem strange? Like a great overripe pomelo or pompelmoose that, by cracking open at the blow-end, squeezes the stem-end closer together. Maybe that happens just as it falls from the tree.

So far as I know I am not mortally ill, but I am going to make arrangements and prepay the burial I want, which is in a cheap biodegradable pasteboard coffin, not one that will last. My grave plot in Ruby's cemetery is next to his, on his left, the way we always slept. Good night, sweet repose, sleep on your back and not on your nose. Here I am, darling. Old, runover, not fixed up, because there won't have been a funeral with the lid up or any kind at all. Nobody will have bid me goodbye or "viewed" me, I'll have that in writing. So you know what the upshot might be? Since no one will have checked anywhere along the line that that might not even *be* me, just as I don't know if whoever it is down there waiting for "meine frau" is really Egon, maybe the two of us won't turn out to be *us* at all. But that won't be so bad, him wandering in the cosmos, me wandering, calling to each other. I *know* we'll get together sometime. We did it before and we can do it again.

Ardyth's Memoir, Part 2

ONE NIGHT HE had gone to bed and was half sitting up against his pillow reading. Out in the kitchen, in the cupboard, was one of those apples of solid chocolate put together in separate sections so it looked like a perfect apple, a big one about the size of a Rome Beauty. On the wrapping it said to put this chocolate apple on a china dinner plate and take a knife and just tap the apple, and it would fall open like a flower in these perfect sections. So, intending to do that, I put it on one of our good Meissen plates and went into the bedroom. I didn't say anything, just portentously—as he was lying flat enough—set the plate on his chest. Looking at me as though to say, Now what? he put his book down, took his glasses off and watched with his world-weary eyes to see what was going to happen. I took the knife, struck the chocolate apple a brisk blow, and—! the plate broke in half. The apple wasn't even dented. One thing I always loved about him was the way he laughed, as if he didn't want to but couldn't help himself.

Notes

The following notes are intended to provide corrections and context for certain mentions and passages in Ardyth's memoir and Egon's journal, as well as some further information about their lives—especially what is known about Egon's life.

Ardyth's letters to relatives and friends, cited in some of the notes, are from a private family collection. Most of her letters did not carry a specific date, only a day of the week.

page 1: "Egon" is pronounced with a "long a" sound and the stress on the first syllable: "*A*-gone."

page 1: "she at fifty-eight and newly widowed": Hiram Parker, the second husband of Ardyth's mother, Lulu "Lula" (Olsen) Kennelly, died January 20, 1940. After Ardyth's father, James Daniel Kennelly, died in Salt Lake City in 1921, Lula, with her young daughters Ardyth and Marion, moved to North Albany, Oregon, to care for the children of her recently widowed brother, a neighbor of the Parker family.

page 2: "farm home in North Albany": The house was located at 820 North Albany Road. In May 1923, when Hiram and Lula married, Ardyth was 11 years old, Marion was 8, and Hiram's daughter by his first marriage, Ruby, was 15.

page 3: "Not what the stars have done . . .": Ardyth is paraphrasing what Emily Dickinson wrote to her friend Maria Whitney in 1883: "Not what the stars have done, but what they are to do, is what detains the sky."

page 3: "Clarene and Freda": Clarene and Alfreda (Freda) were two of Ardyth's nine Olsen cousins, children of her mother's brother George Rudolph Olsen. George and his family lived at

1035 North Albany Road, about an eighth of a mile from the Parker home.

page 3: "moving his eye, ear, nose, and throat practice": The *Corvallis Gazette-Times* of February 9, 1932, reported that Egon had "opened offices in Portland" (p. 3).

page 4: "by Ada Hastings Hedges": Ardyth's typescript had "*Bridge of the Gods* by Ada Hastings Hedges," but that book, first published in 1890, was by Frederic Homer Balch. Possibly Ardyth had seen in the window Hedges' book *Desert Poems*, published in 1930. Ardyth later worked on the WPA Federal Writers' Project in Portland, where she met Hedges, a supervisor on the project.

Advertisements for Egon's book appeared in the *Oregonian* of May 19 and May 23, 1933.

page 6: "*The Enormous Land*": Schnitzler's play *Das weite Land* (1911) was translated as *The Vast Domain*.

page 7: "What title I gave it I don't remember": In the story, called "This Is Where I Live," a seven-year-old girl lost in a Salt Lake City park tries to describe the houses near her own, hoping that the young couple she encounters will help her get home. One of the nearby houses, she tells them, is where "Bertha and Sarah Jew" live. (*The Manuscript*, Winter 1931, pp. 17–19, in Historical Publications of Oregon State University; available at oregondigital.org.)

page 7: "the year my father died": James D. Kennelly, who was a lineman for the Utah Power & Light Company, died on April 21, 1921, when he was electrocuted and fell from a power pole in Salt Lake City. ("Electrical Workman Is Killed in Fall from Pole," *Salt Lake Tribune*, April 22, 1921, p. 22.)

page 7: "living in close proximity": The Kennellys might have been at the house Ardyth labeled "First house we lived in after Oregon sojourn," located behind the "site of the original 2nd ward" on Seventh South between Fourth and Fifth East, according to a map of the vicinity she drew in later years at the behest of her mother. (Map provided courtesy of Ardyth's cousin William Scott Fisher.)

page 8: "experience is the state . . .": The quotation does not appear to be specifically from William James. The *Oxford English Dictionary*, which Ardyth owned at one time, defines "experience" as "the state of having been occupied in any department of study or practice, in affairs generally, or in the intercourse of life."

page 9: "when Huey Long really did die": Long was shot the evening of Sunday, September 8, 1935, and died early on September 10.

page 10: "rode back and forth to Oregon State": Ardyth attended Oregon State Agricultural College (now Oregon State University) in 1929–32, but did not graduate.

page 13: "like bats among birds . . .": The line is from Bacon's essay "Of Suspicion" (1597): "Suspicions amongst thoughts are like bats amongst birds, they ever fly by twilight."

page 14: "when the time came": Ardyth and Howard were married December 11, 1935. They divorced on January 25, 1940. (Ardyth to her literary friend Frederic "Freddy" Jacobson, May 15, 1962.)

page 15: "books like *Goodbye to Berlin*": Ardyth's typescript had "books like *I Am a Camera*," but that was a play and film based on the 1939 book *Goodbye to Berlin*, by Christopher Isherwood.

page 17: "the old pioneer graveyard in Peoria, Oregon": A stone in Pine Grove Cemetery, near Peoria, reads "In Memory of Howard S. Gibbs / Apr 13 1911 / Sept 11 1977 / Died in Tangier, Morocco."

page 17: "a clerk by the name of Mountstuart Elphinstone": In her "little mythology," Ardyth is mixing a trace of fact with her fiction. She had perhaps read in Hubert Howe Bancroft's 1886 *History of Oregon* that by 1834, Astoria (or Fort George, as it was called while under control of the Hudson's Bay Company) "no longer deserved to be called a fort, the defences of every description having disappeared, while at a little distance from the old stockade, now in ruins, was one principal building of hewn boards, surrounded with a number of Indian huts. Only about four acres were under cultivation, and only one white man, the trader in charge, resided there" (p. 11). There was indeed a Mountstuart Elphinstone who lived at the same time, but he was an official in British India.

page 18: "You know, Tupso . . .": *Tupso* is a Chinook Jargon word denoting grass, leaves, fringe, feathers, or fur.

page 19: "smelling like . . . Christmas Night": A perfume that Ardyth liked.

pages 20–21: "the founder's oldest children's names": Lewis A. McArthur's *Oregon Geographic Names* (6th ed., 1992) gives a different explanation for the town's name: "Glenada townsite was platted by Geo. H. Colter about 1890. . . . Since the place was in a circle of the Siuslaw River, it was called 'Glen-Ada,' the Ada being for Mrs. Colter. Why the circle of the river suggested Glen has not been explained." A biography of the town's founder, George Huestis Colter, states that Glenada, "according to his daughters, was named for the beautiful location (Glen) and his wife (Ada)." (Kevin K. Mittge and the Siuslaw Genealogical Society, *Tangled Grass: The Story of Those Buried in the Glenada, Oregon Odd Fellows Cemetery* [Florence, Ore., 2003].) Colter did have a daughter named Ada, but no son named Glen.

page 21: "the *Florence Gazette*": The actual name of the local paper at the time of Ardyth's birth was *The West*.

page 21: "my folks, . . . born and raised in Salt Lake City": James Daniel Thomas Aquinas Kennelly was born in Salt Lake City on January 16, 1880, into an Irish Catholic family; Lulu Amanda "Lula" Olsen was born in nearby Echo, Utah, on March 18, 1882, to a Norwegian father and a Swedish mother (the models for Olaf and Linnea Ecklund in Ardyth's first novel, *The Peaceable Kingdom*).

James and Lula left Utah sometime between 1903, when their daughter Grace was born in Salt Lake City, and the time of the 1910 census, when they are listed in Missoula, Montana; presumably, they were looking for economic opportunities. Sometime in 1910, they moved to Glenada. Ardyth's cousin William Scott Fisher explains, in his 1996 *History of Our Olsen Family Ancestors* (p. 58), that Lula sent word to her brother George Rudolph Olsen in Salt Lake City that a sawmill was going to be built in Florence that would "spark an economic boom," and George and his family arrived in Florence in July 1911. But the sawmill was not built; both families apparently had a difficult time in Glenada, and in mid-1912 they moved to North Albany, where George had found work.

The Kennelly family moved back to Salt Lake City when Ardyth was three years old (at some point after her sister Marion was born, on April 12, 1915). After James died in 1921, Lula, Ardyth, and Marion lived for a time with Lula's mother, the chiropractor and midwife Anna (Johnson) Olsen, in Salt Lake's old Constitution Building; in 1922 they returned to North Albany. (*History of Our Olsen Family Ancestors* is available online at www.familysearch.org; search by the title in the Books section.)

page 23: "our old duplex": Ardyth and Egon's duplex was at 2475 Northrup Street in Northwest Portland. They purchased this house after Ardyth's financial success with her first book, *The Peaceable Kingdom* (1949), and it was here that she wrote her other four early novels.

page 24: "her profound melancholy . . .": Ardyth wrote about the Empress Elisabeth's obsession with thinness and beauty in "The Case of the Hungry Empress," the only surviving full chapter of a book on the history of dieting that Ardyth wrote, or at least began writing. (A partial chapter on Lord Byron has also survived.)

page 25: "emigration and a partnership for Egon": Egon apparently decided to emigrate because of political and economic conditions in Austria at the time. A 1927 article in the Portland *Oregonian* quoted him as saying, "Vienna, a city that might be said to have a 'scientific proletariat,' is under a complete socialistic government, conducted in such a manner that a professional man is taxed so heavily that, regardless of his income, he is utterly unable to keep more than enough for a bare living. Such conditions are bringing about emigration of many of the men in the medical and other professions." ("Socialist Rule in Vienna Said to Hurt Professions," *Oregonian*, April 10, 1927, p. 11.)

The *Corvallis Gazette-Times* of February 17, 1927, reported that Egon, after teaching for seven years at the University of Vienna, had been "engaged by O. A. C. [Oregon Agricultural College, later Oregon State University] to give special lectures in biology and physiology." He had been an "assistant to Professor Neumann, the greatest living authority on the ear, nose and throat. His work on the eye has been done with Professor Dimmer, head of the Fuchs clinic" in Vienna ("Vienna Specialist Added to List of Local Physicians," p. 1).

Egon had arrived in the United States on December 14, 1926, according to his petition for U.S. citizenship (which he obtained in 1934), although in his journal he states that he came in 1925 (see page 83). He returned to Vienna in July 1931 for "post-graduate work in ophthalmology and also did original research on dietetic treatment on sinus diseases," arriving back in Oregon in January 1932 after presenting papers to medical societies in Vienna, Berlin, and St. Louis, Missouri. ("Dr. Ullman Returns," *Corvallis Gazette-Times*, January 18, 1932, p. 6.) Egon was accompanied to Europe by his wife, Margarethe Kubin, whom he had married in 1923.

Egon described his findings on diet in colds when he arrived in New York after his sojourn in Vienna: the "new treatment" consisted of "a steady diet of raw vegetables and the elimination of table salt from food, which, he said, was being used successfully by Viennese physicians.... The theory of the new treatment was that sodium chloride had the property of expelling calcium from the system, and calcium, he said, was the one basic element that was 'anti-phlogistic' or 'anti-inflammatory.' 'The reason for the diet of raw vegetables,' said Dr. Ullman, 'is to provide the body with the necessary minerals in the absence of sodium chloride.'" ("Effective Cold Cure: Diet of Raw Vegetables Used Successfully in Vienna," *The Gazette* [Montreal], January 23, 1932, p. 2.)

page 27: "Egon's father": Dr. Karl Ullmann was born September 27, 1860, in Habern, Bohemia, and died December 24, 1940, in Vienna. (At some point after emigrating to the United States, Egon dropped the final "n" from his surname.) Egon's mother was Gabriele Ella Rosauer, born November 19, 1869, in Vienna; she died February 23, 1942.

page 30: "a young man named Richard Neuberger": Richard Neuberger (1912–1960) was a prominent Oregon Democrat and U.S. senator.

page 30: "a professor named Dr. Goldenweiser": Probably the anthropologist Alexander Goldenweiser (1880–1940), a visiting professor of sociology at Reed College in 1933–39.

page 30: "a man named Dr. Steiner": Probably Richard Morrow Steiner (1901–1975), a pastor of the First Unitarian Church from 1934. His father was Edward A. Steiner, author of *Tolstoy the Man*.

page 31: "after the refugees started coming": Among the Austrian refugees who came to Oregon during or shortly before the war were three siblings of Egon's first wife, Margarethe (Gretl) Kubin Ullmann. A 1939 article in the Portland *Oregonian* describes the lives of these and other refugees on the 235-acre Cedarbrook Dairy farm, near the Tualatin River about seventeen miles southwest of Portland; the farm had been secured for the newcomers by the Oregon Émigré Committee, headed by Max Hirsch. Moritz Eisinger, Selma Kubin's husband, was "head of the clan. . . . Four families, an even dozen men, women and children, comprise this refugee colony on the Onion flat. First members of the group arrived in Oregon late in November, 1938." Moritz had owned "much valuable farm property" in Austria and had been "the government's adviser in cattle breeding and dairy affairs and a buyer of cattle for the state." The plans for coming to the United States "included the families of Hans and Josef Kubin, brothers of Mrs. Eisinger and Mrs. Ullmann"; the Kubin brothers had been involved in horse breeding and selling in Austria. Other members of the Cedarbrook community were the Hungarian farmer Josef Gross and his wife; Hans Kubin's wife, Margarethe, and their daughter, Liesel (Elizabeth); Josef Kubin's wife, Hella, and their son, Karl; and Paul and Gertrud (Trudi) Eisinger. ("'Ja, We Are Happy,' Say Refugees in Oregon: Jewish Folk Turn to the Soil for Livelihood," *The Northwest's Own Magazine* [*Oregonian*], April 16, 1939, p. 9.) Ardyth's letters to her mother and sister from around 1940 contain numerous references to Egon's going "out to the farm," apparently on Sundays; for example, on a Monday in October 1940, Ardyth wrote, "Usually George [George Stern, the Ullmans' boarder] and Egon go out to the farm, but yesterday it rained and they decided to stay home."

In later years, Elizabeth Kubin (later Blane) told an interviewer that none of the people living on the farm had been farmers; they were "solid middle-class business people in Europe" but lost everything they had to the Nazi regime. "Everyone on the farm was traumatized," she added. (Quoted in Polina Olsen, *Stories from Jewish Portland* [Charleston, SC: The History Press, 2011], p. 110.)

According to Max Hirsch, by the end of 1938 about 100 German-Jewish refugees had "made permanent homes in and around Portland." (Shotwell Callvert, "Refugees in City," *The Northwest's Own Magazine* [*Oregonian*], December 25, 1938, p. 10.) In Ardyth's letters to her mother and sister in the 1940s, there are numerous references to two other Austrians with whom the Ullmans were acquainted: one named Bloch (probably Henry J. Bloch, a wood exporter who represented Austria's tourist and state interests by the 1950s); and another named Kriegel (probably Joachim Kriegel, a medical doctor from Vienna who, according to his obituary in the *Oregonian* on January 20, 1969, came to the United States in 1941 and became a dentist; his 1942 draft card names Egon as the "person who will always know your address").

In a mostly fragmentary, late-life outline of what Ardyth presumably intended to become her autobiography, she expanded on Egon's and her own relationship to the Jewish refugees, and on how she believed Egon and the refugees saw themselves:

> The refugees start coming from Hitler's Germany & Austria via London and South America. I meet a few of them—am struck by how educated they are and beautiful manners and begin to realize I am a lout. Also I discover that for all my reading I don't know straight up.
>
> I should write here about how strange the "Jewish" thing was—before the war, during it while Egon served 4 years in the army (Air Force, different chief of EENT units on posts & around the country—I was with him about half the time).
>
> Before the war, while everything was building up, he got all these letters from friends & relatives wanting to get out of Germany & Austria, asking help, he *gave* help in the form of affidavits or something—but we talked about *Jurgen, South Wind* and the Magic Mountain, the Sitwells, etc.—never talked about real things. The refugees, as they appeared, the same (as Egon). Nobody was Jewish. This wasn't just something they were doing *now*—For maybe more than a generation or two, they weren't religious. Egon's father, for instance, when Egon was born wouldn't allow him to be circumcized. They were doctors, lawyers, professors, well-off business men; knew the jokes, the sayings, curled their tongues around the darling talk. They thought the Berliners, the Viennese, etc. accepted them as just like themselves. And the same in Hungary, in France—yes, and in America.

I took a daily paper but I didn't read "all that stuff" in the first section, only the funnies, the Society page which flourished in those days, the book reviews, movie news—

Now I know that Egon & the refugees were in a state of shock because they thought everything had been settled— But it hadn't been—they were right back in the Middle Ages and were absolutely *stunned*. "I don't go to Temple," "I've never been circumcized," "I eat everything," "I've got blue eyes," "—no money," "—a middle name," etc. A lot of good it did them! Why didn't they know? I think I would have known. One trouble was I think that they only associated with each other and thought that was everybody. Anyway, at the time I paid but little attention.

page 33: "The day after Pearl Harbor": In late May or June 1942, Ardyth wrote to her mother, Lula, about Egon's determination to get into the Army. A letter he received from the Army "said that if he passes the examination he will receive his commission within sixty days. You can imagine how happy and excited he is. [. . .] He loves America so terribly and wants so much to help." In March or April of 1943, while Egon was stationed in Salt Lake City, Ardyth told her sister Marion: "Egon is more precious than gold. [. . .] I wish you could see him being a Major in a handsome uniform and winning the war and being so sweet and kind even in the morning when most people (me) are so damned mean."

Egon was later promoted; in late fall 1945, Ardyth wrote to Marion: "Egon came home as a Lt. Colonel on Friday afternoon and I leant down and kissed the silver oak leaf on his overseas cap."

page 34: "conjoining a lot of my thoughts with extension": The reference is apparently to Hume: ". . . the materialists, who conjoin all thought with extension." (*A Treatise of Human Nature*, vol. 1, *Of the Understanding*, pt. 4, sec. 5.)

page 35: "she was left penniless": Lula and her second husband, Hiram Parker, had separated at some point, but she returned to Albany to take care of him when he became ill, several weeks before his death in 1940. Although the couple was still married when he died, Lula apparently received nothing from his estate.

page 35: "WPA Writer's Project": Under the Federal Writers' Project of the Works Progress Administration, Ardyth (writing as Ardyth Gibbs) contributed to the 1940 book *Oregon: End of the Trail*, one of the American Guide series. She also wrote a sketch about Ellendale, Oregon, as part of the Oregon Folklore Studies (available at the Library of Congress website; search on "Concerning Ellendale: Ghost Town").

Ardyth was working under the WPA well before 1940. In an undated letter to Marion—probably from late 1936 or 1937—she mentions that she had "very good luck with my interview on Friday and the old gentleman lent me his father's diary, written in 1859." The Library of Congress's documentation on "Concerning Ellendale" gives the interview date as "Winter, 1937–38"; her sketch was received by the LOC on October 10, 1940, at which time Ardyth was noted as being "no longer on the project."

page 37: "And so she did": Lula's handwritten story of the early-1900s maternity home in which she assisted her mother—Anna M. (Johnson) Olsen, a midwife and chiropractor in Salt Lake City—has been transcribed by William Scott Fisher, in his *History of Our Olsen Family Ancestors*, pp. 27ff.

page 37: "but beautiful was the first requirement": This theme—the torturous burden placed upon women by the "requirement" to be beautiful—was developed in Ardyth's last novel, *Variation West*.

page 38: "the year between her coming to live with me and my marrying Egon": This would have been 1939–40.

page 39: "the head of the music department": Paul Petri (1877–1958) was director of the School of Music at Oregon State College from 1924 to 1947; his parents were born in Germany. His wife, Lillian Jeffreys Petri (1877–1955), was an accomplished pianist and a faculty member as well.

page 39: "the Dean of Women": Kate W. Jameson (1870–1967) was the Dean of Women at Oregon State College from 1924 to 1941; her parents were born in Germany. The 1930 census shows Egon, his wife Margarethe, and two college teachers living at the same address as Dean Jameson. Ardyth took Social Ethics classes from the dean during her college years, and Ardyth and Egon had tea with her (and lunch with the Petris) while visiting in Corvallis immediately after their honeymoon. (Ardyth to Marion, November 11, 1940.)

page 39: "his wife Gretel": Margarethe Kubin Ullmann was born December 31, 1900, in Austria; the 1930 census lists her occupation as "pract. nurse" in a "doctor's office." She applied for a divorce from Egon early in 1940. (*Oregonian*, February 22, 1940, p. 9.)

page 39: "I was with him most of the time": Ardyth's letters to Lula and Marion during the war years show that Egon was initially stationed in Salt Lake City, starting in probably the late summer or fall of 1942. Sometime between probably late 1943 and spring 1944, Ardyth left Egon in Salt Lake City and lived at the Claremont Inn in Claremont, California, while receiving treatment for "undulating fever" from Dr. Joseph F. Griggs, with daily "vaccine" shots. (This was a diagnosis that even Ardyth apparently thought was tied up with her social anxiety; in January or February 1944 she wrote to Lula: "Remember how sick I got in the dining room and had to leave? Well, tonight (temp. 100) I went down as calm as you please. There was an even bigger crowd. [. . .] I actually have got to the stage where I enjoy being with and looking at people again. Finished off with dessert and coffee, then leaned back and smoked. And looked. Finally walked unhurriedly from the dining room. It means that fever or not I've got the damned thing whipped.")

Sometime in early 1944, Egon was transferred to the East Coast, assigned first to Fort Meade in Maryland. In March or April 1944 Ardyth joined him in the East, and they spent some time in Baltimore and Washington, D.C. (where Ardyth was thrilled to see Ford's theatre, the house where Lincoln died, and the site of the bridge that John Wilkes Booth galloped over when escaping—which she would write about in her 1951 novel *The Spur*). Egon was stationed briefly in Carlisle, Pennsylvania, then at Fort Pickett in Virginia and at Fort Eustis, also in Virginia—where Ardyth rented an apartment in Hampton after being unable to find a suitable one in Newport News (see pp. 39–40). When Egon was transferred to Butler, Pennsylvania, and it became clear that he would not receive a permanent assignment, Ardyth went to live with her mother in Santa Monica, California, arriving in August 1944. She returned to Portland around February 1945, and Egon joined her there later in the year. (Letters of Ardyth to Lula and Marion, fall 1942 to August 1944; February 1945; and late fall 1945.)

The *Oregonian* of May 21, 1944 (p. 13), reported that Egon had been "commissioned in the army medical corps August 13, 1942. Before being assigned to Fort Eustis, he had assignments at the army air base, Walla Walla; army air base, Salt Lake City; 99th General hospital, Fort George G. Meade, Aberdeen proving ground, Md., and 104th General hospital, Camp Pickett, Va."

page 40: "made it easy to buy a house": This was no doubt the house that Ardyth and Egon bought in mid-1946, at 1103 NW 21st Avenue in Portland.

pages 40: "he wanted so much to be truly an author": Ardyth wrote to Marion on December 1, 1940, telling her in detail how to praise the letter Egon was sending to her: "Egon has one fault and that's his vanity about writing. [. . .] It's his one peculiarity, so help me to pamper him, will you? It means so terribly much to him."

Egon published a book of poetry titled *Graver than Nonesuch* in 1936, under the name "Victor Egon" and dedicated "to her with whom I am gay"—no doubt Ardyth, since she and Egon had already begun their affair. Egon was mentioned among other Oregon poets in Eleanor Allen, "Oregon Becomes Active Center for Writers," *The Northwest's Own Magazine* (*Oregonian*), March 29, 1936, p. 6.

page 43: Egon wrote his journal—sometimes by hand, sometimes with a typewriter—on loose sheets. The pages were not numbered until someone, presumably Ardyth, did so; so it's possible that Ardyth left out some pages (for example, there are no entries for 1953). Only minor edits have been made here, mainly for clarity and for consistency in spelling and punctuation; and a few irrelevant passages have been deleted.

page 43: "Since last night I knew that Ardyth is a novelist": Ardyth was already quite far into the writing of her first novel, *The Peaceable Kingdom* (with the working title *Love Is a Local Anguish*); in an April 1947 letter to Marion, she says she was on page 309. But on July 10, after a visit to Marion in Modesto, California, she wrote, "I discovered by reading to you from my novel that it simply won't do—and am starting in to do it over, at least in parts. . . . from a totally different angle."

page 44: "that Mother had made for her": Egon's "Mother" always refers to Ardyth's mother, Lula.

page 46: "Ardyth's mother left for Marion's": Marion was living in Centerville, California, by this time, with her husband Kenneth Pettibone and their two young sons.

page 52: "he confines himself to books": In 1952, Egon and Frederic "Freddy" Jacobson (Ardyth's literary friend) were among five Portland men featured, with photos, in a full-page newspaper article about "masculine bibliophiles" (Gwladys Bowen, "Men Also Collect Books," *Oregonian*, January 6, 1952, sec. 3, p. 1).

page 52: "Morris' Postscript": Lloyd Morris's book is *Postscript to Yesterday; America: The Last Fifty Years* (Random House, 1947). Van Wyck Brooks's book is *The Times of Melville and Whitman* (Dutton, 1947).

page 54: "at the Sawards . . .": These men were all colleagues of Egon at Kaiser Permanente Northwest in Vancouver, Washington, in the 1940s: Ernest Saward, medical director; Norman Frink, chief of surgery; Frederick Waknitz, orthopedist; and Lucius Button, surgeon. "Malbin" could have been either Morris Malbin, a radiologist, or his brother Barney, an internist. See Ian C. MacMillan, *Permanente in the Northwest* (The Permanente Press, 2010).

MacMillan describes Egon and how he came to the group practice:

> In 1946 the Medical Group hired its first eye-ear-nose-and-throat (EENT) physician—Egon Ullman. In 1927 Ullman emigrated from Vienna where he had earned a reputation as a distinguished faculty lecturer at the University of Vienna. But he had become disillusioned, believing that Austria's socialist predilections were damaging the medical profession. And so he came to Oregon, accepting a position as special lecturer in biology and physiology at Oregon Agricultural College (now Oregon

State University). [. . .] During World War II, Ullman served as a colonel in the U.S. Air Force. At war's end, he sought an organized practice in Oregon. Although a man of science, Ullman, a dedicated bibliophile, was a lover of the arts, literature in particular. His considerable book collection included an autographed Mark Twain. Erudite and worldly, he loved Mozart, fine food and wine, and had a raconteur's talent for delighting friends and colleagues with stories. But Ullman was no effete; his wide-ranging interests included professional wrestling, whose heroes he likened to Roman gladiators. The day a friend introduced him to wrestler Gorgeous George was a cherished memory (p. 102).

Egon is listed among the twelve members of the original Kaiser Permanente partnership (p. 255). He was considered "something of an eccentric according to his contemporaries," but he was "admired for his prodigious work output" (p. 34).

page 56: "dancing lesson at Murphy's": Probably this was Arthur Murray's dance studio.

page 56: "Beauty is only skin deep . . .": The quotation, from Dorothy Parker, is "Beauty is only skin deep, but ugly goes clean to the bone."

page 57: "the cow Bonnie having been sold": At least in the final version of *The Peaceable Kingdom*, the cow Bonnie was not sold; but her calf, Beauty, was given away at a dramatic moment in the story (p. 207).

page 57: "at George's wedding": Ardyth described the Sterns' wedding in a letter to Lula and Marion the following Saturday, January 17 (see the Index of Names for identification of the people mentioned in Egon's and Ardyth's accounts of the wedding):

> Well, I will start right in at the beginning and tell you about the wedding and not stop to apologize for not writing sooner. [. . .] I worked like a dog to get everything ready—don't think we ever had it so nice. It was just as clean as a pin, the table was

made as big as it would go and all set beautifully, the house was filled up with white asters and lots of greenery, and I had white candles burning. [...]

Aunt Anna had written that they might come up, and I was so glad they did—she helped me so much, pouring coffee, standing by the buffet and helping to serve the cake. We had a great big wedding cake that was supposed to serve 100 people, Mrs. Stern and her sister made 4 cakes (2 like the one she brought to Aunt Laura's wedding and 2 white ones), about 100 of those little horned things like crescent moons and about 100 of another kind of cooky. And I made 2 cakes. And all that was left was about a fifth of the wedding cake!

There were a hundred and fifteen people here. Dr. and Mrs. Steinberg came, Adele and her husband (from Adele's restaurant)—they both asked after you and said to send you their regards—the Everetts, Ungar, his niece, newly arrived from New York, the manager of Young's Gown Shop, Pepel Kubin, his wife and son and one of the other Kubin boys. In fact, just everybody under the sun—Elspeth, her father, the Spitzers, etc. It was a wonderful success—everybody said so—I had so many telephone calls the next day that I was just swamped.

Did I tell you about the punch? I got the recipe directly from George Washington and everybody said no wonder we won the Rebellion. You take 3 bottles of rum, 2 bottles of brandy, 2¼ cups lemon juice, 2 cups thick sugar syrup (3 cups sugar boiled up with very little water) and 16 ounces of peach liqueur and put it in a bowl with a chunk of ice. Add 5 bottles of champagne and 5 bottles of sparkling burgundy. Man, oh, man. You get to feeling like a helicopter. Even Uncle George's hair stood right on end.

Well, we were the merriest old souls you ever saw. Mr. Berger had to make a few forced landings because of the altitude, but on the whole he zoomed around from flower to flower paying court to the ladies like Maeterlinck's bee. I myself got to feeling like a Woman of Distinction, but I see in Time magazine that scientific tests prove that the Irish get 74 times drunker than the Jews because of their cells or something, so that of course accounts for it.

Everybody said it was a wonderful party, not a bit like a wedding reception, and we all had so much fun. Mrs. Stern and George were as proud as could be of it all, and I've had about ten telephone calls from them since, about it.

The reception was very different from the wedding . . . Eva had a pretty cream-colored silk dress on, long white gloves, brown suede pumps, and George made her a fur coat (I can't understand why so ugly—made of uninhibited colt or something, in hot brown) and she had a little white half-hat with a line of gold around it. She's got a nice little figure. Well, George looked like the corpse of the world, just like he was laid out in his coffin. We went up to the apartment and here was Mrs. Stern and her sister in dead black, absolutely unrelieved by any color whatsoever. Mrs. S. didn't even want to wear a corsage, but I made her. Nobody said one word to anyone else . . . Egon and I had to do all the talking.

Well, we went to the Synagogue and it was cold and dark, nobody was there at all. Finally George scraped up the janitor or somebody from the basement, who let us in the library—ice cold, so that everybody's teeth chattered—and there we waited in that horrible ominous silence with nobody saying one word, because for some reason the synagogue even shut us up, Egon and me, and there we stood staring at each other while one of those big clocks like they have in schoolrooms ticktocked. Finally Egon said politely for God Almighty's sake why don't you call the Rabbi and find out what's the matter?—while I glared at him for taking the Lord's name in vain—however, he said it wasn't in vain, because then George called the Rabbi. And we made a mistake, all the time! We weren't supposed to go to the Synagogue. We were supposed to go to his house! So we went up there, to the famous Rabbi Berkowitz, and George and Eva were married in his library.

He lives in an absolute palace, and I must say that was one of the most beautiful rooms I have ever been in, in my life. I stood on one side, and Egon stood on the other, and the ceremony was very beautiful-sounding, wonderfully poetic. And then the Rabbi said the witnesses had to sign the wedding certificate, so of course I rolled up my sleeve and was going to put down my name with a flourish . . . but he gently ignored me, and George's Uncle Alfred, only, and Egon, were allowed to sign. I was bewildered, but found out later that among the Jews, the woman's signature means nothing, she has no standing whatever, so my being there was about the same as if Anne Boleyn had airily drifted in to watch the proceedings . . .

Afterwards, we took Mrs. Stern, the sister and Uncle Alfred home—it was then about 5:35— George and Eva went home also—and then Egon and I stopped in at Jack Cody's and grabbed ourselves some dinner, then went home. Uncle George and Aunt Anna were waiting out in front, had just arrived. We asked them to stay all night, but they left about nine-thirty. I have written her a little note thanking her for assisting as much as she did. She really was a wonderful help after they starting coming in in such hordes. I had Nanny stationed by the punch bowl—she was replaced later by Trudi, as there was some danger of her falling in— I put Lilly at the front door to let the guests in and direct them where to put their wraps. We had a reception line (Egon and I, according to etiquette, not acting merely as host and hostess but also taking the place of Eva's absent or non-existent parents) . . . first me, then Egon, then Mrs. Stern, then George, then Eva . . . but this wavered as the festivities waxed warmer, and soon, alas, the proxy mamma was being caught up in a Viennese whirl, that changed to a rhumba and then to a fox-trot, and she never went back to shake hands anymore but danced the whole evening with everybody but the guy what brung her . . .

They didn't leave for their honeymoon right away—in fact, rather tastelessly, I think, have worked all week. But they are leaving today for San Francisco. Mr. Ungar gave George a complete set of sterling for twelve and $150 a month raise [. . .]

The Hurlimans didn't come, so no colored pictures, but somebody else was taking pictures. I haven't seen them yet.

page 59: "To all things clergic . . .": The quotation is actually from Alexander Woollcott.

page 60: "a fellow by the name of Bob Blauer": Egon's handwriting is unclear, so "Blauer" is a guess. The sentence continues with "a furrier in George's dptmt," which presumably means "department."

page 60: "I comforted her . . .": From Song of Solomon 2:5: "Comfort me with apples, for I am sick of love." Ardyth explained the meaning of this phrase in the caption to her late-life collage titled "Comfort Me with Diamonds, for I Am Sick of Love": "'Sick of love' does not mean I have had it up to here with love. It means I have contracted the hot contagion of love. And diamonds is the coolingest thing in the world."

page 65: "How Mrs. Hansen baked cherry pie": "Mrs. Hansen" was likely Randine Hansen, a good friend of Lula's mother, Anna Olsen. Randine and her husband, Amund Hansen, were the inspiration for the story of Ingeborg and Gustave Jensen in *The Peaceable Kingdom*. The Peacocks were neighbors of the Parkers and Olsens in North Albany, but the woman who lived to be a hundred was more likely their neighbor Susan Austin, who indeed was an invalid late in her life and died in 1938 at the age of 101.

page 66: "the story of the manhunt for Booth": In spring 1948, Ardyth wrote to Marion: "Have got the next book all ready to go—not what I intended at all (as was going on with saga) but had authentic inspiration so will have to turn to and do it." On July 9, 1948, she wrote to Lula: "You wouldn't believe how hard I have been working. I expect to start writing *Black Easter* about August 1st."

page 66: "an apartment on Montgomery Street": This was at 1626 SW Montgomery.

page 67: "Charms and simples": These were probably some kind of wall hangings that Ardyth made or bought. A photograph of the bathroom in another of the couple's residences (probably 1103 NW 21st Ave.) shows a hanging titled "Simples" (medicinal herbs) and illustrating, apparently, "Perdita's simple cupboard," as described in Richard Le Gallienne's book *An Old Country House* (1902, pp. 104–7). The hanging portrays shelves of decorative bottles with labels such as "Wine of Marigolds to Inspire Love."

page 68: "helped Ardyth writing her second book": The *Oregonian* of February 8, 1953, has a photo of Ardyth holding Violet (Gretchen Grondahl, "Tellers of Tales," sec. 3, p. 1).

page 68: "a letter arrived from H.M.": In an undated letter to Lula ("dearest little fellow-author"), Ardyth transcribed the letter ("that made us so happy") from Dorothy de Santillana of Houghton Mifflin:

> Dear Miss Kennelly:
> Your letter has given me almost as much pleasure as your book, and now maybe I can return some of the pleasure of both.
> Houghton Mifflin Company to a body wish to publish your novel, and we are offering the following terms: An advance of $500, payable on the signing of the agreement, against a royalty of 10 percent of the list price of the book (that means the bookstore price) to 5000 copies, 12½ percent to 10,000 copies and 15 percent thereafter.
> If you let me know whether this meets with your approval I will have the contracts made out and send them on for your signature.
> Please tell your mother from me that you did

indeed write your book "like a big author." With best wishes,

    Sincerely yours,
    Mrs. G. D. de Santillana, Managing Editor

It was expected that Ardyth would receive between $75,000 and $125,000 for the book. (Ianthe Smith, "Authoress of Best Seller Former Albany Resident," *Albany Democrat-Herald*, November 12, 1949, p. 4.)

page 69: "Ardyth likes that young, proud, Catholic Florentine now": Ardyth confessed to Marion in a letter of December 13, 1948—and in several more letters the following spring—how she was trying to "win" Nello Spada, an instructor at the University of Portland and the Italian consul in Portland. Ardyth speculated that it was because he reminded her of her father, on whom she had had "such a case," and because as a five-year-old she had been in love with her Aunt Laura's Italian husband Fedele "Fred" Cerra.

page 69: "a Reed student, Falbo": Ernest Salvatore Falbo graduated from Reed College and in 1949 received a Fulbright scholarship to Italy to study nineteenth-century Italian poets. "A literature and language major at Reed, Falbo studied Italian authors independently and wrote the first Reed thesis in Italian." ("Reed Graduate Gets Fellowship," *Oregonian*, December 4, 1949, p. 9.)

page 70: "Ardyth would go down to Santa Monica": Lula was living in Santa Monica, California, at the time. Apparently, Ardyth also sought refuge from phone calls while finishing *Good Morning, Young Lady* in early 1952. Although Egon's journal skips from July 1951 to July 1952, the *Albany Democrat-Herald* of January 26, 1952 (p. 6), referencing "a note in the New York Times," reports that "Miss Kennelly has gone into seclusion to finish her newest book which is scheduled for delivery to the publishers in February." Another, undated clipping from around the same time quotes Egon as saying that Ardyth is "'somewhere' up in Washington state in seclusion until her new book is finished."

page 71: "Dr. George's New Year's Egg Nog afternoon": Roger George, a colleague of Egon's at Kaiser Permanente, was Chief of Obstetrics and Gynecology. (MacMillan, *Permanente in the Northwest*, p. 34.)

page 71: "Professor Woodbridge": Probably Benjamin Mather Woodbridge Sr., a professor of Romance languages at Reed College from 1922 to 1952. (Obituary for Benjamin Mather Woodbridge Jr. in *Reed* magazine, August 2007.)

page 73: "Ardyth put the finis to the Booth": Ardyth's letter of Saturday, February 5, 1949, to her mother says, "I just finished the book five minutes ago," so either Ardyth or Egon got the date wrong. Ardyth's letter continued, "I haven't the faintest idea whether the thing is good or bad, it doesn't seem like it could be good, to be written so quick. [. . .] I can say without lying it was the damnedest hardest job I ever did in my life."

page 74: "a letter from Diggory Venn": Richard H. "Diggory" Venn was the public relations director for Houghton Mifflin. The pictures requested would have been for the jacket of *The Peaceable Kingdom*, which was then in production.

page 74: "the pictures which Kassowitz made": Ernst Kassowitz (1888–1985) emigrated from Vienna to the United States in 1935; he had a photography studio in Portland in 1937 (according to the city directory) but by 1940 had moved his studio to Seattle.

page 74: "Dr. MacRae, Dr. Jones . . .": These professors were likely Donald MacRae, English, Reed College, 1944–73; Richard Hutton Jones, history, Reed College, 1941–82; John W. Scheberle, C.S.C., English, University of Portland, 1934–61; and Charles A. Lee, C.S.C., English and speech, University of Portland, from about 1938.

page 75: "Dr. Mossman": Frank Mossman began training with Egon in EENT at the Vancouver Permanente clinic in 1946. The next few years saw a serious division among the members of the Permanente Medical Group, with Egon siding with the conservative faction of physicians and Mossman with the progressive faction. (MacMillan, *Permanente in the Northwest*, pp. 39–43.)

page 75: "Mr. Potassio": Egon is likely referring to Mauro Potestio, a son of Italian immigrants; he graduated from the University of Portland in 1950 and had a career in education.

page 75: "Paul Brooks": Brooks was the editor-in-chief of the

General Books Department at Houghton Mifflin.

page 75: "stop the pain in her heart": In a letter of April 16, 1942, Ardyth—who seems to have suffered from depression and anxiety since her youth—tells Marion that she hasn't had "a black Irish mood for months," and in a postscript says, "Dr. Evans would be amused to read this letter I see upon looking it over. All the ancient guilt here for having been born, all the eternal apology for the crime of living, all the passionate longing to do better!"

page 76: "a syndicated article on anonymous photographs": The St. Louis *Globe-Democrat* of January 1, 1950, under the headline "Imagination Is Funny" (p. 47), published six tintype photos of unknown people along with life stories that Ardyth made up for the subjects of two of the photos. Readers were invited to "join in the hobby by making up their own versions of the other tintypes and comparing them with the author's."

page 76: "a place for Marion, Mother and the boys": Marion at that time had two children—Michael, age 12, and Timothy, age 9. Lula was usually living with either Ardyth or Marion.

page 77: "as soon as the Literary Guild pays": *The Peaceable Kingdom* was the Literary Guild selection for December 1949. Ardyth wrote in her memoir of her two years in New York City in 1963–64 (forthcoming from Sunnycroft Books): "In the forties and even quite a while later, there were only two book clubs in America, the Book of the Month Club and the Literary Guild, and in Portland amongst our bookish cohorts the one that gave you the brownie points was the former. The Literary Guild was a great deal better than a poke in the eye with a sharp stick, of course, but not something that because of, you could throw your weight around."

page 77: "Ardyth Kennelly Day": On December 13, 1949, Ardyth autographed *The Peaceable Kingdom* at a "silver tea" in Albany, arranged by the Albany Women's Club. She was also honored at a luncheon with the Albany Chamber of Commerce board. More than 500 people attended the "autographing tea," and Ardyth donated her royalties ($250) to a fund to build the Albany Memorial Stadium. ("Author C. of C.'s Guest," *Albany Democrat-Herald*, December 14, 1949, p. 1; "500 Attend Benefit Tea Here Featuring

Ardyth Kennelly," *Greater Oregon*, December 16, 1949, p. 4; "Authoress Gives Stadium Money," *Albany Democrat-Herald*, March 24, 1950, p. 1.) A second "autographing tea," again sponsored by the Albany Women's Club, was held November 12, 1956, after the publication of Ardyth's fifth novel, *Marry Me, Carry Me*. ("Ardyth Kennelly Honored at Autograph Tea," *Albany Democrat-Herald*, November 17, 1956, p. 4.)

page 77: "I am still plowing through Parrington's *Main Trends*": The title of Vernon Parrington's history, published in 1927, is *Main Currents in American Thought*.

page 79: "the horseback party at Borghild's": This probably refers to Borghild Lundberg Lee, a Norwegian immigrant and poet living in Portland at the time.

page 81: "I have to ask Mrs. Bristol why": Edith L. Bristol was manager of the book department at J. K. Gill in downtown Portland from 1925 through the 1950s, according to her obituary in the *Oregonian* (April 26, 1983).

page 82: "when I was in Claremont": See note to p. 39.

page 83: "a gentleman and his wife": The couple must have been Dr. Stefan (Stephen) Simon Kien (1862–1961) and Ella Rosenfeld Kien. Their son was George Kien (1903–1986).

page 84: "the *N.Y. Times, Harper's* and *The Atlantic* ignore the book": In fact, the *New York Times Book Review* published a review of Ardyth's "intensely human story" on November 13, 1949 (p. 56). Dozens of favorable reviews were published in major newspapers in the next several weeks; and Ardyth received a brief profile in *Life* magazine in the January 30, 1950, issue ("Four New Writers: Unknown Names Fill the Publishers' Lists," p. 35).

page 87: "cobwebs obtained from Florida": Ardyth extensively redecorated the duplex purchased in 1950 with money she earned from *The Peaceable Kingdom*, and in late 1954 she undertook another remodeling project (see Egon's entries for October 13, 1954, and January 18, 1955). She wrote an article to accompany photos of the couple's upstairs apartment that appeared in the April 1956 issue of the *Ladies' Home Journal*, titled "Just a House That Puts Its Arms Around You" (pp. 198–99). The "cobwebs" appear to be a wall decoration above some stairs; Ardyth's caption reads: "Our brass spider web was copied by a metalworker from a picture of an absolutely perfect web made by a spider doped with lysergic acid."

page 91: "she speaks of Dorney Leaf": This is the protagonist of Ardyth's novel *Good Morning, Young Lady*, published in 1953.

page 93: "we both believe in God": In the typescript, Ardyth wrote "?!" after this phrase, and again after the phrase "deeply religious," which is in line with her expressions in other contexts of her lack of conventional religious belief.

page 93: "Ardyth has begun her fourth novel": This is *Good Morning, Young Lady*, which was her third novel to be published (in 1953). She had written *Up Home*, a sequel to *The Peaceable Kingdom*, in presumably 1949–50, but it languished with Houghton Mifflin for more than three years until being serialized in the *Ladies' Home Journal* in 1955 (see Egon's entry for January 18, 1955).

page 94: "the Holbrooks": "Portland's Stewart Holbrook (1893–1964) became a leading American journalist and historian by writing what he called 'lowbrow' or 'non-stuffed shirt history.' His writings, sense of humor and social criticism also made him a sort of combination of Will Rogers, Mark Twain and H.L. Mencken for Portland and the Pacific Northwest." (Brian Booth, "Stewart Holbrook," Oregon Cultural Heritage Commission website, accessed April 3, 2023.) Bennett Cerf (1898–1971) was a publisher and founder of Random House; he was also known as a television personality and for his compilations of jokes and puns.

page 95: "Dr. O. Chambers": Othniel R. Chambers (1894–1951) was the head of Oregon State College's psychology department from 1929 to 1951.

page 95: "cowboy ballad of Wyoming": The traditional song "Goodbye, Old Paint" has many variations. The lines Egon quotes serve as the epigraph to *Good Morning, Young Lady*.

page 98: "See's candies": Egon wrote "Susi's candies," but he no doubt meant See's candies, a well-known favorite of Ardyth's.

page 98: "edited by Mark Van Doren": The 1951 edition of Dickinson's letters was edited by Mabel Loomis Todd, with an introduction by Mark Van Doren.

page 98: "How strange . . .": Egon is paraphrasing Dickinson's lines.

page 99: "Mary Drayton": The playwright Mary Drayton's dramatization of *The Peaceable Kingdom*, starring Teresa Wright and titled *Salt of the Earth*, was performed March 13–15, 1952, at the Shubert Theatre in New Haven, Connecticut; after unfavorable reviews, it closed at the Wilbur Theatre in Boston only a week later, never making it to its anticipated April 3 premiere on Broadway. See *Record-Journal* (Meriden, Conn.), March 1, 1952, p. 5; "Opening," *Boston Globe*, March 16, 1952, p. 44; "Theater Notes," *Brooklyn Daily Eagle*, March 13, 1952, p. 11; and *Boston Globe*, March 22, 1952, p. 16 (which advertised the "last 2 times" for the play at the Wilbur Theatre). The play was rewritten and performed the next year, under the title *Second Fiddle*, at the Westport, Connecticut, Country Playhouse in June; at the Pocono Playhouse in Mountainhome, Pennsylvania, in July; and at the Cape Playhouse in Dennis, Massachusetts, in August. See "Betty Field Stars in Mormon Comedy," *New York Times*, June 2, 1953, p. 35; "The Curtain Rises," *Morning Call* (Allentown, Penn.), July 12, 1953, p. 30; "'Grundy' Readied for Upstate Test," *Daily News* (New York, N.Y.), July 23, 1953, p. 59.

Ardyth's book *The Spur* was also dramatized, airing on NBC's Philco Television Playhouse on September 23, 1951. See the IMDb listing, at www.imdb.com/title/tt0674449, accessed June 21, 2023.

page 99: "'Her' story being played on Broadway": "Her" refers to Lula (as Ardyth clarified by adding "Mother's" above this line in the typescript). *The Peaceable Kingdom*'s main character is Linnea Ecklund, a midwife and a second wife in polygamy, both of which Ardyth's maternal grandmother indeed was. One of Linnea's children, Gertrude, is based on Ardyth's mother.

page 100: "was never loved by his mother": In a letter of February 18, 1987, to her cousin Francis Olsen, Ardyth wrote that Jimmy and Grace were "never appreciated, understood, loved or helped enough, either one of them, poor kids."

page 101: "she ran away with an Italian barber": Grace married Peter "Pete" Sciara in 1919.

page 101: "Grace suddenly turned up in Portland": This was not unplanned, as Egon apparently thought. Ardyth wrote to Marion in California, around the time of Ardyth and Egon's marriage in October 1940, that she had been corresponding with Grace and wanted to bring her to live with herself and Egon in Portland, and take care of her for the rest of her life. Ardyth remembered Grace fondly from her childhood, as the one whose hand "first guided my hand in the forming of letters A, B, C, D, E. I could always read, I'm sure, even before I went to school—somebody, she, must have taught me. From my first consciousness she was my great kind clumsy-footed friend than whom I was always one year older, even at five and six." Grace had been Ardyth's "constant companion (save for you) until I was nine years old and I'm sure she did nothing but *foster* whatever potentialities I may have had or have now—not knowingly, but with a blind forbearance."

However, Ardyth felt it would be "unfair" to Egon (who had, like her Grandma Olsen, "a horror of ugliness and stupidity") to ask him to live with Grace as she was—"dirty, fat, frowsy beyond description, unutterably vulgar and with a mentality of not more than eight years." Ardyth asked Marion to take Grace (who was presumably also living in California) for six months in order to "help me camoflage that ugliness and stupidity, make it less blatant, so that when she came here, life with her would be endurable for him."

When Grace arrived in Portland in early 1941, Ardyth and Lula secretly put her up at the YWCA for a few days. They got Grace some new clothes, and Ardyth was happy with how she looked (except for her teeth). Ardyth wrote to Marion, "Egon seems entirely undisturbed by her presence. [. . .] He told me in confidence that he was glad to see such a vast difference in types produced in one small family, both in physique, mental powers, etc. He said it was that kind of family where each child could be called a distinct type and completely unlike the other that could produce a genius. (Forgive careless grammar.) I didn't go into it and ask him whether he meant Grace, Jimmy, you or me but presume he meant me as he is still rationalizing our marriage and is pathetically insistent, for his own ego's sake, that I am a veritable Titan of intellect!"

page 101: "no one has ever heard of her": Grace's fate after she left Portland has remained unknown to the family.

page 101: "Then came Ardyth": Egon typed these words in red ink.

page 102: "the Ice follicles": Egon no doubt meant the Ice Follies, a touring ice show.

page 104: "*Letters and Literary Correspondence* . . ." The actual title is *The Literary Life and Correspondence of the Countess of Blessington* (published in 1855).

page 104: "I can never be real fond of it": Following this sentence in the transcription of the journal, Ardyth wrote "??!" In Egon's original journal, the sentence ends at the bottom of the page; Ardyth wrote immediately below it, continuing on the reverse side of the sheet: "Egon: So many of your statements about me are NOT TRUE—especially when you say I have said something. I never ONCE have said what you said I said—it's all LIES. If I should die before you, don't ever publish a word of your 'Boswellian' rambling (my God, was he as inaccurate as you? it scares me) about me, because if you do, I'll *haunt* you. Boo! Love & kisses, Ardyth Kennelly. Oct. 26, 1953." Under Ardyth's message, Egon wrote: "Ardyth: Maybe I can't remember every word. But I could *almost* tell what words passed, if not quite. Yet I have not put onto these pages, Ardyth, a single thing that I have not actually, whole and real, in my memory. What remains there must be the essential truth for *me*, no matter how slight it may turn out to be. Don't you think that all that was not ours finally escapes us? I do. I always mistrust, in written or recounted memories, those long, interesting conversations that we sometimes enjoy very much. Because talk, real talk between people, is as unexpected and surprising to them as it is uttered as any moment in nature. It flows through one like wind. One simply *cannot remember* one's own real talk. One cannot remember the quick, evanescent, exact movements of one's own independent soul. The most one can do is to recall the general feeling or mood of a long conversation in after years. Love and more kisses, Egon." Egon added alongside his paragraph: "When I saw this note of you first: August 26, 1955." Almost forty years later, Ardyth wrote "Sorry, sweetheart" alongside Egon's paragraph, and one final note on the original journal page: "June 18, 1992— I take this note all back—he didn't really lie— This is more or less how it was— Now I'm 80 and still after 30 years can hardly bear it without him. His 'weibchen.'"

page 105: "The relationship between the two": In a letter to Marion of April 16, 1942, Ardyth explains at least one of her reasons for wanting to please her mother: "It's because she won't wear her lower teeth I can deny her nothing, I look at her and remember Jean Starr Untermeyer's 'Autumn (To My Mother),' I feel a bitter guilt for all maidens grown old, as though I myself had allowed the devastation, the pretty dulled hair, the easy tears, the fierce reminiscent sentimentality, the sorry little gums. And then I can't do enough to make up for it. It's the same with you, Marion. I read it in your letters, your concern, our twin wishes to buy a banana split, a stamp, a show, 'a little turban,' with grocery money, stocking money, no money, to beg her forgiveness, to buy the forgiveness of every lady rose-colored once, yellowing now, for the lost stupendous heartbeat, frittered lover, discarded kiss. Humbled curls, and sweethearts deep in the ground cost 'a thousand pounds a minute,' like the passengers said to Alice in Through the Looking Glass." In the same vein, she wrote: "Remember how I cried because Kenneth had to have his first molar filled? That was the symbol of all my grief—the golden lads and girls coming to dust before my very eyes."

page 105: "In yesterday's Sunday magazine section": The photos Egon refers to accompanied a short article by Nancy Bedingfield, "Platter Parties" (*Oregonian*, April 29, 1951, sec. 3, p. 1). Dr. Richard Steiner was a Unitarian minister in Portland.

page 108: "I hate them like I hate my blood vessels": In the margin of the original journal page, Ardyth wrote, "Not true," and in the margin of the typescript she drew a line beside this sentence and wrote "never said."

page 109: "the Winsor girl": The protagonist of Kathleen Winsor's semi-autobiographical novel *Star Money* (1950) is a woman who struggles with self-doubt and other personal problems despite

Notes

having had overnight success with her first novel—as Winsor did with her 1944 book *Forever Amber* and Ardyth did with *The Peaceable Kingdom*.

page 109: "the son of the owner": Heinrich Walter Skrein's father was Stephan Skrein, a journalist and editor who worked for (but did not own) the *Wiener Allgemeine Zeitung*, among other publications.

page 115: "Ardyth full of plans for fifth book": *Marry Me, Carry Me* was Ardyth's fifth book. *The Unwilling Hyacinth*, mentioned in Egon's next entry (July 20, 1952), was presumably its working title.

page 116: "Mr. Forsyth's office": This was probably the lawyer James P. Forsyth, Jr.

page 116: "letter to Egon's cousin Claire Bunzell": This letter is an original, typed page with Egon's handwritten signature, but it's unknown whether this was a letter that was never mailed, a second copy, or perhaps a translation from German for Ardyth. Nor is it clear why Egon stated that the date was "Sunday the 16th of May" but handwrote "3rd April 1954" at the top.

page 116: "About three weeks ago": Here Ardyth wrote in the margin of the typescript, "Trying to deal with so-called writer's block —but it wasn't that—the 'talent' just ran out."

page 116: "a burning city at night": Possibly this refers to the fire resulting from the 1906 San Francisco earthquake, which Ardyth describes in *Marry Me, Carry Me*.

page 119: "*The Sky Is Not Cloudy All Day*": This was likely a working title for *Marry Me, Carry Me*.

page 120: "The departure of Byron . . .": This is probably Egon's own translation of a passage from Heinrich Heine's letter of June 25, 1824, to Moses Moser.

page 120: "It is easy to work . . .": These lines are by Emily Dickinson.

page 120: "Charlotte Mish has begun painting Ardyth": The *Oregonian* of February 20, 1955 (p. 9), noted that the portrait of Ardyth had just been completed.

page 120: "Charlotte Mish and Graziella Boucher": Charlotte Mish (1896–1974) was a well-known Portland artist who had worked in the WPA's Depression-era Federal Art Project in Portland (and once painted Ardyth's cat, Violet). Together with her cousin Graziella Boucher, a fervent animal-welfare activist, she founded the Animal Defenders League of Portland in 1957. (Early Deane, "Ageless Champion of Animals 'Bones' Up Officials on Needs," *Oregonian*, May 21, 1978, p. 1.)

page 122: "the Ullmans flew to Las Vegas": Margarethe and her new husband, a film comedy writer, lived in Hollywood. (Elwood Ullman was apparently no relation to Egon.)

page 122: "*Up Home* is appearing": The book was published on September 8, 1955. Houghton Mifflin reported that as of that date, *The Peaceable Kingdom* had sold more than 450,000 copies, while *Good Morning, Young Lady* had sold 349,849 copies; both of these books were selections of the Literary Guild. (Charles Alexander, "Albany Author, 799,849 Copies," *Albany Democrat-Herald*, September 10, 1955, p. 7.)

page 122: "*Albrecht von Graefe: The Man in His Time*": Egon's 55-page article was published in the *American Journal of Ophthalmology* in three parts, October–December 1954. Egon, as both a medical doctor and a scholar of literature, began the biography with a quotation from Balzac. Given the native fluency and liveliness of the writing, Ardyth may well have helped Egon write it. In a letter to Marion of September 8, 1940, she writes that she "helped Egon put the last touches to his re-written diet book to meet a deadline." (The book was *Diet in Sinus Infections and Colds*, originally published in 1933.)

page 122: "The first time in three and a half years": Lilly had moved with her daughter, Anna Alinde ("Nany"), to Los Angeles in December 1951; she worked there as a housekeeper, according to her 1953 petition for naturalization.

page 124: "the Grotto": A Catholic shrine in Northeast Portland with trails and gardens.

page 125: "How unimportant": Ardyth wrote "?!" here.

page 125: "the Goldsboroughs": John B. Goldsborough was a physician and also a photographer. He is credited with at least one of the photographs of the Ullmans' home in the April 1956 issue of the *Ladies' Home Journal* (see note to p. 87).

page 125: "he tried to appease me": It was not until the 1960s that interventions for heart attacks were developed. At the time of Egon's attack, only rest was prescribed, with morphine for pain relief.

page 127: "which had rejected her": In 1963, probably early May, Ardyth wrote from New York to her Portland literary friend Freddy Jacobson that New York was "the one place where—in all my life—I haven't felt like an exile, a displaced person. [. . .] now I realize Portland was like a cold, forbidding stepmother—gave me a roof over my head, enough to eat—even vitamins—but no love; and you could never please her."

page 127: "The Peacock and the Bride": This children's story was never published, and the manuscript did not survive—at least not past 1968, when it is mentioned in two letters to Ardyth from her correspondent Sybil Leek (May 13 and May 24, 1968).

page 128: "Simone de Beauvoir's *The Other Sex*": The correct title is *The Second Sex*.

page 128: "Not what the stars have done . . .": See note to p. 3.

page 128: "You know, today for the first time . . .": In the typescript, Ardyth wrote beside this sentence, "I can't imagine saying such a thing."

page 129: "Read during my illness": This list appears to have been written out (by hand) all at once; possibly it is a rewritten copy of a list that Egon started on August 13 (thus the date at the top) and added to through September.

page 129: "*Cybernetics . . . Self Search*": The correct title of Wiener's book is *The Human Use of Human Beings: Cybernetics and Society*; Reik's books are *The Haunting Melody* and *The Search Within*.

page 130: "Our need of achievement . . . is so great": Ardyth wrote "never!" beside these lines in the typescript.

page 131: "Alice Iltz": The 1956 Portland city directory lists Clarence and Alice Iltz at 2473 NW Northrup, so this couple must have been either renting the other half of Ardyth and Egon's duplex, or living right next door.

page 131: "I never, never saw her as flushed with success": Following this sentence, Ardyth wrote in the typescript, "True. The triumph of my life."

page 131: "That is why she *never* thinks of herself as *literary*": Ardyth wrote beside this sentence, "Thank you, darling."

page 132: "President Eisenhower's attack": Egon apparently got the date of this entry (September 23) wrong, as Eisenhower's heart attack was not until September 24.

page 133: "The subject was her future plans with writing": In the typescript, Ardyth wrote beside this paragraph, "Spinning my wheels."

page 133: "In fact, I shall put up as my motto . . .": In the typescript, Ardyth wrote here "Never did I say this."

page 134: "without analyzing myself and without much self-observation": In the typescript, Ardyth wrote here, "Thank God."

page 134: "Beauty Is Only": This, along with "Uncle Sam" (mentioned in Egon's entry for December 16, 1955), is another story that was never published and did not survive.

page 135: "My cousin Ernesto Rosenthal": Sometime in the late 1950s, after the death of Ernesto's wife in spring 1956 (see Egon's entry for April 3, 1956), Ernesto visited the Ullmans in Portland. Ardyth saw him again in New York City in 1964, when they went to the World's Fair together. In her memoir about her two years in New York (forthcoming from Sunnycroft Books), Ardyth tells the story—which she heard second-hand—of what happened when Ernesto and his business partner found the last woman left in the sultan's deserted harem in Constantinople around 1921.

page 136: "Michael's triumph": In the typescript, Ardyth added "Won Nat. prize for (High School) essay." In May 1956, Ardyth's nephew Michael Massee, representing Seattle's Franklin High School, won the national high school championship in the Hearst Newspapers' Tournament of Orators. ("Bassler Nosed Out for Title in National Oratorical Contest," *Asbury Park Press* [N. J.], May 17, 1956, p. 17.)

page 137: "I am sympathetic only with the dead artist": In the typescript, beside the rest of this paragraph, Ardyth wrote "Not."

page 138: "William Moyes": Bill Moyes wrote a radio-TV and local-gossip column, "Behind the Mike," for the *Oregonian* newspaper for many years, occasionally mentioning Ardyth and Egon; but by this time (1956), Moyes was writing for the *Oregon Journal*. The final title of the April 1956 *Ladies' Home Journal* article showing Ardyth's decoration of their home was "Just a House That Puts Its Arms Around You."

page 140: "and was finished on February 16, 1957": Egon added this and the remainder of the sentence at a later date, as indicated by his handwritten words on the otherwise typewritten page.

page 140: "We went to see Paul Petri": Paul Petri was formerly the director of the School of Music at Oregon State College. His wife, Lillian, had died the previous year.

page 148: "a medical convention being held": The International Congress of Ophthalmology met September 12–17, 1954, in New York City. ("World Eye Specialists to Meet at Waldorf," New York *Daily News*, September 12, 1954, p. 11M.) Helen Keller spoke at one of the dinners (see her speech in the Helen Keller Archive at www.afb.org/HelenKellerArchive, accessed June 23, 2023). The Ullmans' trip east lasted about six weeks, from late August to mid-October.

page 148: "like I would never work again": Ardyth in fact never stopped writing, but she did not find a publisher again during her lifetime. Her 1963–64 letters from New York City to Freddy Jacobson in Portland mention her attempts—apparently none of them successful—to sell her work there, through her agent Theron Raines.

In the late 1960s, Ardyth destroyed a number of her manuscripts. The only ones known to have survived from (probably) that decade are a novel of "millionaire housekeeping," set in New York City in the early twentieth century, which she titled *Promoting the Elegant Conduct of a Grand Private Residence* (forthcoming from Sunnycroft Books); and two chapters, dealing with Lord Byron and the Austrian empress Elisabeth, of a book on the history of dieting—at one point probably called *Weighty Matters*, a title mentioned in Ardyth's letter of July 26, 1964, to Freddy.

From 1977 to 1994, Ardyth wrote her greatest novel, *Variation West*, published in 2014 by Sunnycroft Books. In 1992 she finished a book-length "history of the world" and also wrote the current memoir. In 2001 she wrote another memoir, of her 1963–64 sojourn in New York City. One of her last significant writings was the outline of a dark-humor play titled "Last Rites for Barbie," sent in a letter of April 8, 1996, to her friend Brian Booth, a Portland lawyer and founder of the Oregon Institute of Literary Arts.

page 149: "more dull and baffled than before": This is the last line of H. Phelps Putnam's poem "Ballad of a Strange Thing," from which Ardyth also quoted on pages 30–31.

page 153: "first fine careless rapture": From Robert Browning's "Home-Thoughts, from Abroad."

page 156: "An African Grey parrot": Sometime in the later 1960s, Ardyth did acquire an African Grey parrot, which she named Mojo. (See Barbara Jordan, "Parrot's Idiosyncrasies Please Pet Owner," *Oregonian*, March 14, 1973, sec. 2, p. 1.)

page 164: "The first time I ever saw Egon": This was probably near the beginning of 1931. The Albany newspaper *Greater Oregon* noted on February 6, 1931 (p. 2), that Ardyth, who had been "seriously ill with sinus trouble," had returned to the college several days earlier; but the March 13 issue (p. 3) states that although she was now improving, she had been absent from school since the beginning of the term. Ardyth's college transcript shows that she withdrew from the winter term on February 11.

page 168: "someone's poem in Untermeyer's anthology": The poem "Rain at Night" is by Helen Hoyt.

page 168: "on Groundhog Day in 1962 he died": One of Egon's colleagues found him "slumped over his desk in his second floor office at Bess Kaiser Hospital. Cardiologist John Wild tried to resuscitate him without success." MacMillan, *Permanente in the Northwest*, p. 103.

page 170: "Clyde Peacock's corner field": The dig at Peacock's Corner (as the field was known to local people) began in March 1923, when Ardyth was almost eleven. The Peacock property was only a short walk from where Ardyth was presumably living at the time, the home of her uncle George R. Olsen on North Albany Road. Before the flood-control dams were built on the Willamette River tributaries in the 1950s, the river regularly flooded up to Peacock's Corner. (See "New Evidence of Ancient Race Is Found near City," *Albany Daily Democrat*, March 21, 1923, p. 1.)

page 173: "laying out a graveyard": This is Willamette Memorial Park in Millersburg, just north of Albany.

page 173: "Mr. and Mrs. Gregory and their five children": Arthur D. and Edith Self Gregory, immigrants from England, were close neighbors of the Parker, Kennelly, and Olsen families in North Albany; but by 1924 the Gregorys had moved to Millersburg.

page 179: "when the news helicopter flew over": Ardyth's typescript read "when the *Oregonian*'s helicopter flew over"; but there does not appear to have been any such incident reported in the *Oregonian*, and it seems unlikely that a newspaper would have published a photo of a suicide victim. Possibly Ardyth heard such a story elsewhere and mixed fact with fiction here (as she did in the story of Tupso and Mountstuart Elphinstone). Perhaps only coincidentally, Ardyth, at the time she was writing this memoir, lived in a downtown apartment building in Portland (1331 SW 12th Avenue) that has four floors and what appears to be a flat roof.

page 183: "I never got back on track with the writing": In a 1986 letter to Freddy, Ardyth wrote: "Even though it's been so long I still have a hard time working without Egon to ward everyone off, do the grocery shopping, answer the phone & all he used to do, bring home books, be my dear companion etc.—spoil me." See also note to p. 148.

page 183: "Egon is still taking care of me": Ardyth received Egon's military pension after he died.

page 183: "Hardly anything is left": In a letter to Freddy of early May 1963, Ardyth wrote from New York that she was flying home to Portland, but "it's only to sell the house, car, books & everything except a few keepsakes." On December 24 of that year, she wrote to him, "I felt sorry not to go through the book-burning *with* anybody (except Ruby's Wesley who helped start the fire, then had chores to do) & have our gay Walpurgis night, but doing it in one of the home fields [near her childhood home in North Albany], over the old gully, down by the grape patch, I realized I'd have about burst, trying to be merry & hostessy—for it was a sad, sad thing—my tears nearly put out the fire—all those days & years, Egon's & mine, all our hopes & schemes—well, you can imagine what I was thinking as the fire burned. Now I know why the devil always carries a pitchfork. It was a hard job (physically) & took more than an hour of assiduous tending. And big ashes blew about as big as big black leaves off some mournful tree & when it was all over it just looked like a place where some hoboes had gathered to warm themselves & make some coffee & then move on & I guess that's all the whole thing really was from beginning to end."

page 183: "I made thirteen collages": Ardyth continued making large collages and mixed-media pieces for years. Her work was exhibited in Portland at the Elizabeth Leach Gallery in 1996 and the Mark Woolley Gallery in 2000. (See Randy Gragg, "Reclusive Raconteur," *Oregonian*, July 21, 1996, p. F1.)

page 184: "there won't have been a funeral": A memorial gathering for family was held in Albany shortly after Ardyth's death on January 19, 2005.

Index of Names

The following list identifies some of the persons mentioned in Ardyth's memoir or Egon's journal. Much of the biographical information comes from records found on Ancestry.com and from historical newspapers, as well as family records.

Adele: *see* Nussbaum, Adele.

Aunt Anna: *see under* Olsen, George.

Aunt Fanny: Fanny (Olsen) Clive (1880–1972) was one of Ardyth's maternal aunts. *p. 37*

Aunt Laura: Laura (Olsen) Jackson (1884–1977) was one of Ardyth's maternal aunts. Her fourth marriage, to Robert Lee Humphrey, took place in Portland in 1947. *pp. 37, 100, 102, 132, 169, 201, 206*

Aunt Tekla: Tekla (Olsen) Hogge (1894–1992) was one of Ardyth's maternal aunts. *pp. 71, 105*

Berkowitz, Rabbi Henry J.: He served as rabbi at Temple Beth Israel in Portland from 1928 to 1949. *pp. 58–59, 202–3*

Bright, Verne (1893–1977): An Oregon poet, newspaper reporter, and English teacher. *pp. 92, 100*

Bunzell, Claire (Clara) Elizabeth Ullmann: Egon's first cousin on his father's side. Claire (1889–1973) emigrated to the United States in December 1940 with her husband, Emil Bunzel (1880–1969), who at the time of his naturalization in 1947 changed his name to Emil Fredrick Bunzell. The couple owned a grocery in southeast Portland and later moved to Los Angeles. *pp. 57, 63–64, 116–17, 215*

   Claire and Emil's daughter, Marietta, studied at Reed College in Portland and married the anthropologist Robert Francis

Spencer. The couple lived in Minnesota, where she became a pioneering social worker in the field of post-adoption services. (See her obituary by Chris Serres, "A Native of Austria, She Worked to Change Adoption in the U.S.," Minneapolis *Star-Tribune*, April 25, 2017, p. B4.) *pp. 105, 117, 133*

Claire: *see* Bunzell, Claire.

"Daddy": *see* Kennelly, James Daniel.

Devers, Eva: George Stern's bride. She was born Eva Deutsch in Breslau, Germany, in 1917; she emigrated to El Salvador in 1938 and came to the United States in 1941. *pp. 54, 57–60, 202–4*

Eisinger, Paul and Gertrud ("Trudi"): Natives of Vienna who arrived in the United States in December 1939; they are listed in the 1940 census as living in the "Jewish refugee colony" with Moritz Eisinger and other relatives (see note to p. 31 about the Cedarbrook dairy farm). Paul's 1945 petition for naturalization gives his occupation as "office clerk." *pp. 116, 117, 193, 203*

Emil: *see under* Bunzell, Claire.

Eva: *see* Devers, Eva.

Everetts: Ardyth's dentist, Frank G. Everett, and his wife, Leonie. He had changed his name from Franz Ehrenfest, presumably sometime after emigrating from Vienna in 1939. *pp. 105, 201*

Freddy: *see* Jacobson, Frederic.

George: *see* Stern, George; *or* Olsen, George.

Gibbs, Howard Scott: Ardyth's friend from Albany, whom she married December 11, 1935, and divorced January 25, 1940. Howard, an artist, died in September 1977, at the age of 66. *pp. 3, 10–17, 35, 41, 50–51, 105, 112, 189*

Goldsborough, John Bayman and Hazel: John (or Jon) Goldsborough (1913–1977) was a physician and also a photographer. He was born in Illinois, but the couple was living in Portland by 1953. *pp. 125, 126, 147, 166, 217*

Grace: *see* Kennelly, Grace.

Index of Names 225

Holbrook, Stewart and Sybil: Stewart Holbrook (1893–1964) was a popular journalist and an author of "lowbrow" Northwest history. *pp. 94–95, 97–98, 115, 210*

Howard: *see* Gibbs, Howard.

Hurlimann, Max: A Swiss émigré of 1929 who worked at the Eastman Kodak Company. He retired in about 1959 and then volunteered in the print shop of the University of Oregon Health Sciences Center, until 1978. ("Co-workers Honor 'Late Bloomer,'" *Oregonian*, July 29, 1978, p. A9.) *p. 204*

Jacobson, Frederic "Freddy" Oral: Freddy (1916–1990) was a literary friend of Ardyth's, although according to Ardyth's family members, he was often quite critical of her work. He was a postal clerk, an aspiring poet, and a book collector. His mother was Mary "Mamie" Barlow Jacobson (c. 1883–1964). *pp. 51–52, 54–55, 60, 70, 73, 74, 79, 95, 99–100, 102, 103, 105, 137, 199*

Jimmy: *see* Kennelly, James Arthur.

Kennelly, Grace Lulu: Ardyth's older sister, born March 17, 1903; died sometime after 1940. Her married name was Sciara. *pp. 41, 101, 190, 211–13*

Kennelly, James Arthur (Jimmy): Ardyth's older brother, born February 18, 1901; died June 20, 1977. *pp. 41, 100–101, 211–12*

Kennelly, James Daniel (in full, James Daniel Thomas Aquinas Kennelly): Ardyth's father, born January 16, 1880, in Salt Lake City; died in a work accident on April 21, 1921. *pp. 7, 21, 38, 41, 64, 175–76, 181, 187, 188, 190*

Kennelly, Laura Marion (known as Marion): Ardyth's younger sister, born April 12, 1915, in Albany, Oregon; died November 12, 2011, in Vancouver, Washington. Marion's married names were, successively, Pettibone, Massee, Arbury, and Brownell. *pp. 2, 3, 36, 37, 41, 46, 64, 72, 76, 77, 82, 85, 87, 88, 91, 102, 116, 123, 133, 145, 173, 175, 187, 191, 198, 199, 208, 212, 214*

Kien, Stefan (Stephen) Simon (1862–1961): Born in Moravia, Stefan, a physician, immigrated to the United States in 1942 together with his wife, Ella Rosenfeld Kien; she was born in Vienna in 1880 and died in 1958. Their son, George, also a physician, was born in

Vienna in 1903 and immigrated to the United States in 1938; he died in Vancouver, Washington, in 1986. *pp. 83–84, 116, 209*

Kubin, Pepel: This was possibly a nickname for Josef Kubin, a brother of Egon's first wife, Margarethe. Josef, with his wife Hella (Helen) and son Karl, came to the United States as a refugee in late 1938 with Egon's help. They lived initially on the Cedarbrook dairy farm (see note to p. 31), along with Josef's brother Hans, sister Selma, and Selma's husband, Moritz Eisinger. *pp. 193, 201*

Laura: *see* Aunt Laura.

Lilly: *see* Von Flesch, Lilly.

Marietta: *see under* Bunzell, Claire.

Marion: *see* Kennelly, Laura Marion.

Mish, Charlotte (1896–1974): A Portland artist (painter) and, with her cousin Graziella Boucher, animal-rights activist. *pp. 120–21, 216*

"Mother": *see* Olsen, Lulu.

Nanny: *see under* Von Flesch, Lilly.

Nussbaum, Adele: The proprietor of Adele's Restaurant "arrived in Portland from Russia in 1914 with two brothers and opened Adele's Restaurant on SW Park a year later. . . . Adele's was a popular meeting place for Jews in the community." ("Series 1: Adele's Restaurant, 1915–1960," in collection "Oregon Jewish Businesses, 1840–2012," Oregon Jewish Museum and Center for Holocaust Education, Portland.) *p. 201*

Olsen, George Rudolph (1886–1975): Ardyth's maternal uncle, who lived very near Ardyth's childhood home in North Albany (the Parkers were at 820 North Albany Road, the Olsens at 1035 North Albany Road). George's second wife was Anna (Spjut) Olsen (1886–1961). *pp. 59, 65, 105, 173, 174, 187, 190, 201, 203, 221*

Olsen, Lulu "Lula" Amanda: Ardyth's mother, born March 18, 1882, in Echo, Utah; died July 13, 1966, in Albany, Oregon. Her first husband was James Daniel Kennelly, and her second husband (Ardyth's stepfather) was Hiram Parker. *pp. 1, 21, 35, 36–38, 39, 41, 44, 46, 56, 60–61, 65, 67, 70–73, 76, 82–83, 85, 87, 88, 92, 93, 99, 100–102, 105,*

109, 113, 115, 132, 148, 151, 157, 161–62, 163, 165, 173, 175, 177, 181, 187, 190, 191, 195–96, 197–98, 199, 206, 208, 212, 214

Parker, Hiram: Ardyth's stepfather, born June 7, 1867, in Plainview, Oregon; died January 20, 1940. He was a farmer and lumberman. *pp. 2, 41, 165, 176, 181, 187, 195–96*

Parker, Ruby Rebecca: Ardyth's stepsister, born June 6, 1908, in Scio, Oregon; died of cancer August 13, 1964. Ruby was also Ardyth's cousin-in-law, by virtue of having married Ardyth's cousin (George) Francis Olsen, the oldest son of George R. Olsen, in 1926. Ruby later divorced Francis and married Wesley Muller, in 1945. *pp. 3, 172–73, 183, 187, 222*

Petri, Paul and Lillian: Paul Petri (1877–1958) was director of the School of Music at Oregon State College. His wife, Lillian Jeffreys Petri (1877–1955), was a member of the music faculty. *pp. 39, 140, 196, 197, 219*

Ruby: *see* Parker, Ruby.

Spencer, Marietta and Robert: *see under* Bunzell, Claire.

Spitzers: Ernst Spitzer, a physician, and his wife Emma, an optometrist, both of whom were born in Vienna and emigrated to the United States in November 1938. *p. 201*

Steinberg, Dr. and Mrs.: These were probably the surgeon Joseph D. Sternberg and his wife Josephine. Joseph was born in Albany but living in Portland by 1910; his brother Albert remained in Albany through the 1930s as owner of the Albany Tanning Company and the Sternberg Saddlery. A 1940 letter of Ardyth to Marion mentions "Dr. Joseph Sternberg, Al Sternberg's brother." *p. 201*

Steiner, Richard M. and Deborah: Richard Steiner (1901–1975) was pastor of the First Unitarian Church in Portland from 1934 to 1966. *pp. 30, 105, 192, 214*

Stern, George (Georg): George Stern boarded with the Ullmans in 1940 and remained friends with them in later years. Born in Vienna in 1910, he was a third-generation furrier. He emigrated to the United States in August 1938, working first for Nicholas Ungar Furs and then for himself as a fur designer. He married Eva Devers (Eva Deutsch) on January 11, 1948, and Ardyth and Egon hosted their wedding reception. *pp. 54, 55, 57–60, 193, 200–204*

George's parents were Josef and Rosa (Pisker) Stern; they came to the United States in December 1940 and January 1941, respectively. Rosa's sister, Frieda, and Frieda's husband, Alfred Kann (Uncle Alfred), arrived in 1947. *pp. 57–60, 73, 201–3*

Stern, Mrs.: *see under* Stern, George.

Tekla: *see* Aunt Tekla.

Trudi: *see* Eisinger, Paul and Gertrud.

Ullmann, Karl: Egon's father, born 1860 in Habern, Bohemia (today Habry, Czech Republic); died 1940 in Vienna. *pp. 27, 34, 39, 83–84, 110–11, 158, 159, 180, 181, 192, 194*

Egon's mother was Gabriele Ella Rosauer, born 1869 in Vienna; died 1942 in Vienna. *pp. 69, 83, 110–11, 139, 162–63, 166–67, 192*

Uncle Alfred: *see under* Stern, George.

Uncle George: *see* Olsen, George.

Ungar, Nicholas: A longtime Portland furrier, with whom George Stern worked at times. Nicholas was born in Budapest, Hungary, in 1884 and came to the United States in 1904. *pp. 201, 204*

Von Flesch, Lilly Helene Ullmann (1895–1984): Egon's sister, who left Vienna (after being held in a concentration camp near the end of the war) and arrived in Portland in September 1947. She was accompanied by her twenty-six-year-old daughter, Annelinde (or Anna Alinde) Von Flesch, called Nanny or Nany by the family. Lilly was previously married to Walter Skrein; in 1918 the couple had a son, Philip Skrein. Philip was listed on Lilly's 1951 naturalization petition as living in Vancouver, B.C. *pp. 70, 71, 85, 90, 109–111, 117, 122, 203, 215, 216*

www.ingramcontent.com/pod-product-compliance
Lightning Source LLC
Chambersburg PA
CBHW051545010526
44118CB00022B/2579